BUDD SCHULBERG

A Bio-Bibliography

Nicholas Beck

The Scarecrow Press, Inc.
Lanham, Maryland, and London
2001

SCARECROW PRESS, INC.

Published in the United States of America
by Scarecrow Press, Inc.
4720 Boston Way, Lanham, Maryland 20706
www.scarecrowpress.com

4 Pleydell Gardens, Folkestone
Kent CT20 2DN, England

British Library Cataloguing-in-Publication Information Available

Library of Congress Cataloging-in-Publication Data

Beck, Nicholas, 1932–
    Budd Schulberg : a bio-bibliography / Nicholas Beck.
        p.   cm.
    Includes bibliographical references and index.
    ISBN 0-8108-4035-9 (alk. paper)
        1. Schulberg, Budd. 2. Authors, American—20th century—Biography. 3.
    Screenwriters—United States—Biography. 4. Schulberg, Budd—Bibliography. I. Title.

PS3537.C7114 Z58 2001
818'.52099—dc21
[B]   2001020590

Printed in the United States of America

♾™ The paper used in this publication meets the minimum requirements of
American National Standard for Information Sciences—Permanence of Paper for
Printed Library Materials, ANSI/NISO Z39.48-1992.

CONTENTS

ACKNOWLEDGMENTS

I am grateful to my good friend John Ahouse, curator of American literature at the Doheny Library at the University of Southern California, for his many favors during the long preparation of this work. I also extend my thanks to John's colleague, Ned Comstock, at the USC Cinema Library, and to John's person Friday, Dace Taube. I am indebted as well to the kind people at five other exemplary Southern California institutions: the indispensable Margaret Herrick Library of the Academy of Motion Picture Arts and Sciences in Beverly Hills; the Frances Howard Goldwyn Hollywood Regional Branch of the L.A. Public Library; the periodicals department at the John F. Kennedy Memorial Library on my own former campus, California State University, Los Angeles; the Southern California Library for Social Science and Research and the Paul Ziffren Sports Resource Center of the Amateur Athletic Foundation of Los Angeles in the beautiful West Adams district of this city.

I would not have proceeded without the assistance and friendship of Bart Auerbach, Maurice F. Neville, Julian Bud Lesser, and Sonya Schulberg O'Sullivan; and I could not have proceeded without the patient help of a gifted and generous computer whiz, Nancy Ng.

I thank the following for permission to reprint copyrighted material: Sylvia Shorris and Marion Abbott Bundy for quotations from their interview with Sam Jaffe, copyright 1994 *Talking Pictures: With the People Who Made Them*. Reprinted by permission of The New Press. To Victor S. Navasky for quotations from *Naming Names,* copyright 1980. Reprinted by permission of the Viking Press and Penguin Putnam, Inc. To Elia Kazan for a passage about Marlon Brando in *A Life,* published in 1988 by Alfred A. Knopf, a division of Random House, used by permission of the publisher.

I owe a special debt to another friend, Matthew J. Bruccoli, who inadvertently got this project started in the first place.

Finally, I must thank Budd Wilson Schulberg for steadfastly answering my every question and helping in so many other ways.

Nicholas Beck
Hollywood

February, 2001

INTRODUCTION

For more than six decades, Budd Wilson Schulberg has known success in virtually every category of American writing. Raised in the Hollywood of the 1920s as the privileged son of a pioneer studio mogul, Schulberg achieved fame as novelist, short story writer, playwright, Oscar-winning screenwriter, and boxing historian. His 1941 creation, Sammy Glick, the all-American antihero of *What Makes Sammy Run?* is listed in many dictionaries as code for any ruthless self-promoter. Terry Malloy, the hapless dock worker of Schulberg's 1954 movie *On the Waterfront,* who "coulda been a contenda," has made it to *Bartlett's Familiar Quotations*; Manley Halliday, the faded Jazz Age novelist of *The Disenchanted*, seems destined to be forever famous as the "thinly-disguised" portrait of F. Scott Fitzgerald (despite Schulberg's protestations that he is a composite of many gifted writers who lost their way in Hollywood).

Schulberg, who was as comfortable in the company of Fitzgerald as he was in the presence of David O. Selznick or Muhammad Ali, also became a central figure in the entertainment industry's political turmoil of the 1940s and '50s, fleeing first from the Communist Party's attempts to control his writing, then testifying as a cooperating witness before the House Committee on Un-American Activities, and finally emerging as a leader of the nation's non-Communist Left. Schulberg chronicled these events in the country's leading newspapers and intellectual journals.

Despite warnings from his editors and friends that his interest in the violent and often corrupt sport of boxing could harm his reputation as a serious writer, Schulberg the fight fan has haunted the country's gyms and arenas and has written countless newspaper and magazine pieces about the great and not-always-great boxers of the world.

He has also known, and written about, many other American writers and their difficulties in maintaining or recapturing early success. In addition to Scott Fitzgerald, with whom he collaborated on a disastrous 1939 movie assignment, and Fitzgerald's not-so-good friend Ernest Hemingway, who apparently regarded Schulberg as a rival, Schulberg in his early Hollywood days knew Nathanael West, William Saroyan, John Steinbeck, William Faulkner, John O'Hara, Irwin Shaw, and many other distinguished novelists and playwrights who were doing studio work. Two of Schulberg's books, *The Four Seasons of Success* (1972) and its expanded revision, *Writers in America* (1983), deal with some of these men and the derailing of their serious writing by the lure of Hollywood money.

The bibliographical portion of this book is the first attempt to compile a comprehensive list of works by and about Budd Schulberg, and thus it must be regarded as a working bibliography.

1

A PRINCELY CHILDHOOD

Budd Wilson Schulberg was born on March 27, 1914, in a three-room apartment on 120th Street in the mostly middle-class Jewish section of upper Manhattan called *Harlem*. His father was Benjamin Percival ("B.P.") Schulberg (1892–1957), a rising young publicist and photoplay editor for Adolph Zukor's Famous Players Company, soon to be known as *Paramount Pictures*.[1] His mother was twenty-one-year-old Latvian-born Adeline ("Ad") Jaffe (1892–1977), who would one day found the Malibu Colony and become one of Hollywood's top talent agents.[2]

In 1922, B.P., Ad, little Budd, and sister Sonya (born in 1918) followed the motion picture industry to Los Angeles where, by 1925, B.P. was head of production at Paramount–Famous Players–Lasky Corporation at a salary that would grow steadily to more than $10,000 a week. Budd Schulberg, an authentic Hollywood prince, would grow up in a mansion in the exclusive Windsor Square enclave of already swank Hancock Park, just down the block from producers Harry Rapf and Sol Lesser.

During the next seven decades, Budd Schulberg would join and then leave the Communist Party, witness his father's self-destructive decline, work with F. Scott Fitzgerald on a disastrous film project, create a famous literary caricature (and outrage the film capital's pioneer studio moguls), testify as a cooperating witness before the notorious House Committee on Un-American Activities, win a best screenplay Academy Award, add phrases to the American lexicon, chronicle the careers of the great prizefighters, and defy Horace Greeley by becoming the only major American novelist to start in Hollywood and work his way East. Schulberg was a natural who, by age seven, knew the only thing he wanted to be was a writer.[3]

Despite a severe stammer that would afflict him into adult life, young Schulberg was a fine student in grade school and during a brief

1

stay in military school.[4] At Los Angeles High School, he became editor of the *Blue-and-White Daily* and was a member of the tennis team. He spent a year at Deerfield Academy in Massachusetts between 1931 and 1932 before going on to Dartmouth College. In Hanover, he wrote a one-act play called *Company Town,* coauthored a musical called *Banned in Boston,* contributed to the campus literary magazine, and as editor of *The* (Daily) *Dartmouth,* infuriated the campus community and alumni by supporting striking marble workers across the river in Proctor, Vermont.[5]

At the Hanover Inn, in late fall 1935, Schulberg met Random House and Modern Library publisher Bennett Cerf (1898–1971). Years later, Cerf would remember Schulberg as a "shy, self-effacing and incredibly vague youngster"; at their initial meeting, he complimented Schulberg on his writing and invited him to the Random House offices in New York, where Schulberg was introduced to editor Saxe Commins.[6] Commins, whose clients included William Faulkner, Eugene O'Neill, and Irwin Shaw, would become Budd Schulberg's editor and friend.[7]

NOTES

1. B.P. was one of filmdom's master phrasemakers. He crowned Mary Pickford "America's Sweetheart"; created the slogans "Famous Players in Famous Plays" and "If it's a Paramount Picture, it's the best show in town"; and characterized old friend Louis B. Mayer as the "Czar of All the Rushes." He wrote the scenario for Mary Pickford's *Tess of the Storm Country* (1914) and the subtitles for *The Prisoner of Zenda* (1914); and in 1918, he devised the plan for the creation of United Artists, through which Charlie Chaplin, Douglas Fairbanks Sr., Mary Pickford, and D. W. Griffith would increase their profits by producing and distributing their own films. B.P. got nothing on paper, however, and was frozen out when U.A. was formed the following year. From 1922 until 1924, B.P. shared the Schulberg-Mayer Studio with Louis B. Mayer in Eastlake (later Lincoln) Park in the Lincoln Heights section of Los Angeles. (Lincoln Park is the present-day site of the city's Hispanic shrine, the Plaza de la Raza.) In 1924, when Mayer merged with Metro Pictures and became part of MGM, B.P. took his Preferred Pictures to Paramount.

2. Ad Schulberg, who paid Budd twenty-five cents for every "classic" he read as a child, later became his agent. She is remembered in the Film Colony not only as a leading theatrical and literary agent but also as a cofounder of the Hollywood Progressive School, which stood across Highland Avenue from the Hollywood Bowl.

"She could be formidable," Schulberg said, "but I always admired her and was fond of her." Still, he joked, "I once saw her kiss one of her clients, Rex Reed; she treated him like a son, me like a client."

3. "B.P. read to us aloud on Sunday when we were children," Schulberg recalled. "Twain, Poe, Conrad, Galsworthy. We had a typewriter in the house in Hancock Park and it took the place of a piano. We all used it, my sister Sonya and my brother Stuart."

4. Despite Schulberg's diligence and good grades, he and boyhood pal Maurice Rapf managed to get themselves expelled from Temple B'nai B'rith (by none other than Rabbi Edgar Magnin) for "blasphemous and unforgivable" behavior and for "mocking" their faith. Schulberg would also confess (in his 1981 autobiography) that he and Rapf once pelted Greta Garbo and Norma Shearer with ripe figs from a strategically located tree at MGM, where the two privileged boys regularly played among the backlot sets.

5. The Proctor family was one of Dartmouth's major financial contributors.

6. Bennett Cerf, *At Random: The Reminiscences of Bennett Cerf* (New York: Random House, 1977), 119.

7. One of Cerf's favorite "Schulberg stories" was about a night, many years later, when the writer was driving from his Pennsylvania farm to a formal dinner in New York City. His maid had asked him to deliver a dachshund puppy to a friend who ran a beauty parlor in Harlem; Schulberg, who had forgotten his driver's license, somehow lost the address of the beauty shop, forgot about the dinner, and was picked up by the police while driving aimlessly around Harlem. Finally, the officers called Cerf, who identified the bewildered Schulberg and arranged for his release. Bennett Cerf, "Trade Winds," *Saturday Review,* 14 October 1950, 5.

2

TO RUSSIA, WITH MAURY

In the summer of 1934, Schulberg and L.A. High School and Dartmouth classmate Maurice Rapf (son of MGM producer Harry Rapf) took a fateful three-month trip to the Soviet Union under the sponsorship of the left-wing National Student League (costing them only $350 each). With "five or six others" from Dartmouth in a group of about fifty American students, they attended the English-language Anglo-American Institute, where they learned about Marxism and communism and became thoroughly radicalized. They were particularly impressed with the antifascist spirit in Russia, and at the fact that anti-Semitism was illegal. In Russia, they met Princeton student Ring Lardner Jr., son of the famous American humorist; at the time, Lardner Jr. was anti-Marxist and anti-Soviet, but he later would join the Communist Party in Hollywood, along with Schulberg and Rapf.

When Rapf and Schulberg returned to Hollywood at the end of the summer, heads shaven in proletarian solidarity (and perhaps to discourage head lice), these two sons of famous fathers took a ribbing in the Los Angeles newspapers. Their embarrassed dads reacted by subjecting them to grillings from some of the top executives in the film capital, including Louis B. Mayer, David O. Selznick, former university professor Albert Lewin (who told them that their radicalism was a betrayal of their "producer class"), and especially Irving Thalberg, whom Budd Schulberg regarded as "Hollywood's almost official head-Rabbi."

Already, however, Schulberg's blue-blood pedigree was in jeopardy. After seven years (1925-1932) at the Paramount helm—during which he had turned out 1927's *Wings* (the first feature motion picture to win the Academy Award for best picture), *An American Tragedy* (1931), and *Dr. Jekyll and Mr. Hyde* (1932)—his father had been fired. Although he had developed the careers of Gary Cooper, Fredric March, Cary Grant, Clara Bow, and Sylvia Sidney, and brought Marlene Dietrich and Emil Jannings to America, B.P.'s prodigious gambling, drinking, and womanizing had finally cost him his job and forced him to become an "independent" producer. At the same time, an open affair with Sidney, begun in 1931, had ended his marriage to Budd's mother.[1]

NOTES

1. Sylvia Shorris and Marion Abbott Bundy, *Talking Pictures: With the People Who Made Them* (New York: New Press, 1994), 32–40. B.P.'s brother-in-law, Hollywood superagent Sam Jaffe (1901–2000), who later represented Humphrey Bogart, Jennifer Jones, Fritz Lang, Stanley Kubrick, and many others, loved Schulberg, who had given him his first job as a messenger at Famous Players–Lasky in 1916. But Jaffe came to believe that Schulberg simply couldn't handle Hollywood's temptations. "The destruction of Schulberg is a whole story in itself," Jaffe recalled in 1985. "When he was working well—that is, when he was normal and well—he would come home with his scripts, have dinner, and everything was great. I think Schulberg in those days made $6,500 a week, so you can imagine how that kind of money affected him. Ben couldn't take that kind of success. He went crazy. He gambled, he screwed, and he drank. He was screwing every girl that came along. He was handsome, he was intelligent, but the business was going down, and he was fired. He ruined himself." Schulberg's last production was *City without Men,* a low-budget B picture in 1943 for Columbia, with story and screenplay cowritten by son Budd. In 1949, broken in purse and spirit, B.P. placed an ad in *Variety* that read, in part, "This is the only industry I know. I am able to work as hard as anybody in it. Sure I have made some mistakes. . . . Who hasn't? What is the judicial code of the industry? Life imprisonment for a misdemeanor and execution for violating a parking law? Must we always wait until a production pioneer is found dead [referring to D. W. Griffith, who had died the previous year in Hollywood's Knickerbocker Hotel] in a Hollywood hotel room before reflecting on an 'indifferent and forgetful' industry?" B.P. died, after a stroke, in 1957. In Budd Schulberg's short story *Somebody Has to Be Nobody* in the October 18, 1941, *Saturday Evening Post,* studio boss A. D. Nathan (clearly B. P. Schulberg) waits at the Hollywood nightspot Ciro's for a call from New York to learn if he's been fired. The story was dramatized as "A Table at Ciro's" on PBS in 1987, with Darrin McGavin as Nathan.

3

THE PARTY

When Budd Schulberg graduated summa cum laude and Phi Beta Kappa from Dartmouth in June 1936 with a degree in sociology, he returned to Hollywood and almost immediately went to work as a junior writer at Selznick International Pictures.[1] He also joined a Communist "study group" that gradually became part of the Communist Youth League. It was in 1937, he believes, that he joined the party. At Selznick, he was finally teamed with Ring Lardner Jr. and assigned to do "polish work" and "add dialogue" on the script for the Janet Gaynor-Fredric March film, *A Star Is Born* (1937). The two veterans of the Anglo-American Institute in Russia, according to Hollywood lore, came up with Gaynor's memorable concluding line: "This is Mrs. Norman Maine!" Next, they wrote the final sequences for the highly successful Carole Lombard-Fredric March comedy, *Nothing Sacred* (1937), after Ben Hecht (who received credit as screenwriter) walked out in a dispute with Selznick.[2]

Despite his studio work and Party duties, Schulberg also found time to write short stories, which he hoped to sell to mass-circulation magazines such as *Saturday Evening Post, Collier's,* and *Liberty.* His father put him in touch with Carl Brandt, a respected veteran agent who knew the magazine market, and Brandt was able to place one story in *Liberty* at the end of 1937 and nine others in *Liberty, Collier's,* and *Story* in the following year. The first *Liberty* story, published in the issue of October 30, 1937, was *What Makes Sammy Run?*[3] Two of the 1938 stories dealt with the same lead character, Sammy Glick (née Glickstein), and another was a story about Sammy's "mentor," nice guy Al Manners (later Manheim). Sammy Glick was the ultimate antihero, a ruthless overachiever, a disloyal self-promoter whose code of conduct could best be summed up by his own quip, "Going through life with a conscience is like driving your car with the brakes on." Sammy starts as a New York City copyboy but quickly works his way to Hollywood, where he climbs—almost entirely on the backs of others—to the top of the studio heap. Few people in the film industry seemed to notice the stories, but magazine editors were very interested and asked Schulberg for more adventures of this supreme Hollywood Heel.

"The magazines came and went quickly, and people didn't pay that much attention," Schulberg recalled in 1998. "The people in my own social group seemed to like them, as I recall, and my father was proud that I was getting things published. I had the time to write them, and the Party didn't ask to see them in advance."

Schulberg initially was an enthusiastic Party member, according to Maurice Rapf. "Budd got Scott Fitzgerald to say he thought he (Fitzgerald) was a Communist, and he persuaded Dorothy Parker that she should be more organized about her left-wing activities," Rapf said. "She hadn't read the Marxist stuff as diligently as Budd and I had."[4] Schulberg recalls only that he got Parker to agree to "pay the 10 percent tithe" to the party and to receive reports of the weekly meetings. About this time, Jack Moffitt, a writer for the *Hollywood Reporter,* did a story that claimed that Ring Lardner Jr., Budd Schulberg, and Maurice Rapf controlled the Communist Party in Hollywood, to which Sam Goldwyn was said to have remarked, "If they are the ones who are running it, we've got nothing to worry about."[5]

Not long after joining the Party, Schulberg and Rapf were approached by a man named Stanley Lawrence ("the first real American Communist I had known," Schulberg recalled), who ordered them to report to Ventura County, northwest of Los Angeles, where they were put to work in the fields, organizing local farmworkers virtually in front of menacing farm owners and their hired thugs. "It was pretty scary and dangerous stuff," said Schulberg, "and when the Hollywood Party people found out about it, Lawrence was reprimanded for using us as regular CP organizers when we had such value with our 'inroads' to the Hollywood Establishment."[6]

"During the years 1937-1939, I would say I was still in favor of the immediate issues the Communists seemed to be following then," Schulberg remembered. "But by 1939, I was definitely backsliding. I was upset first by the Moscow Purge Trials and then by the Nazi-Soviet Non-Aggression Pact. I avoided as many meetings as I could and as many responsibilities as I could, and I was already having trouble with [local party head] John Howard Lawson. I'd worked with Jack and I admired him, but now I was having trouble with him over my book, even over the right to write the book."[7]

Schulberg had made virtually all of the major characters in the Sammy Glick stories Jewish, but most of their names were changed for magazine publication. "I honestly can't remember why we changed the Jewish names in the magazine manuscripts (from Manheim to Manners, and Fineman to Boyce, etc.), or why, or who suggested it," Schulberg said. "Maybe it was Carl Brandt, or the *Liberty* editors, or both. Maybe Brandt just thought there were too many Jewish names in the first story. But I don't think it was because anybody thought we might fuel anti-Semitism."[8]

By May 1939, Schulberg had come to believe that the party was inimical to art. About the same time, local party leaders—who had earlier ignored his Sammy Glick short stories—began to tell him that the stories had been "too realistic . . . too depressing, decadent, and didn't show sufficiently the positive force of the workers." Finally, he was told that he couldn't turn Sammy into a novel without permission. "I was told that I should submit an outline to Lawson to determine if the novel's contribution to the Party would justify time off from my weekly assignments," Schulberg said. "At that time, if you wanted to travel East, you had to ask [the Party] for a leave. Party rules were strict; often you would be assigned to another group in the area where you were going. By then I just wanted to write my novel and I was defiant toward the Party," Schulberg said. "I decided I was 'out,' and so my wife and I just got in the car and left Hollywood and drove to Norwich, Vermont. At that time it seemed like a very daring thing to do."

NOTES

1. At Selznick, he was first teamed with Marshall ("Mickey") Neilan as a writing partner. "Mickey's rise and fall provided the springboard for some of my stories," said Schulberg. Neilan had been a top director in the silent days and had been married to leading lady Blanche Sweet.

2. Schulberg learned early to deal with setbacks as well as successes in Hollywood. His first produced screenplay (coauthored with Samuel Ornitz), *Little Orphan Annie* (Paramount, 1938), received this comment in the November 24, 1938, issue of *Variety*: "A stupid and thoroughly boresome story, combined with mediocre direction, makes this a leading candidate for the poorest picture of the season." Interestingly— given both B.P.'s and Budd's interest in fighting— Schulberg injected a boxing angle into the film, with Orphan Annie persuading her tenement neighbors to pay the training expenses of a local fighter. Several of his other early film efforts might have fared better if they had been filmed with their original casts. *Weekend for Three* (1941), for which he had written the original story (heavyweights Dorothy Parker and husband Alan Campbell did the screenplay) was to have starred Irene Dunne and Cary Grant, with Garson Kanin directing. Instead, the leads were played by Jane Wyatt and Dennis O'Keefe, and Irving Reis directed. *Government Girl* (1943), which Schulberg adapted from an Adela Rogers St. John short story, at one point seemed set for Joseph Cotton, but Sonny Tufts somehow got the part, to the distinct displeasure of costar Olivia De Havilland, who tried unsuccessfully to get out of the film. Even his father's final film, *City without Men* (1943), which Budd cowrote (story and screenplay), was to have starred Jean Arthur in 1939; Sam Goldwyn instead sold the property to Columbia. Schulberg said he finally left Selznick International in 1939 after the producer declined to read two scripts he had cowritten with Lardner and, at the same time, refused Schulberg a salary raise from $75 to $100 a week.

3. In the summer of 1937, Schulberg wrote to his friend William Saroyan: "I wrote a story last week which I am sure is the best I ever did. It is about a Hollywood writer, and called *What Makes Manny Run.* . . . I was bowled over when I heard I had sold my story about Manny Glick to *Liberty* for five weeks salary. . . . The *Manny* story . . . incidentally, is now *Sammy,* because *Liberty* was afraid Manny Cohen of Paramount would think it was him." (Typed Letter Signed [*TLS*], Schulberg to William Saroyan, 1937). Years later, Schulberg admitted that it was his father, and not the magazine, who had suggested the name change. The man who replaced B.P. at Paramount in 1932 was Emanuel "Manny" Cohen; "and my father, although he liked the story, was afraid Cohen might see it as an act of petty revenge on the part of the Schulberg family," said Schulberg. "Otherwise, *Manny Glick* might have gone into the language. It was a lucky switch, as once made, I found I much preferred *Sammy.*" See *Budd Schulberg: An Exhibition in Observance of the 50th Anniversary of What Makes Sammy Run?* (Los Angeles: University of Southern California, 1991), 2. By then, however, Cohen already had been fired (in 1935) at Paramount and replaced by Ernst Lubitsch.

4. Nancy Lynn Schwartz, *The Hollywood Writers' Wars* (New York: Knopf, 1982), 152.

5. Patrick McGilligan and Paul Buhle, *Tender Comrades: A Backstory of the Hollywood Blacklist* (New York: St. Martin's, 1997), 521.

6. Maurice Rapf, *Back Lot: Growing Up with the Movies* (Lanham, Md.: Scarecrow Press, 1999), 121-122. Lawrence regularly delivered Communist Party material to Rapf at the family home, until a suspicious Harry Rapf finally ordered him not to come back. Maurice Rapf said the party organizer "Brimmer" in Fitzgerald's *The Last Tycoon* was based on Lawrence. Rapf became convinced that Lawrence was an FBI plant, and Rapf and Schulberg were later told that Lawrence had died mysteriously while serving in the Abraham Lincoln Brigade during the 1936-1939 Spanish Civil War. Schulberg later told Victor Navasky that he heard Lawrence was shot as a traitor (*Naming Names,* New York: Viking, 1980), 244.

7. The brilliant but dogmatic Lawson (1894-1977) had been a cofounder (1933) and first president of the Screen Writers Guild. His career came to a halt in 1948, when he tangled with the House Committee on Un-American Activities and was sentenced to a year in jail. He was thereafter blacklisted in Hollywood. The Screen Writers Guild was certified in 1939 as the collective bargaining agent of all writers in the motion picture industry. In 1954, it became the Writers Guild of America (West and East), with offices in Los Angeles and New York. It represents writers in the motion picture, broadcast, cable, interactive, and new media industries.

8. Schwartz, *Hollywood Writers' Wars,* 168. One Schulberg friend who *did* think the stories were anti-Semitic was screenwriter Richard Maibaum (1909-1991), who authored the script for the 1949 (Alan Ladd) *The Great Gatsby* and the screenplays for thirteen James Bond films. Maibaum recalled urging Schulberg (as Schulberg prepared to turn the short stories into the novel) to change Al Manners back to Al Manheim. "At least it wasn't quite so bad to have this Jewish bastard described by another Jew," Maibaum said.

4

JIGEE

Schulberg's wife was the strikingly beautiful Virginia "Jigee" Ray (born in 1915); their marriage, on New Year's Eve 1936, more or less determined the immediate group of writers and filmmakers with whom Schulberg would associate in the two years before he and Jigee left Hollywood. Jigee, still remembered as a Hollywood legend, had been active in "progressive" circles since her days at Fairfax High School in West Hollywood, where her closest friends were Amber Dana (later to marry screenwriter Waldo Salt) and Marian Edwards (who would wed novelist Irwin Shaw). She had appeared, uncredited, as Cupid in a Sonja Henie film at Fox, and had danced in several films at Warner Bros., including *The King and the Chorus Girl*. Her sister Anne's husband, comedy producer-director Melvin Frank (*Mr. Blandings Builds His Dream House*), remembered Jigee: "All of the Jewish communists were attracted to her, because she was a gorgeous gentile princess accessible to Jewish communists because *she* was a communist."[1] The author Nancy Lynn Schwartz said that seventeen men she interviewed admitted to having loved Jigee, among them Ring Lardner Jr., who almost destroyed his own first marriage (to David Selznick's secretary Silvia Shulman) in a protracted and fruitless pursuit. The outspoken Jigee was active in the party with her husband and with screenwriters Maurice Rapf, Lardner, Albert Maltz, and Robert Rossen; and with their wives—who apparently didn't much like her, according to Schwartz.[2]

NOTES

1. As a child, Jigee's sister Anne could not pronounce "Virginia" and so gave birth to the unusual nickname.

2. Schwartz, *Hollywood Writers' Wars,* 91–95. The exquisite, brown-haired Jigee had such a powerful and lasting effect on the men who admired her that she was immortalized as "April" in Lardner's *The Ecstasy of Owen Muir,* as a character in Irwin Shaw's *Two Weeks in Another Town,* and as "Jigee" in Arthur Laurents' 1945 play, *A Clearing in the Woods.* Although Laurents says the Barbra Streisand character ("Katie Morosky") in his 1973 screenplay for *The Way We Were* is based primarily on a student he had known at Cornell, she is also partly Jigee. Even Groucho Marx, according to biographer Stefan Kanfer (*Groucho: The Life and Times of Julius Henry Marx,* Knopf, 2000) was in love with Jigee, and wrote to his son Arthur in 1943 to say that he hoped to marry her. Jigee bore Schulberg a daughter, Victoria, in 1940 and left him in 1942; they were divorced in 1943, and she married the non-Communist screenwriter and novelist Peter Viertel (*Saboteur; The Sun Also Rises; White Hunter, Black Heart*). She left the Party in 1945, testified before the HCUA on June 6, 1956, in Los Angeles, and (as part of a complicated deal she believed would save Viertel's commission in the Marine Corps reserve) named names. In December 1949 and January 1950, she had had a "flirtation" with Ernest Hemingway, first aboard the *Ile de France* and then at the Ritz Hotel in Paris; aboard the ocean liner, Hemingway saw to it that she could come from her tourist-class cabin to lunch in first class with him and his fourth wife, Mary; in Paris, he got her a reduced rate at the Ritz and gave her almost $2,000 in cash from an unexpected royalty payment, to the annoyance of both Mary Hemingway and Peter Viertel. When the Hemingways went on alone to Venice, Mary was told by her husband that Jigee had tried to lure him away. Ernest, Mary Hemingway later wrote, said Jigee had told him: "She (Mary) obviously doesn't appreciate you; we'll have a ranch with horses in California and you can give up the heat of Cuba. I understand your sensibilities." (See Mary Welsh Hemingway, *How It Was* [New York: Alfred A. Knopf, 1976], 247–252; Peter Viertel, *Dangerous Friends* [New York: Doubleday, 1992], 95–97.) In 1959, Jigee divorced Viertel, who had left her for French model Bettina Graziani. On January 31, 1960, she died in Los Angeles at age forty-five, from burns suffered when she dropped a lighted cigarette into the pocket of her negligee. Viertel later married actress Deborah Kerr.

5

SAMMY

Bennett Cerf had told student editor Schulberg, "When you write a novel, I want it." In 1939, having seen the several Sammy Glick stories in *Liberty* and *Collier's*, he asked Budd if the stories might be "the seeds of a novel." Schulberg, already thinking on the same lines, replied in the affirmative, and Cerf offered a $500 contract with a $250 advance. At the same time, he reminded the twenty-five-year-old Californian not to expect a big sale when the book was published. "People who read novels have no interest in Hollywood, and people who go to the movies don't read novels," he said. Cerf was so certain of this that he told Schulberg that Random House would limit the first printing to 2,500 copies.[1] Nevertheless, Schulberg eagerly went to work in modest lodgings across the Connecticut River from Dartmouth. When the advance money ran low, he paused to write short stories that Carl Brandt was able to sell quickly; when he completed the book, he rushed to New York to show it to Cerf and Saxe Commins.[2]

The Schulbergs returned to Hollywood in March 1940. Budd had already mailed a copy of the manuscript to his father, who by now was growing uneasy about the book. The previous December he had written to Budd, "I think the writing is swell, really fresh and vigorous," but he added, "I think honest and vigorous as the writing is here, that it is too honest and that it means the end of you in Hollywood."[3] Once back in Hollywood, Budd told screenwriter Richard Collins that he had considered himself "out" of the party since leaving the previous year. "For some reason, though, partly out of curiosity and maybe because leaving the Party seemed almost like leaving the Roman Catholic Church, I went to see Lawson, and then V. J. Jerome [a cultural commissar sent to Hollywood by the Party in 1936].[4] I was told that my entire attitude was wrong," Schulberg testified more than a decade later. "That I was wrong about writing; wrong about this book, wrong about the Party; wrong about the so-called peace movement at that particular time . . . a kind of harangue.[5] When I came away, I felt, maybe, almost for the first time, that this to me was the real face of the Party. . . . I felt I had talked to someone rigid and dictatorial who was trying to tell me how to live my life, and as far as I remember, I didn't want to have anything more to do with them."[6]

The buildup to telling Collins that he was leaving the party had been a lengthy one, Schulberg remembered. "It was like a three-stage rocket. First, you argue inside yourself. I'd write notes to myself about the Moscow show trials, the Hitler-Stalin Pact. Second, you go out of the Party, but you feel that to make it public would play into the hands of reaction; you are still anti-fascist and you don't want to shore up the reactionaries if you can help it. Third, you realize that you have not been true to yourself because you have not spoken out on something you knew was a scourge." Later, to former Communist Arthur Koestler, he said, "I hate the communists, but I don't like to attack the left." Koestler's reply was, "They're not left, they're East."[7]

In February 1941, after spending time in Ensenada, Mexico, tinkering with a proposed sequel to *Stagecoach* for Sam Goldwyn, Schulberg returned to Hollywood to await publication of his novel. It came on March 7, just twenty days before his twenty-seventh birthday. The book's striking dust jacket carried a heavyweight blurb from F. Scott Fitzgerald (excerpted from a letter written to Cerf just eight days before Fitzgerald's death on December 20, 1940): "It is a good book, utterly fearless and with a great deal of beauty"; and from John O'Hara: "Here is a fine book by Budd Schulberg, the novelist." Later printings quoted Dorothy Parker: "It has understanding, pity, savagery, courage and sometimes a strange high beauty. . . . It is good to be present when such things happen." Damon Runyon praised the book in his column, and Walter Winchell touted it on radio (and claimed he knew who "Sammy" was). Cerf came to think of it as "probably the best book about Hollywood ever written."[8] A decade later, he would publish it again in Random House's Modern Library. To Cerf's (and certainly Schulberg's) astonishment, the book went through ten printings in 1941, was condensed in *Reader's Digest* that July, and was selected as "Best First Novel of the Year" by the *New York Times.*

The most astonishing review of all ran in the April 2 issue of the Communist *People's World* and the April 7 issue of *The Daily Worker*. The papers' film critic, Charles Glenn, lavished praise on the book: "American bibliophiles and critics have been awaiting the Hollywood novel. While they may argue its merits and demerits, I've a feeling that all critics, no matter their carping standards, will have to admit they've found the Hollywood novel in Budd Schulberg's *What Makes Sammy Run?*" Young Glenn, an admirer of Schulberg, had run into Budd in Stanley Rose's Bookshop on Hollywood Boulevard shortly before the book was to be published; he asked Schulberg if he could read the galleys, and then, without clearing his notes with Lawson or Jerome, submitted his review. "I jumped the review date by a few weeks," Glenn said. "I thought the book was good, and I didn't think it was anti-Semitic." In fact, he thought it was a masterpiece of social realism. When his reviews appeared, however, Glenn was immediately called on the carpet by Lawson ("and spent the most tortured hour and a half I'd ever spent") and ordered to write a retraction.[9] On April 23 and 24, the same two papers ran his retraction, which read, in part: "On the basis of quite lengthy discussion, on the book, I've done a little reevaluating. . . . To say that I felt more than a trifle silly when these weaknesses were called to my attention is putting it a bit mildly."[10]

Meanwhile, Dorothy Parker, an ardent anti-fascist and Screen Writers Guild (SWG) loyalist who remained close to many party members, countered the Party's charges that the book was anti-Semitic: "Those who hail us Jews as brothers must allow us to have our villains, alas, as any other race."[11] Schulberg defended himself against the same charges by reminding readers and critics that every one of Sammy Glick's victims was also Jewish: father, brother, Al, Julian Blumberg, Sidney Fineman. Sammy and the others, said Schulberg, "suggest the wide range of personalities and attitudes under one ethnic umbrella."[12]

The reaction among the studio bosses was almost volcanic. Schulberg was suddenly called into Samuel Goldwyn's office, where the incensed mogul demanded, "What have you done?" Goldwyn, Budd would soon learn, believed that Sammy Glick's initials were code for Sam Goldwyn. When Schulberg tried to explain that this reprehensible character was merely a composite, Goldwyn told him he was fired and ordered him off the lot. At a meeting of the MPPAA (Motion Pictures

Producers Association of America), Louis B. Mayer lit into his old colleague. "B.P., I blame you for this," he shouted. "How could you let him
do this? We should deport him." To which B.P. replied, "He was raised
here; where would you deport him TO, Catalina Island?" Privately, however, B.P. told his son, "You'll never work in this town again. How will
you live?" The day he was fired, Budd stopped for a drink at the original Lucy's, a Paramount watering hole, where he was confronted by
actress-turned-columnist Hedda Hopper. "Humph, I read the book," she
said as she stormed out. "How *dare* you!" Most Hollywood hands
thought Goldwyn, with his suspicions, was on to something and that
Sammy Glick was based on a real person in their midst.

NOTES

1. It was a considerable irony for Schulberg that Cerf had been married for seven
months in 1935–1936 to Sylvia Sidney (1908–1999), whose affair with B.P. Schulberg
had caused the separation of Budd's parents.

2. On the first day in the city, after returning to his hotel room, Schulberg discovered to his horror that he had lost the only copy of the manuscript. "I nearly went
mad," he said. "I told myself if it's lost for good I'm going to quit writing." He began to retrace his every step that day. "Finally I went back to a stationery store on
Madison Avenue and there was the proprietor reading it. He said it was amazing,
since he had been born on Rivington Street (Sammy Glick's birthplace)." (Edwin
McDowell, "What Authors Do to Protect Manuscripts," *New York Times,* 16 September 1982.) Since then, Schulberg sends copies of everything he writes to his
agent, his sister, and occasionally even to friends.

3. TLS, December 15, 1939, B.P. Schulberg to Budd Schulberg.

4. Jerome was later a Smith Act defendant.

5. Until Hitler invaded the Soviet Union in June 1941, the party line on the
"peace movement" was to oppose U.S. entry into the war in Europe.

6. See Appendix A, U.S. Congress. House Committee on Un-American Activities. *Annual Report for Year 1951.*

7. Victor Navasky, *Naming Names* (New York: Viking Books, 1980), 246.

8. Bennett Cerf, *At Random: The Reminiscences of Bennett Cerf* (New York: Random
House, 1977), 119.

9. Nancy Lynn Schwartz, *The Hollywood Writers' Wars* (New York: Alfred A. Knopf,
1982), 168. "I have never ceased regretting the retraction," Glenn said. "Ten years
later I wanted to apologize to Budd, but I didn't have the guts."

10. See *People's World,* April 2, 1941, 5; *People's World,* April 24, 1941, 5; *Daily Worker,* April 7, 1941, 7; *Daily Worker,* April 8, 1941, 7; *Daily Worker,* April 23, 1941, 7. The April 2 and April 24 *People's World* stories are reprinted in their complete form in Appendices B and C.

11. Schulberg, introduction to the Modern Library *What Makes Sammy Run?* (New York: Random House, 1952), ix. The party apparently believed that even the slightest hint of anti-Semitism by its members would discourage Jews from joining the Party.

12. Maurice Rapf claimed that Schulberg sent galley proofs of the novel to him, to F. Scott Fitzgerald, and to Ring Lardner Jr., and promised that if any of them found the book to be anti-Semitic, he would not publish it. Schulberg acknowledges that he sent the proofs, but says that under no circumstances would he have considered not publishing. In any event, Rapf in 1941 did not think that the book was anti-Semitic. Years later, however, he stated, "But you know, what really happened with that book was that (Josef) Goebbles pirated it and published it in Germany as anti-Semitic literature. So it was anti-Semitic. Five hundred thousand copies were published in Germany. . . . It was considered effective anti-Semitic propaganda by the Germans. So I was wrong; Fitzgerald and Lardner were wrong"; see McGilligan and Buhle, 495-539. There is no evidence that Rapf's assertion is true, however, and the *Gesamtverzeichnis des deutschen Schrifttums* ("Complete Catalogue of German Books") indicates that nothing of Schulberg's was printed in Germany until 1956, when a translation of *The Harder They Fall* appeared. Rapf did not repeat the charge in his 1999 autobiography, *Back Lot: Growing Up with the Movies.*

6

THE CONTENDAS

The leading contender for the title of the "real" Sammy Glick was without question writer-producer Jerry Wald (1911–1962), but there were plenty of other worthy candidates, including playwright Norman Krasna (1909–1984), producer Milton Sperling (1912–1988), and even Twentieth Century-Fox production head Darryl F. Zanuck (1902–1979).

Like Sammy, Wald had started on a New York newspaper, got a radio column, and somehow ("innocently," his brother Malvin said in 1998) was involved in 1934 with another writer in submitting as their own a script someone else had written.[1] In 1948, he was awarded the Irving Thalberg Memorial Award, by which time he was also known for collaborating on scripts without asking for screen credit. Wald wrote and produced *Mildred Pierce* (1945) and *Johnny Belinda* (1948). Malvin Wald, also a screen (*Naked City*) and television writer, said Maurice Rapf insisted that Sammy was based on B.P. Schulberg, and that Budd was really retaliating against his father for causing the family breakup. "Preposterous," replied Budd Schulberg. "If B.P. had had more of Sammy's attributes, maybe he'd have survived in Hollywood." Added Schulberg, "the Sidney Fineman character actually was a 'cleaned-up' version of B.P."

Norman Krasna (*Fury, Indiscreet*) also had a news background and had been a film critic and drama editor on several New York papers. In 1950, he and Jerry Wald became partners in a production company.

Milton Sperling (*Marjorie Morningstar, The Court-Martial of Billy Mitchell*) started as a messenger boy in Paramount's Long Island City studios and in 1939, married Harry Warner's daughter, Betty. Schulberg was a guest at the wedding and later admitted to having "used" the ceremony in describing Sammy Glick's wedding in the novel. Still, he was startled some twenty-five years later when, during a friendly discussion in Sperling's den, the producer suddenly remarked, "I want you to know that I understand and don't resent that you were writing about me [as Sammy]." Schulberg, meanwhile, has maintained for more than sixty years that Sammy was "not a single person but a pattern of behavior."[2]

In 1942, Schulberg got a unique compliment for the "accuracy" of his portrait of Sammy. It came from Dr. Franz Alexander, associate professor of psychiatry at the University of Illinois and director of the Institute for Psychoanalysis in Chicago. Writing on the social dynamics at play in the second generation ("re-tribalization," as it came to be known) of many immigrant families in America, Dr. Alexander might have been describing the family from which Sammy Glick had recently fled.

> In most cases the father has lost his prestige in the family for he has had to struggle for his existence, has not learned good English, has been a mediocre provider, and has sometimes been an object of ridicule to his son's contemporaries. . . . His slow ways, especially his cultural interests, are attributed to laziness. The family's future is bound up in the son, for whom everything must be sacrificed. . . . A common solution is that the son usurps the father's place in the mother's affections as well as in economic importance and acquires an inordinate ambition. He wants to justify all his mother's hope and sacrifices and thus appease his guilty conscience about his father.
>
> I am impressed by the accuracy with which [Budd] Schulberg has described this type, a victim of cultural conditions, in his recent novel . . . and how well he has portrayed the hero, Sammy Glick, the "frantic marathoner" of life, "sprinting out of his mother's womb, turning life into a race in which the only rules are fight for the rail, and elbow on the turn, and the only finish-line is death."

Sammy, said the doctor, was "a ruthless careerist, obsessed by the one idea of self-promotion, a caricature of the self-made man, and a threat to Western civilization."

Sammy, already a part of the language, had entered the pantheon of American literary characters with Sinclair Lewis's George Babbitt and Ayn Rand's Howard Roark. Now he was being described in university textbooks and discussed in ivory towers.[3]

NOTES

1. *Twenty Million Sweethearts* (First National, 1934). According to Malvin Wald, brother Jerry wrote the original story. Jerry Wald's agent, Paul Finder Moss, then simply added his own name as "coauthor," sold the story to Warner Bros., and obtained an attractive contract to write (with Wald) the screenplay. When the two newcomers to Hollywood realized they didn't know *how* to do a screenplay, Moss (without the knowledge of the studio, or of Jerry Wald, according to brother Malvin) summoned a former Penn State classmate, Julius Epstein, to Hollywood and put him to work (in a tiny North Hollywood apartment) on a script. Moss later submitted Epstein's screenplay with his and Wald's bylines; but the talented twenty-four-year-old Epstein, who later became famous as an Oscar-winning coauthor of *Casablanca, Arsenic and Old Lace,* and *The Male Animal,* also hadn't known how to write a screenplay. When the studio rejected the script, it assigned two staff writers to do a complete rewrite. The pair, Warren Duff and Harry Sauber, received credit for the shooting script, and Wald and Moss got story credit, although their reputations took a beating when the story began to leak out. The film, a cheerful musical directed by Ray Enright, starred Pat O'Brien, Dick Powell (playing a character based on crooner Russ Columbo), and Ginger Rogers.

2. The "Kit Sargent" character, who leaves Sammy Glick for Al Manheim, was thought to have been based on novelist and short story writer Tess Slesinger (1905–1945). Slesinger and husband Frank Davis were nominated (after her death) for an Academy Award for their screenplay for *A Tree Grows in Brooklyn* (1945). Rapf said that the Manheim character, the "sympathetic Jewish voice who carries the story," was based on his (Rapf's) cousin.

3. Franz Alexander, *Our Age of Unreason* (New York: Lippincott, 1942), 237–238.

7

FITZGERALD AND
WINTER CARNIVAL

Schulberg first met F. Scott Fitzgerald in January 1939 when producer Walter Wanger paired them to write a screenplay for a "college" picture, *Winter Carnival,* parts of which were to be shot at Dartmouth. Schulberg had already written a ten-page treatment and Wanger, a Dartmouth alumnus, hoped Fitzgerald, a Princeton man, could add some vintage flourish. Budd had read and liked Fitzgerald's novels but he thought Fitzgerald was dead; he was astonished when Wanger said, "If he is, he must be the first ghost who ever got $1,500 a week."[1] Fitzgerald's contract at MGM had recently run out and he had just finished a few days' work on *Gone with the Wind* for David Selznick. Neither man knew the other was about to write a "Hollywood" novel. Schulberg was eager to start work on the novel *What Makes Sammy Run?* and Fitzgerald was making plans for *The Last Tycoon,* the book he would not live to finish. The two men hit it off immediately, so much so that they largely ignored the film project in favor of talking about writers and what current college students were doing and thinking. Fitzgerald, Budd recalled, "was fascinated with the details of my childhood, asked to meet my father," and posed seemingly endless questions about "old" Hollywood.

When Wanger learned that only ten pages of script had been written, he ordered both men to head for Dartmouth, hopefully to be inspired by the winter weather in Hanover. Fitzgerald was reluctant to go, but Schulberg was excited at the chance to get back to his old campus. B.P. thought the assignment was such a step up for Budd that he delivered two bottles of champagne to their plane at Lockheed Air Terminal in Burbank. Schulberg noticed that Sheilah Graham was also on the flight, though he was not aware of her relationship with Fitzgerald. Nor was he aware of Scott's alcoholism, and he committed the near-fatal error of urging Fitzgerald to share the champagne. The older writer, uneasy about making the flight, obliged, became drunk, and was still drunk when they got to New York, where he headed for the nearest bar. When Schulberg finally managed to get him on the train to Hanover, Fitzgerald somehow obtained more alcohol en route and was in a sorry state when they reached New Hampshire on February 10. Once there, he continued to drink, caught a serious cold, made a fool of himself in front of faculty and students and, along with Schulberg, was fired (and ordered out of town) by Wanger. When Schulberg and the now clearly ill Fitzgerald returned to New York on February 12 on the Montrealer, no hotel would accept them in their disheveled condition. In desperation, Schulberg took Fitzgerald to Doctors Hospital. Then he notified Sheilah Graham, who—after three days—got Fitzgerald to a hotel room, nursed him for another week, and finally took him back to Los Angeles.

When Wanger returned to New York, Schulberg sought him out and was rehired. Schulberg suggested to Wanger that Maurice Rapf, who by coincidence was in Hanover on his honeymoon, be hired to replace Fitzgerald. "Wanger fired me after six weeks," Rapf remembered. "And Lester Cole came on. I shouldn't have gotten screen credit on the film— and really didn't want it because it was a terrible movie—but all three of us [Budd, Cole, and Rapf] got it."[2] The film's stars were Ann Sheridan and Richard Carlson.

"I don't think I was ever aware, when I first met Scott and he seemed so interested in Hollywood, and how I was raised, that he was writing a novel about Hollywood, or that he was writing a novel at all," Schulberg said in 1998.[3] "I just thought he was curious." Although Schulberg acknowledges that he used the Fitzgerald *Winter Carnival* incident as the "spine" of his 1950 novel *The Disenchanted,* it hadn't occurred to him to use Fitzgerald as a basis, or partial basis, for a fictional character until about 1948. "I did keep notes about Scott and *Winter Carnival,*" he said, "but I didn't really think about *The Disenchanted,* or the Manley Halliday character, until a year or more after I had published *The Harder They Fall.*" Schulberg has insisted for nearly fifty years that—like Sammy Glick—Manley Halliday is not entirely Scott Fitzgerald, but "a combination of a dozen or more talented writers who frittered their careers away in Hollywood."

Fitzgerald used Schulberg as a character in one of his *Esquire* short stories, *The Lost Decade*, in 1939. Only 1,100 words, it is one of Fitzgerald's most haunting stories. In it, a once-famous architect, Louis Trimble (Fitzgerald), tours Fifth Avenue with Orrison Brown (Schulberg), a young news magazine employee (and recent Dartmouth graduate). Trimble has "been away" (drunk) for almost twelve years, and is reacquainting himself with the sober world. Fitzgerald identifies Brown/Schulberg as a "curly-haired man who a year before had edited the Dartmouth *Jack-a-Lantern* [sic]."[4] Schulberg found Fitzgerald "a remarkably endearing man. He really had no pretension. His interests were vast, his memory remarkable. I obviously liked him enormously." And Fitzgerald clearly liked Schulberg. Deeply embarrassed by his sad performance in Hanover on *Winter Carnival*, Scott continued to send suggestions about the script to Budd long after he had been taken off the picture.[5] Schulberg, meanwhile, is proud of his role in the so-called Fitzgerald Revival of the early 1950s. "[T]he timing of my novel, *The Disenchanted*, and the [Arthur] Mizener biography *[The Far Side of Paradise]* appearing in the same season—and even my review of the Mizener book in the Sunday *New York Times*—touched off the popular revival of Scott's work that happily goes on and on," he wrote to a friend in 1986. In 1941, Schulberg and John O'Hara were asked to collaborate on a completion of *The Last Tycoon,* but they declined on grounds that the work of a writer like Fitzgerald should not be tampered with.[6]

NOTES

1. Budd Schulberg, "In Hollywood (In Memory of Scott Fitzgerald: II)," New Republic (3 March 1941), 312.

2. Maurice Rapf, *Back Lot: Growing Up with the Movies.* Lanham, Md.: Scarecrow Press, 1999, 113–122. "My fate is to be tied to a movie clinker named *Winter Carnival,* which is listed in December 1939 by the *New York Times* as one of the ten worst films of that year and a movie that is run almost annually on the Dartmouth campus, where I teach, because it immortalizes a traditional Dartmouth winter event," wrote Rapf. "I could be asked about *Song of the South* or *Cinderella* (both of which I also wrote)—and sometimes I am—but, for some reason, curious movie buffs are more interested in the saga of the ubiquitous and now campy *Winter Carnival.*"

3. It is Budd Schulberg's childhood that "Cecilia Brady" (the narrator) describes as her own at the opening of Fitzgerald's *The Last Tycoon*. In the book, Rudolph Valentino has come to Cecilia's fifth birthday party, just as Jackie Coogan attended one of Budd's real birthday celebrations. Both Cecilia and Budd had been "brought up" in pictures, but "not on the screen"; each was a "producer's child"; and each finally went East, Cecilia to Bennington and Budd to Deerfield and Dartmouth.

4. Somehow Schulberg, who also wrote for *Esquire*, was not aware of the story until 1991. "I don't know how I ever missed it," Schulberg said. "It's a fascinating little vignette." The next year (1940), when Fitzgerald wrote a screenplay (for Lester Cowan) based on his own story *Babylon Revisited*, he changed the name of the child from Honoria to Victoria, in honor of Budd's newborn daughter, Vicki.

5. A part of Fitzgerald, however, apparently saw Schulberg as a literary rival; about the time he sent the glowing letter to Bennett Cerf about *What Makes Sammy Run?* he also wrote in his notebook, "Bud [*sic*], the untalented." Andrew Turnbull, *Scott Fitzgerald* (New York: Scribner's, 1962), 320. In a small way, perhaps, Fitzgerald's friendship with Schulberg was like his ambivalent relationship with Sheilah Graham who, after Fitzgerald's death, found that he had written on the back of her framed photograph, "picture of a prostitute."

6. Scribner's finally published it in its unfinished state, together with *The Great Gatsby* and five of Fitzgerald's short stories, with the help of critic and novelist Edmund Wilson. Wilson, one of Fitzgerald's closest friends at Princeton, added a summary of the unwritten chapters, along with some of Fitzgerald's notes.

8

BOYS IN THE BACK ROOM

Schulberg was friendly with countless other novelists in Hollywood in the years before World War II.[1] He lunched with them at Musso and Frank's Grill, drank with them next door in the back room of Stanley Rose's storied bookshop,[2] and met them across the street in the building that housed the fledgling Screen Writers Guild headquarters.[3] He and O'Hara were best friends from about 1937 until 1950, "when John took offense at something so trivial that no one can remember what it was," Budd said. "It was probably something like borrowing his car and forgetting to fill the tank, but that was the end." Until then, Budd was often called upon to coax O'Hara out of bars and restaurants when he had had too much to drink. "For some crazy reason, John thought I was, or could have been, a great fighter; and all I had to say was, 'OK John, let's go,' and he'd meekly follow me out, when nobody else had been able to handle him," Schulberg said. Schulberg also had a playful friendship with the cocky but charming Bill Saroyan (1908–1981), and he admitted that he wrote the first Sammy Glick story in *Liberty* without quote marks around the dialogue because he was following the style of "William Saroyan and other groundbreakers of the 1930s."[4]

Schulberg's close friendship with novelist and screenwriter Irwin Shaw (1913–1984) was strained for a time in 1941 when Schulberg learned that his wife, Jigee, had begun an affair with Peter Viertel and that Shaw was aware of it, but had chosen not to tell Budd.

NOTES

1. In addition to Saroyan, Shaw, William Faulkner, and Nathanael West, this group of novelists included Guy Endore, Michael Blankfort, Aben Kandell, Jo Pagano, Daniel Fuchs, Tess Slesinger, and John Fante.

2. "Stanley served lousy orange wine, which Faulkner, Hammett, Dottie Parker, and Charlie Brackett drank by the gallon," Schulberg recalled.

3. The Hollywood Center Building (1655 N. Cherokee Avenue) is still standing, just off the corner of Hollywood Boulevard. The story of Sammy Glick in Hollywood is told against the backdrop of the SWG's bitter but successful 1938 campaign to gain certification as the sole bargaining agent for screenwriters. The guild, formed in 1933, fought for a minimum wage for writers and for a rational system to determine screen credits. Until then, credit had been decided by studio executives or producers and frequently was unfair or inaccurate. In a desperate attempt to defeat the SWG, the studios had formed a "company" union called *Screen Playwrights;* the struggle between the two organizations destroyed many friendships.

4. Schulberg was not in awe of the older and more famous writer, and in an undated TLS (probably penned in 1939 or 1940), he told Saroyan of a recent visit to Stanley Rose's establishment, during which Rose asked him to go over several Saroyan essays and stories, written with an eye toward a book about Hollywood. Schulberg wrote, "I belong to the great school of admirers of yours who think you are half as good as you think you are, which is better than most. . . . So now you see where we stand." And in reference to a particular story, "That article seemed so shallow to me that if I tried to jump into it I would break my legs."

9

PAPA

Schulberg had several brushes with Ernest Hemingway, most of them unpleasant. The first occurred in Key West in 1947, when *The Harder They Fall* was near the top of the bestseller lists. At a cocktail party given in honor of "Papa" by their mutual friend Toby Bruce,[1] Hemingway confronted Schulberg and demanded to know what Budd knew about prizefighting "for Christ's sweet sake?" Drinking, and probably jealous of his own reputation as an "expert" on boxing, Hemingway tried to bully Schulberg, grilling him about various boxers' records while trying to "belly-bump" him into a corner. When Schulberg wouldn't be intimidated, answered virtually all of the questions, and asked a few Hemingway couldn't answer, the older man lost interest and withdrew. Three years later, the ever-optimistic Bruce arranged for the two writers to meet in Cuba, but when Schulberg reached the Ambos Mundos Hotel, he was warned that Hemingway had reversed course, did *not* want to see him and was "outraged" that Budd, in *The Disenchanted,* (and Arthur Mizener in *The Far Side of Paradise)* had once again "invaded his territory" (regarding F. Scott Fitzgerald). Schulberg also learned that Papa had called him a "gravedigger."[2] In 1954, however, at the height of the praise for *On the Waterfront,* Schulberg (back in Key West) spoke to Hemingway by telephone and found him surprisingly "magnanimous." "'You've done a lot of good work,' he told me," Schulberg said, "and he was very nice." By then, of course, Hemingway was back on top after the success of *The Old Man and the Sea* in 1952. Their final meeting occurred early in 1960 in a Havana restaurant. Hemingway suddenly appeared and upbraided Schulberg for not attending Jigee's funeral. "One thing we do, we bury our dead," Hemingway told Schulberg, who had been in Mexico and had not learned of his first wife's death until after she was buried.[3]

In a 1999 letter to author, restaurateur, and former bullfighter Barnaby Conrad, Schulberg described his feelings about Hemingway: "What a jackass 'Papa' was about fellow writers. Always found it odd he could be so sensitive in some areas, & write so well, and so myopic & dog-in-the-manger in others. He could lap up praise all right. What bugged him was anyone venturing into areas he felt were his by eminent domain, bullfighting for you, boxing for me, War for Irwin (Shaw). I never forgave him, aside from my own slights, for his ingratitude & boorishness to Scott (Fitzgerald), who went to bat for him early on in a way EH would never have reciprocated."[4]

NOTES

1. In 1957, Schulberg gave Bruce the part of "Joe Bottles" in the film *Wind across the Everglades*.

2. See Schulberg's *Sparring with Hemingway: And Other Legends of the Fight Game* (Chicago: Ivan R. Dee, 1995), 24–25. Hemingway apparently had not read *The Disenchanted*, or at best had only skimmed it, for in a June 2, 1951, letter to Malcolm Cowley, he wrote, "For money Schulberg made Zelda [Fitzgerald] out to be Jewish. Which would have been fine. But she wasn't." In an early chapter of *The Disenchanted*, the "Zelda" character, Jere, playfully misleads the patrician "Fitzgerald" character, Manley Halliday, into thinking she is Jewish; she drops the guise in the next chapter, but Hemingway hadn't read that far. Papa would jump the gun again in May 1952 in another letter to Cowley: "I'm sorry the Fitzgerald boom is over. But it was so violent it would be hard for it to last."

3. Schulberg, *Sparring with Hemingway,* 29–30.

4. Autograph Letter Signed (ALS), January 25, 1999.

10

THE MANLY ART

Schulberg's enduring love-hate relationship with boxing began on an unhappy note in 1921 when, at age six, he accompanied his father to the original Madison Square Garden to see every Jewish kid's hero, Benny Leonard, defend the world lightweight title against Richie Mitchell. When the ticket-takers turned away little Buddy because he wasn't sixteen, Schulberg had to wait almost a dozen years to see his idol in action. On October 7, 1932, Dartmouth freshman Schulberg hopped a train to New York only to see Leonard, in the final bout of his career, get knocked out by Jimmy McLarnin.

Budd later saw plenty of boxing in Los Angeles, one of the country's great fight towns in the late 1930s and early '40s, and he regularly attended matches at the old Vernon Arena, the Olympic Auditorium, and Hollywood Legion Stadium, often rubbing shoulders with ringsiders like Al Jolson, Charlie Chaplin, and Lupe Velez.[1] He thought little of flying cross-country to witness a big match, and was in New York in June 1941 when Joe Louis came from behind to beat Billy Conn.[2]

In late 1942, not long before he entered the U.S. Navy, Schulberg began work on a boxing story he called "Gigante," based partly on the career of 1933-1934 heavyweight champion Primo Carnera. In it, the boxer is mercilessly exploited by his managers and finally is killed in the ring. Five years later, Random House published the story in novel form as *The Harder They Fall* and it was an immediate success.[3] Former champion Gene Tunney said it was the best novel about boxing he had read since George Bernard Shaw's *Cashell Byron's Profession*, called it "brilliant, witty, and amusing," and ventured the opinion that it was the equal of Hemingway's short stories "The Killers" and "Fifty Grand."[4] The *New Republic* said, "Schulberg contemplates the boxing spectacle with the eye of a scientist, the heart of a sardonic moralist, and the frank interest of a fight fan." Schulberg hoped to follow this triumph with a nonfiction book called *Machiavelli on Eighth Avenue* about boxing promoter Mike Jacobs, but his Random House editor, Saxe Commins, fearing Schulberg's stature as a serious writer could be harmed, talked Budd out of it. Instead, it was serialized in five parts in *Collier's* as "Champions for Sale: The Mike Jacobs Story" in the spring of 1950. Despite Commins' fears, for the next half-century—and with no apparent damage to his reputation—Schulberg continued to write about the sport he loves, either as *Sports Illustrated's* first boxing editor, as ringside reporter for the *New York Post* and *Newsday*, or as feature writer for boxing journals such as *Boxing Illustrated, International Boxing Digest,* and the most recent boxing journal, *Fight Game.* In 1969, he was one of 102 indignant writers and celebrities (ranging from painter Jasper Johns to Igor Stravinsky) who demanded that Muhammad Ali (who had been "stripped" two years earlier of the heavyweight championship for refusing induction into the military) be allowed to defend the title. In 1972, Schulberg authored a book on Ali, *Loser and Still Champion: Muhammad Ali.* In 1984, he scripted and coproduced (with fight film collector and Mike Tyson comanager Jim Jacobs) the two-part documentary "Joe Louis: For All Time" for ABC–TV; and in 1995, he published *Sparring with Hemingway and Other Legends of the Fight Game,* a collection of his nonfiction.

Asked in 1973 to predict whether boxing would survive, Schulberg summed up his feelings in a letter to Barnaby Conrad:

> In this rapidly changing world it may be foolhardy to predict what will happen to any form of human expression in 1975, much less 1995. But I doubt that boxing will be as dead as some people like to think. After all, it's been around in one way or another since the days of ancient Crete, and I seriously doubt that Watergate, cassettes, or any other of our present or future phenomena will bring about its demise. Despite all our scientific advances, there still seems to be an element that persists in the human spirit, the element of contention, competition and proving oneself through courage and grace. It's true that the small boxing clubs are gone, and that there are fewer professional boxers today than there were a generation ago. On the other hand, free television and close circuit television bring boxing to scores of millions, even hundreds of millions, who never would have watched a boxing match thirty years ago. I have my nights

when things go wrong in the ring and I'm not very proud of my devotion, or is it addiction, to the prizefight world. But there are other times, just as there are in the bull ring, when one feels not debased but exhilarated, intensified and increased by the lonely battle fought with unflinching skill. I don't know—I'll do my damndest to be here to see it—but I have a feeling that the positive qualities we find in boxing today will still be needed fifteen or twenty years from now.[5]

More than a quarter of a century later, however, in a letter to *New York Daily News* sports columnist Bill Gallo, Schulberg repeated an oft-expressed concern for fighters: "As these troops of sick and needy ringmen march across my mind, I can't help asking: couldn't the fight game borrow a page from the theater or the film industry and organize some program of constructive aid for those veterans who gave freely, perhaps too freely, of their blood and courage and skills when they were prime, but have since run out of health, money, eyesight, coordination—and maybe hope?"[6]

NOTES

1. See Schulberg's "Mosley-De La Hoya and My Old Hometown, L.A." *Fight Game* (November 2000), 52–57, for his recollections of growing up during the city's heyday as a boxing center second to none.

2. In the 1950s, when Schulberg was involved in the production end of his own film projects, he saw to it that former fighters he was fond of appeared in his films. Abe Simon, Tony Galento, and Tami Mauriello (each of whom had fought title bouts with Joe Louis) were in *On the Waterfront,* as was Lee Oma, who challenged Ezzard Charles for the heavyweight crown. Galento was also in *Wind across the Everglades.* In 1947, Schulberg became the manager of Trenton, N.J., heavyweight boxer Archie McBride. In a moderately successful career that lasted until 1967, McBride faced a number of top fighters, including world champions Floyd Patterson and Ingemar Johansson. Schulberg described his managerial career in "Confessions of an Ex-Fight Manager" in the magazine *Fight Game* (July 2000), 54–57. When Schulberg wed his third wife, actress Geraldine Brooks, in 1964 in Beverly Hills, his best men were former world flyweight champion Fidel La Barba and the original California "Golden Boy," Art Aragon.

3. Boxing old-timers used to say that turn-of-the-century heavyweight champion Bob Fitzsimmons, when warned that challenger James J. Jeffries was "big and strong," replied, "That's all right. The bigger they are, the harder they fall."

4. Gene Tunney, "Caneravorous Fight Racketeers." *Saturday Review of Literature* XXX, no. 32 (9 August 1947), 9–10.

5. TLS, Schulberg to Conrad, December 11, 1973.

6. Letter from Schulberg to Bill Gallo, mentioned in Gallo's column, March 5, 2000.

11

WORLD WAR II AND
THE DISENCHANTED

After the Japanese attack on Pearl Harbor, many of Hollywood's eligible party members and other "premature antifascists" found that their left-wing pasts often made them "unfit" for military service. Maurice Rapf, who said recruiting officers invariably asked if he'd been in the Communist Party, tried unsuccessfully to get into the Marine Corps' photographic unit, the OSS, and the U.S. Navy's Industrial Sound Division. Ring Lardner Jr. was rejected (always after security checks) by the Marines, the OSS, and the Office of War Information.[1] Even Dorothy Parker, who merely wanted to work as a war correspondent, was denied a passport. Schulberg, however, was somehow able to enter the U.S. Navy on March 10, 1943, with a direct commission. He served in John Ford's Office of Strategic Services photographic unit in Washington, D.C., where he was later joined by his brother Stuart (born in 1922), a Marine Corps officer. "We were with our unit in London, Paris, then into Germany, and finally winding up in Berlin when Hitler quit," Schulberg said. "Gen. ['Wild Bill'] Donovan [founder of the OSS] assigned me to head a unit to uncover and assemble film and still photographs that could be used as evidence against major war criminals at Nuremberg."[2]

In February 1943, after his divorce from Jigee, Schulberg had married stage and film actress Victoria "Vicki" Anderson, who would bear him two sons, Stephen (born in 1944) and David (born in 1946). When Schulberg was released from active duty on March 17, 1946, they purchased the fifty-five-acre Inghamdale Farm in Bucks County, Pennsylvania, where among the neighbors were Richard Rodgers, Oscar Hammerstein II, Moss Hart, and George S. Kaufman, and where Budd began to mull over the book that would become *The Disenchanted* (1950).

"One day I drew up a list of writers who had achieved something in the 1920s and then had lost their way and gone off on difficult tangents," Schulberg said. "I think I stopped at 12. My father had preferred 'literary' writers, and it was exciting for me, as a kid, to meet them. But then, maybe ten years later, I would find them dull and talking a certain way, and yet nothing produced. They always swore they would make some money and then stay out of Hollywood, but they never did." Manley Halliday, the hero of *The Disenchanted*, "seems like F. Scott Fitzgerald," Schulberg said, "but he partakes of many writers I knew who had talent and who went to Hollywood and who got short circuited."[3]

Schulberg's list ("Did I Say 12, or 20?") includes Sidney Buchman (1902–1977), who wrote the screenplay for *Mr. Smith Goes to Washington* and cowrote *Here Comes Mr. Jordan*; Horace McCoy (1897–1955), *They Shoot Horses, Don't They?* and *Kiss Tomorrow Good-Bye*; Samuel Hoffenstein (1890–1947), coscreenwriter of *An American Tragedy* and *Dr. Jekyll and Mr. Hyde*; Edwin Justus Mayer (1896–1955), *To Be or Not to Be*; Sinclair Lewis (1892–1950), *Babbitt, Dodsworth, Main Street*, etc.; Dorothy Parker (1893–1967), *A Star Is Born*; Dashiell Hammett (1894–1961), *The Thin Man*; Joe Mankiewicz (1909–1993), *Cleopatra and All About Eve;* and brother Herman Mankiewicz (1897–1953), *Citizen Kane;* John V. A. Weaver (1893–1938), a poet and playwright, and film critic for *Vanity Fair;* Schulberg's own father, B.P.; and even novelist William Faulkner (1897–1962).[4] To these names, he adds Marshall "Mickey" Neilan (1891–1958) who, although not a writer, had a "rollercoaster" career as a Hollywood director; and playwright Vincent Lawrence (1890–1946), *Sea of Grass, Gentleman Jim, Test Pilot,* who once had three shows running at the same time on Broadway.[5]

The Disenchanted, heavily praised by James M. Cain in the *New York Times Book Review*, was quickly named a Book of the Month Club selection and then was picked as one of the three outstanding works of fiction for 1950 by the American Library Association and the National Book Critics. By February 1951, it had gone through six printings. Eight years later, the play *The Disenchanted*, written by Schulberg with poet and *New York Times Book Review* editor Harvey Breit, opened at the Coronet Theatre and played 189 performances. It starred Jason Robards Jr. as Halliday, George Grizzard as the Schulberg-like Shep Stearns, Rosemary Harris as Jere Wilder Halliday,[6] Salome Jens as Georgette, and Jason Robards Sr. as Burt Seixas.[7] It was clearly one of the top shows on Broadway during the 1958–1959 season; but Archibald MacLeish's *J. B.,* directed by Elia Kazan, captured the Pulitzer Prize, and Lorraine Hansberry's *A Raisin in the Sun* won the New York Drama Critics Circle Award. Robards Jr., however, was cited by the Critics Circle for his "outstanding contribution to the art of the theater."[8]

Schulberg would return to the unique problems of writers, notably in *The Four Seasons of Success* (1972) and in its revised version, *Writers in America* (1983). In perceptive essays (that first appeared in *Esquire*) about Fitzgerald, Saroyan, John Steinbeck, Tom Heggen, and Nathanael West, Schulberg skillfully probed the American writer's dilemma in achieving, maintaining, and recapturing critical success.[9]

NOTES

1. He finally was able to enlist in the Army Signal Corps and served a short tour making training films in Astoria, N.Y.

2. Schulberg to author, 1999. One of Schulberg's more ironic tasks was to locate famed documentary filmmaker Leni Riefenstahl, who had made *Triumph of the Will* for the Nazis in 1934 and *Olympiad* in 1936. Schulberg, who had helped organize a boycott of Riefenstahl when she visited Hollywood in 1939, did not believe her claims that she was "apolitical" and ignorant of what Hitler and the Nazis were up to. When he found her in Bavaria, he took her to Nuremberg as a material witness. See Budd Schulberg, "Nazi Pin-Up Girl," *Saturday Evening Post* (30 March 1946), 16. In 1973, Riefenstahl called Schulberg the leader of a "Hate Leni" cult. For Schulberg's reply to the allegation, see Appendix D (letter to *Variety,* 23 May 1973), 247. In April 1946, Schulberg received a commendation from the U.S. Army.

For meritorious service rendered the Office of Strategic Services and this unit from 15 July 1945 to 25 November 1945, Lieutenant (j.g.) Schulberg, a member of the Field Photographic Branch, with tireless devotion to duty, great vision and initiative, directed the collection, under the most difficult conditions, of vast quantities of photographic evidence of German war guilt and crimes against humanity. This evidence, which includes tens of millions of feet of motion picture film, not only assisted materially in the prosecution of the major war criminals but also has tremendous value to the United States Government intelligence and research agencies for the establishment of a permanent photographic record of European political and military developments during the past two critical decades. By this commendation, Lieutenant (j.g.) Schulberg is hereby authorized to wear the Army Commendation Ribbon by direction of the Secretary of War.

3. Harvey Breit, *The Writer Observed,* (New York: World Publishing Co., 1956), 140.

4. An incident in the novel *The Disenchanted* in which the frail and fatigued diabetic Manley Halliday asks squeamish Shep Stearns to administer his insulin injection was borrowed from Schulberg's own life, but it was Edwin Justus Mayer, not Fitzgerald, who told Budd he might one day need such a favor. Schulberg also said he once invited John V. A. Weaver to Dartmouth, "and he too disgraced himself with the English Department and fell off the train at White River."

5. Of all the writers he knew, said Schulberg, "Vincent Lawrence was the one who taught me to write."

6. Many readers and theatergoers assumed that the character of Manley Halliday's wife, Jere, was based on Zelda Fitzgerald, with perhaps a little of Jigee added in, but Schulberg told the author he drew more on his second wife, Vicki.

7. In 1983, Anthony Burgess (*A Clockwork Orange*) said that he had read the novel sixteen times, and he included it in his list of the *Ninety-Nine Best Novels* of the century. See Anthony Burgess, Introduction to *The Disenchanted* (London: Allison & Busby, 1983), 5.

8. More than four decades later, in January 1999, a French-language adaptation of the play opened a five-week run at the Silva Montfort Theater in Paris. The one-character play, directed by Francois Bourgeat, starred (as Manley Halliday) Jean-Pierre Cassel (known to American audiences as the bumbling King Louis XIII in the films *The Three Musketeers* [1973] and *The Four Musketeers* [1974]). Schulberg was in the audience on opening night.

9. In *Writers in America*, Schulberg expanded the introduction and epilogue, and lengthened the material on Saroyan.

12

THE HOUSE COMMITTEE

In the spring of 1951, the House Committee on Un-American Activities began its second round of hearings into subversive activities in the motion picture industry. The first HCUA hearings into Hollywood, in 1947, had resulted in the jailing (for contempt) of the so-called Hollywood (or "Unfriendly") Ten.[1] One of the first witnesses called in the new round was screenwriter Richard Collins (*Song of Russia, Riot in Cell Block 11*), the husband of actress Dorothy Comingore of *Citizen Kane* fame. Collins had been blacklisted in 1947, was now a "cooperating witness," and on April 12 named, among other former Party members, Budd Schulberg.[2] Schulberg, by then firmly anti-Communist, had already voluntarily made known his Communist Party past "to an investigative agency of the Federal Government"; he responded by telegram to the HCUA on April 14, stating that his "opposition to communists and Soviet dictatorship" was well-known and that he would cooperate with the committee. He testified on May 23, 1951.[3]

"My willingness to testify was a complicated thing," Schulberg said in 1998. "I knew I couldn't take the Fifth, or the First (although it passed my mind), and by then I had joined with Arthur Koestler, in New Hope [Pennsylvania] in the Funds for International Freedom, and I was now tithing ten percent of my salary to FIF, just as I had to the Party back in the 1930s." His apparent intention was to identify only those named in previous testimony, but one of the seventeen he cited was Tilly Lerner, and she was named *only* by him. "I'm not really sure how that happened," he said.

Schulberg scoffed at the notion that the Hollywood Communists were merely civil libertarians, and he said to Victor Navasky in 1980 that he had testified because he felt guilty for unwittingly contributing to

41

intellectual, artistic, and racial oppression. He told Navasky that the CP was a totalitarian society and that his guilt was what he and others had done to the Czechs, not to Ring Lardner, Jr.[4]

> You're called by HUAC, and you don't want to act to endorse its thought control, but you know the greatest thought control you've experienced was from the Party. I expressed doubts [about naming names]—it would be inhuman not to. But I truly felt the Communist Party was a menace. It was hard for me to see myself doing anything to help the Communist Party. It was especially a menace for the left and liberals. The CP uses them for protective coloration.
>
> I thought what was happening in Russia was more repressive than anything we were doing in this country, and I didn't trust people who didn't want to fight it. All of that affected what I did before the Committee.[5]

Schulberg told Navasky, "They question our talking. I question their silence. There were premature anti-fascists but there were also premature anti-Stalinists."[6]

Ring Lardner Jr., who shared an Academy Award for writing *Woman of the Year* in 1942 and won again in 1970 for *M*A*S*H,* believed that his old friend named names because he was afraid he'd be blacklisted. "But he shouldn't have been," Lardner said. "By that time he had a couple of books and didn't need Hollywood."[7] After Schulberg's testimony, he and Lardner were still cordial when they met, but they were no longer close.[8] "Ring and I were civil to each other, and once, in the 1960s, we agreed to meet in New York [at "Blake's," a reporters' hangout on 43rd Street, used by Schulberg as background in the early chapters of *Sammy*] to resolve our differences by talking them out," Schulberg said. "It began well, but then we started to argue and decided to call it off."

Lardner (1915–2000) had a slightly different recollection of the meeting at Blake's, which he remembered as spontaneous. "Budd and I were standing at a bar at the same time and we got into what became quite a public discussion. All these newspapermen were hanging around, and they started listening. Budd was justifying what he did, and I told him he wasn't very consistent, because he had said he was doing this out of patriotism and because those people should be exposed, and yet he had deliberately not named several people who were very close to him, relatives. So he admitted that. We argued the whole thing for a couple of hours. I've seen him a couple of times since. On those occasions we speak, but nothing warm."[9]

Maurice Rapf, one of those not named by Schulberg, agrees that Budd need not have testified. "He didn't have to appear, but his father and others talked him into it," claimed Rapf, who did not see or speak to Schulberg for the next twelve years.[10] Screenwriter Walter Bernstein (*Fail-Safe, The Front*), who had known Schulberg at Dartmouth and after, was another Party member not named by Schulberg, although he said he felt "personally betrayed" at the time by the testimony.[11]

In June 1971, when Hollywood Ten screenwriter and director Herbert Biberman *(Salt of the Earth)* died, his *New York Times* obituary stated in a separate paragraph that he had been identified as a CPUSA member by Schulberg, causing Schulberg to complain to the *Times* that he was being singled out as Biberman's *only* accuser and that it was not only unfair but inaccurate. In fact, two other witnesses, Meta Rosenberg and Edward Dmytryk, had named Biberman before Schulberg testified (and more than a dozen others identified him after Schulberg's appearance). Further, Biberman had been named as a Communist in 1942 before the California Committee on Un-American Activities and had served six months in jail after his 1950 conviction for contempt of Congress.

In support of these facts, Schulberg's third wife, actress Geraldine Brooks, submitted to *The Times* a day later a memo which she said was "to be appended to *The New York Times* obit of Biberman in order to represent true historical fact rather than lie through innuendo so that readers of *The New York Times* in the future shall not be misled as were readers of the original obit."[12]

What may have particularly rankled the Schulbergs was that Alden Whitman, the *New York Times* reporter who wrote the Biberman obituary, naming only Schulberg among the accusers, had himself invoked the First Amendment when asked by the Senate Internal Security Subcommittee about his own Communist past.

If Lardner chose not to snub or insult Schulberg, others did. In Navasky's chapter, "The Informer as Victim," he reports that on the day the Biberman obituary appeared, Schulberg went to the Lion's Head Inn in Greenwich Village only to be met by a local character who asked him what he was doing there and expressed mock surprise that Schulberg wasn't sitting shivah (in Hebrew, to "mourn for the dead") for Biberman.

Navasky said Schulberg took a punch at the man but missed and another patron broke it up. Schulberg also suffered through a cocktail party encounter with Lillian Hellman, who disputed his claims that Russian dissident writer Isaac Babel and others had been killed in Soviet camps by shouting "Prove it!" "Prove it!" And one night when Schulberg and Harvey Breit were leaving Sardi's, they met blacklisted playwright John Wexley, a neighbor of Schulberg's, who shook hands with Breit but pretended Schulberg was not there.[13]

NOTES

1. Writer-director Billy Wilder quipped that "maybe two" of the Unfriendly Ten had real talent. "The others were just unfriendly."

2. As late as 1949, the California Senate's Fact-Finding Committee on Un-American Activities still listed Schulberg as a member, or recent member, of three organizations cited by the U.S. Attorney General as Communist fronts: the American Committee for Protection of Foreign Born, the League of American Writers (in 1942), and the National Federation for Constitutional Liberties. The extent of the California committee's fervor is indicated by the fact that in its annual report that year it noted ominously that Schulberg was a "supporter of Henry Wallace," the former U.S. vice-president who had been the Progressive Party's nominee for President in 1948. See *Un-American Activities in California, 1949,* 482–512.

3. Schulberg's full testimony appears as Appendix A.

4. Victor Navasky, *Naming Names* (New York: Viking Books, 1980), 242. In August 1951, Schulberg wrote a lengthy piece for *Saturday Review* about his meetings with Lawson and Jerome, about how Charles Glenn was forced to withdraw his praise for *What Makes Sammy Run?* and about the violence used by the Soviets against Russian writers "who dare assert their independence and individuality." The magazine decided to hold it until after the HCUA had concluded its hearings, and the article finally appeared in the August 30, 1952, issue (pp. 6–7, 31–37) as *Collision with the Party Line.* After his testimony, Schulberg said he began to think of himself as an "independent liberal." He said, "My politics haven't changed, except for no longer thinking that the Communist Party would be the vanguard of social change to improve the lot of people on the bottom." Asked by columnist Army Archerd (*Variety,* 11 February 1999) if he'd make a different decision today about his testimony, Schulberg said, "It's an interesting and delicate subject. I still feel very strongly anti-communist." But he added that he believed many innocent people ("along with the real ones") had been harmed by the hearings and the subsequent blacklisting.

5. Navasky, *Naming Names,* 243–246. Schulberg, replying to a question by *Cineaste* editor Dan Georgakas about Navasky's 1980 *Naming Names,* said, "There simply isn't space (within the interview format) to cite all the misquotations and questionable paraphrases. Under the guise of 'fair play,' it's a hatchet job"; and "His [Navasky's] pretense of balance is overstated." See Dan Georgakas and Lenny Rubenstein, eds., *The Cineaste Interviews on the Art and Politics of the Cinema* (Chicago: Lake View Press, 1983), 360–379.

6. Navasky, *Naming Names,* 246.

7. In fact, Bennett Cerf had already assured Schulberg that his testimony would not matter to Random House, either way.

8. Lardner's second wife, Frances Chaney, would neither shake hands with nor speak to Schulberg.

9. Griffin Fariello, *Red Scare: Memories of the American Inquisition. An Oral History* (New York: Norton, 1995), 265–266.

10. Rapf quit the party in 1946 "out of boredom" and because he believed he couldn't be a filmmaker and a good Communist at the same time. He continued to think of himself as a Communist, however, and even today speaks of the nobility of the cause of the Hollywood Communists of the 1930s. Although twice elected secretary of the Screen Writers Guild, he left Hollywood for good after being blacklisted in 1947.

11. Patrick McGilligan and Paul Buhle, *Tender Comrades: A Backstory of the Hollywood Blacklist* (New York: St. Martin's Press, 1997), 48. Bernstein reread the record in 1997, however, and said he found Schulberg's testimony "quite interesting." "Whereas I didn't believe (Elia) Kazan's or (Robert) Rossen's changed positions for a moment, I could understand it in Budd." Bernstein said the party attacks on *What Makes Sammy Run?* had been "very disturbing" to Schulberg. Of those who testified, Bernstein said, "only Schulberg represents anything of himself."

12. Navasky, *Naming Names,* 241. Navasky later found Ms. Brooks' "appendage" to the Whitman obituary in the *New York Times'* Schulberg file. It read, in part, "The fact was that Biberman, as one of the most outspoken of the original Communist leaders, had been mentioned by many previous witnesses before the Committee. Schulberg simply corroborated a list of names that had already been corroborated many times over."

13. Navasky, *Naming Names,* 241–243, 377.

13

THE WATERFRONT
IN MULTIMEDIA

Schulberg was now working on a screenplay based on Malcolm John-son's 1948 Pulitzer Prize series "Crime on the Waterfront" in the *New York Sun*.[1] He had purchased the rights to the series, and in early 1952 discussed them with Broadway and Hollywood director Elia Kazan (*Gentleman's Agreement, Streetcar Named Desire, Viva Zapata*).[2] Kazan (born in 1909), whose films were distinguished by their sense of social justice, owed Darryl F. Zanuck a picture at Twentieth Century-Fox, and Zanuck said he was willing to take a look. Schulberg had already done some nine months of research on the docks (mostly on the West Side of Manhattan where the luxury line piers were dominated by the "Bowers Mob," and later at Hoboken, N.J., and at Red Hook in Brooklyn), where he gained the friendship of the longshoremen by drinking with them, talking box-ing, and showing sympathy for their cause. He became involved with the crusading waterfront Jesuit priest, Father John Corridan[3]; and he per-suaded one veteran dockworker (Arthur Brown, "Brownie") to live for a time with him in Saxe Commins' home in Princeton, N.J., so that the longshoreman could check the authenticity of the language in the script.[4]

To this day, a familiar story in Hollywood says that when Kazan and Schulberg finally had a definitive meeting with Zanuck in 1953, Zanuck rejected the film and said, "I'm afraid, boys, all you've got here is a lot of sweaty longshoreman." Zanuck's files appear to dispute this account and even to indicate that he was initially eager to make the film, which by then was called *Waterfront*.[5] Zanuck did meet twice with Schulberg in February 1953, after which he wrote to both Schulberg and Kazan say-ing that he felt he and Budd had "solved all of the story differences be-tween us," with the exception of whether Terry Malloy would have a teenage son in the story. But Schulberg says that Zanuck's memos are "not accurate." Said Schulberg in 1999: "I did see Zanuck. He had some wild ideas, like, 'It needs something more, like what if Marlon is working for the FBI?' And, of course, he said he wouldn't do the film unless we could deliver Marlon."[6] Schulberg continued: "Then, the next day, Zanuck sent us transcripts of both meetings; but they included *only the things that Zanuck had said, and none of my replies.*" Still, on February 12, 1953, Zanuck wrote again to Budd and Gadg (Kazan's nickname): "if you come to me with this story in its present state and you say, 'I have got Marlon Brando for this picture,' then it is a clear-cut and simple decision for me to make." Said Schulberg: "But, of course, we *did not have* Marlon, and I had not (and would not have) followed Zanuck's 'line' with regard to the script; so I warned Gadg on our train trip west not to be too optimistic; and the meeting with Zanuck was a fiasco."

As it turned out, it was precisely at this moment that Twentieth Century-Fox committed itself to the newly debuted wide-screen CinemaScope process and to a series of "spectacles" that could fill the wider screen. Zanuck later cited this radical changeover as his reason for rejecting the project. "I had no alternative but to back away from intimate stories even though they were good stories," Zanuck wrote to Kazan after Columbia had released the film to rave reviews the following year. Zanuck told Kazan he had just read a July 11, 1954, *New York Times* story by Schulberg, in which Budd (without naming Zanuck) said the studio boss had lost his courage and had run out on a "touchy" subject. "I cannot accept the idea that I lost my courage or gave you a quick brush-off," the indignant Zanuck wrote. "I spent more time on your project than I do on some of the pictures that we actually produce. In addition to this I invested $40,000 in the property. If this is a brush-off then I have a wrong interpretation of that phrase."

After the film had been turned down at Fox, it was also rejected by Warner Bros. ("Jack Warner wanted Kazan for a film, but not *this* one," said Schulberg), MGM, Paramount, and twice by Columbia. Schulberg was ready to throw in the towel, but Kazan told him, "Budd, believe me, before I take another picture out here, I give you my word I'm gonna do your script if I have to get a hand-held camera and shoot it myself on the docks, with our longshoremen and actors from the [Actors] Studio. I'll make it on a shoestring, but I'll make it." Then Schulberg ran into independent producer Sam Spiegel at the Beverly Hills Hotel and showed him the script. Spiegel liked it and the project was revived, first at United Artists (with Frank Sinatra as Terry), and finally at Columbia with Brando.[7] It was shot, in thirty-six days, for a bare-bones $906,000, with Brando and Kazan each receiving $100,000.[8] The film captured a total of eight Oscars (and twelve total nominations), including best picture for 1954 and best story and screenplay for Schulberg.[9] Brando won the best actor Oscar, and Eva Marie Saint (in her film debut) won for best actress in a supporting role.[10] Rod Steiger, Karl Malden, and Lee J. Cobb all were nominated for best supporting actor. *On the Waterfront* opened in October 1954 and grossed more than $9.5 million in its initial release.[11]

Predictably, Schulberg and Kazan almost immediately were accused in 1954 of using *On the Waterfront* as an apologia for testifying; and indeed it seems to be accepted as fact in many film studies programs and among most film critics that the motion picture is a calculated rejoinder to Arthur Miller's play *The Crucible,* which extolled those who refused to give into hysteria during the Salem witch trials. In his autobiography, the defiant Kazan said yes, "when critics say that I put my story and my feelings on the screen, to justify my informing, they are right," but Schulberg is just as adamant that he had no such motivation.[12]

"Knowing me," Schulberg wrote in a letter in 1992, "can you imagine a situation in which Kazan, provoked by Miller's attack on him and other friendly witnesses via '*The Crucible,*' comes to me to write an answer, in dramatic form, glorifying informers? It's a gratuitous insult. I seem to be fighting a losing battle in explaining that the Terry Malloy role was not based on Kazan's testifying to HCUA but rather the testimony of the rebel longshoremen. Even taken at face value, was Brando betraying his *friends?* My God, if they were watching the film, Terry (Marlon) was testifying because the people he took for friends at the opening had been revealed as stone killers who would use him as a pawn in a cold-blooded murder to frighten others from joining in a protest movement." Schulberg, who had attended all forty of the New York Waterfront Crime Hearings, said it was the dock rebels, taking their lives in their hands to testify against their violently corrupt union and stevedore bosses, who provided him with the ideal climax for the film. "Snitch may be a dirty word, but standing up for the truth, paying the price of the whistle blower, is the other

side of that coin," he said. "To see the film as a metaphor for Mc-
Carthyism is to trivialize their courage."[13]

In a letter published in part in the *Los Angeles Times Book Review,*
Schulberg went further:

> The best you can say for the revisionists with their convenient theories
> dipped in their own political prejudice (let's hear it for anti-anticommunism!)
> is that Kazan's direction may have been energized by some sense that the cli-
> max justified his own position before HUAC. Not that the energy that
> Kazan poured into all his work needed much extra stimulation. Kazan may
> have said that it gave him some extra satisfaction to direct Brando as Terry
> testifying against the labor racketeers with whom he was aligned at the open-
> ing of the film. He may have drawn some self-justification in mounting those
> scenes. But to isolate that emotion as the inspiration for our film is to put the
> cart before the horse.[14]

Ironically, Marlon Brando would later position himself in the fore-
front of those maintaining that the film *was* made to justify Kazan and
Schulberg's testimony. "I was reluctant to take the part [of Terry Malloy]
because I was conflicted about what Gadg had done," Brando wrote in
his 1994 autobiography.[15] "I decided to do the film, but what I didn't realize then was that *On the Waterfront* was really a metaphorical argument
by Gadg and Budd Schulberg: they made the film to justify finking on
their friends."[16]

Even more surprising was Brando's claim that he and Rod Steiger
(who played Terry Malloy's mobster brother) had "improvised" the memorable "I coulda been a contenda" scene in the taxi. After a "creative
fight" with Kazan, said Brando, "Rod and I improvised the scene and
ended up changing it completely." This assertion prompted Schulberg to
demand that his old publisher, Random House (which also had published
the Brando book), request a retraction from the actor. Schulberg also sent
letters to leading newspaper book review editors, expressing his belief that
"he [Brando] transformed himself so completely into Terry Malloy that
he actually came to believe he was making it up as he went along."[17] To
radio and television host Larry King, who was about to do a TV interview with Brando, Schulberg faxed a document that read, in part: "At-
tached is a copy of the 5-page scene written more than half a year before
Marlon arrived. One afternoon when Marlon had to leave [the set] early,

before the reverse close-up on Steiger could be shot, Kazan read his [Brando's] lines off-camera from my script."[18] Added Schulberg: "I hold no malice toward Marlon, whom I respect as a human being who truly cares about the causes he has upheld. . . . But a regard for truth and film history requires [a] retraction." Finally, to Brando personally, he wrote, "The last thing I want to do is get into a hassle with you. I've always felt we shared a lot of feelings for people in common and I really felt in sync with you the last time I was in L.A. when you called me at the hotel. But these things you've written re: *Waterfront* really hurt my pride, my sense of values and respect for the truth. So I do ask you to reconsider statements that strike me as misinforming and preconceived. I look forward to talking to you, and despite these stated differences, I wish you well."[19] Brando did not reply, nor did he issue a retraction.[20]

The actor had also claimed that Kazan and Schulberg met with the Mafia to ask permission to make the film. Not true, said Schulberg in his letter to King. "Would the mob give permission to a film attacking organized-crime control of the harbor?" Schulberg said that Kazan had regular Hoboken police protection from the mob during the shoot, and that once, when mob "enforcers" crowded Kazan against the pier, "Lt. (Joe) Marotta, brother of the police chief, called them off."[21]

Although insistent that the taxi scene was "played exactly as written," Schulberg still had praise for Brando's performance. "Marlon could hurt or help a scene," said Schulberg. "He was awfully creative and often *could* improve the lines." Schulberg also acknowledged that Kazan "improved" the love scene between Brando and Eva Marie Saint. "He took something away from the *verbal* interplay, but the way it was staged and shot gave it greater emotional impact."[22]

In 1955, a year after the film premiered, Random House published Schulberg's novel *Waterfront*. The novel was originally to have been published simultaneously with the release of the motion picture, but Schulberg's energies had to be focused on the film and the book was temporarily put aside.

"It's really accidental that the novel wasn't done first," Schulberg told his friend, *New York Times Book Review* editor Harvey Breit, in 1955. "I thought of it as a novel first. I studied the waterfront as I would for a novel. But the timetable wouldn't allow me to get to it first, that's all. I spent so much time, almost five years, on the waterfront, eating in people's houses, drinking at their bars, that when the picture was over—in spite of its success—I still felt my job wasn't over. I had more to say."[23]

What Schulberg wanted to do in the novel was to give equal time (along with the Brando character, Terry) to the character based on waterfront priest John Corridan, who had suffered not only for opposing the mob for also for defying his archdiocese. In the novel, the waterfront priest, Schulberg wrote in *Saturday Review*, "is brought to stage center, is allowed to share the action with Terry and to dominate the thinking of the book. The novel has not only time but the obligation to examine this with great care. . . . The violent action line of Terry Malloy is now seen for what it is, one of the many moral crises in the spiritual-social development of Father Barry."[24]

Describing for Breit the essential difference between motion pictures and novels, Schulberg said,

> The film, for definition, is tightly disciplined and is best when it concentrates on a single theme. It is related more to the short story than to the novel. It has no time for what I would call essential digression. A film is forced to go from significant episode to significant episode. It can't wander as life sometimes wanders, or pause as life always pauses. A picture has a relentless order; a novel has an order, but it's less restrictive, less your master. I don't agree with the critics who wanted more social analysis in the movie [*On the Waterfront*], but I do it in the novel; it's the novel's job to do it. I'm glad the book is coming out after the effect of the film has waned.

The novel was well received. *New York Times* book critic Orville Prescott called the book "a harsh, grim, indignant, sympathetic story that loses little in dramatic impact because its major characters and story are familiar"; and in a separate review in the *Times Book Review,* another writer said the book was "white-hot fiction with all the menace, suspense, narrative flow, fresh characterization, and social message anybody could reasonably expect in a novel. . . . It's the best of Schulberg, a full-fledged performance by a gifted American writer."[25]

Despite the praise and the critical success of the novel, however, it was clear that the book and its expanded focus had been lost in the acclaim for the movie, and Schulberg was still anguished over the limitations the motion picture had placed on his ability to explore the ordeal of his waterfront priest.[26]

At some point in the mid-1980s, Schulberg and his old Dartmouth collaborator and friend, veteran radio and television writer Stan Silverman, decided there was another way to tell the equal stories of Terry Malloy and Father Barry/Corridan. They determined that the stage could combine the best drama of motion pictures with the expanded detail possible on the stage.

"As far as I'm concerned, the main reason for doing the play is to tell that story," Schulberg said. "What the priest went through as a result of his work on the waterfront—we didn't have time to get into that in the movie. He caught as much hell as the kid (Malloy) did. Now, the roles are virtually equal. All that was in the novel. The play is based as much on the novel as it is on the movie."[27]

Schulberg and Silverman first began working on a two-act adaptation. Some five years and many revisions later, they opened it at the Cleveland Play House in 1988. They tried it off-Broadway at the Theater Row Theater in 1993, and finally put it into a small Chicago theater in fall 1994. Buoyed by good notices in all three venues, they began thinking about Broadway. Late that year, they obtained funding and assembled an attractive cast that included former amateur boxer and *ER* lead character Ron Eldard as Terry,[28] Penelope Ann Miller as Edie Doyle, and veterans Kevin Conway and David Morse as mob boss Johnny Friendly and Father Barry, respectively. During rehearsals for the Broadway opening at the Brooks Atkinson Theater, an enthusiastic Schulberg took the entire cast of thirty-five down to Father Corridan's old Church of St. Francis Xavier in lower Manhattan "so they could absorb the atmosphere of a place where dockworkers gather."[29]

But the Broadway production, which finally opened on May 1, 1995, ran into an unhappy and crippling series of setbacks in rehearsals and during preview performances. The original director, Gordon Edelstein, was replaced; Terry Kinney, who was to have played Father Barry, suddenly left the cast, and James Gandolfini (later to hit it big as the lead character on *The Sopranos*), who was to appear as Charley Malloy, the part made famous by Rod Steiger, was replaced by Michael Hanney. The final blow landed during the Saturday preview matinee before opening night when, with a number of critics attending, cast member Jerry Grayson (playing "Barney," one of the lead goons) suffered a heart attack on stage in the closing moments of Act 1.

The remarkable difficulties notwithstanding, the play was hammered by the critics. In the *New York Times* Vincent Canby said it was "overproduced . . . ostentatious" and weighed down by "stage mechanics." The play, he added, was "simply not strong enough to function on its own," and Schulberg was "not the kind of playwright who writes naturally for, and profits mightily from, the limitations imposed by the stage."[30] The acerbic John Simon seemed to sum up the show's reception in the May 22, 1995, issue of *New York Magazine:* "This Budd is not for you."

The play closed after sixteen previews and only eight performances. It lost an estimated $2.5 million, believed to be the worst loss for a non-musical play in Broadway history.

NOTES

1. First called *The Bottom of the River,* then *The Golden Warriors.*

2. In January, and again in April 1952, Kazan, who had joined the Communist Party in the summer of 1934 and resigned from it in the spring of 1936, stunned his old comrades when he appeared before the HCUA as a "friendly" witness; in the second appearance, he named eight names, all from his Group Theatre days in the early 1930s.

3. Corridan, called "Father Pete," and known for his opposition to gangsterism and terror on the New York waterfront, was codirector of the St. Francis Xavier Labor School, at 30 West 16th Street in Manhattan. The school had been founded in 1936 to combat communism by promoting Catholic social principles.

4. Schulberg wrote the lead part of Terry Malloy with John Garfield in mind, but in May 1952 Garfield suffered a fatal heart attack.

5. See Rudy Behlmer's *Memo from Darryl F. Zanuck: The Golden Years at Twentieth Century-Fox* (New York: Grove Press, 1993), 224–230.

6. Schulberg and Kazan's first attempts to sign Brando for the Malloy part had been unsuccessful, even though Brando had been directed by Kazan in *A Streetcar Named Desire,* both on Broadway and in the film version, and in *Viva Zapata.*

7. Despite Brando and the powerful cast, Harry Cohn apparently believed the film would be a failure. When Kazan first showed him the completed picture, Cohn left the studio projection room without saying goodnight, or any other word.

8. Liner notes, Studio Heritage Collection, Columbia Pictures.

9. Spiegel maintained that *On the Waterfront* would have won the Golden Lion award at the 1954 Venice Film Festival had the voting not somehow been "rigged."

In a September 28, 1954, letter to Barnaby Conrad, Schulberg wrote: "Our producer Spiegel the Eagle says we really won the Venice thing as everybody got up and yelled for the w.f. and the golden lion going to *Romeo &* etc. was a put-up job. I guess we'll survive it, as will Venice." At the same time, the film did win the Venice Festival Award, as well as the New York Film Critics Award, the Foreign Correspondents Award, and the Screen Writers Guild Award.

10. Malcolm Johnson, the reporter whose twenty-four articles (starting in November 1948) in the now-defunct *New York Sun* had inspired the film, was by then retired and living in Macon, Ga. Early on, he had received a small amount of money for the rights to his stories, and he got a small credit in the closing titles; Schulberg felt the recognition was insufficient and paid him an additional fee out of his own pocket. Johnson's former colleague, *New York World Telegram & Sun* columnist Inez Robb, told of a telephone call she received from him: "Ah'm glad the story is on film, and is good, and Ah don't feel badly about not being mentioned during the awards. If my friends look real fast, they'll see Ah got a screen credit on the picture. And, hell, they spelled my name correctly."

11. At the eleventh hour, Columbia Pictures changed the release title from *Waterfront* to *On the Waterfront* when it was discovered that the former title already had been used for a television series.

12. Elia Kazan, *A Life* (New York: Knopf, 1988), 500. Wrote Kazan, "When Brando, at the end, yells at Lee Cobb, the mob boss, 'I'm glad what I done—you hear me?—glad what I done!' that was me saying, with identical heat, that I was glad that I'd testified as I had. I'd been snubbed by friends each and every day for many months in my old show business haunts, and I'd not forgotten nor would I forgive the men, old friends some of them, who'd snubbed me, so the scene in the film where Brando goes back to the waterfront to 'shape up' again for employment and is rejected by men with whom he'd worked day after day—that, too, was my story, now told to all the world. So when critics say that I put my story and my feelings on the screen, to justify my informing, they are right. That transference of emotion from my own experience to the screen is the merit of those scenes."

13. TLS, Schulberg to author, October 27, 1992.

14. *L.A. Times Book Review,* December 11, 1994; full text of letter in possession of author.

15. Kazan, *A Life,* 471. "Marlon's alienation was not so final that he wouldn't make *On the Waterfront,*" Kazan pointed out.

16. Marlon Brando and Robert Lindsey, *Brando: Songs My Mother Taught Me* (New York: Random House, 1994), 193–199.

17. Schulberg says it was his father who first uttered, "He coulda been a contenda" in reference to a fighter B.P. believed could have been "another Benny Leonard."

18. Fax, Schulberg to Larry King, October 6, 1994; see also Kazan, 516. According to Kazan, Brando's contract allowed him to leave the set each day at 4 P.M. in order to visit his analyst in Manhattan. On page 525 of *A Life,* Kazan describes how he read Brando's lines to an "annoyed" Steiger, who believed that the director was "slighting" Steiger's "side" of the scene.

19. Photocopy of handwritten note (undated, 1994), in possession of author. Schulberg has said that he thought he and Brando had developed a rapport during the shooting on the docks, and that once, when they spoke of how a scene had been played, the actor joked, "Y'know, it's so fucking cold out here, there's no way you c'n overact." Schulberg also provided Brando with a coach, the recently retired middleweight boxer Roger Donoghue, to show him a fighter's proper body language.

20. However, Steiger's close friend and biographer, Tom Hutchinson, in *Rod Steiger: Memoirs of a Friendship* (New York: Fromm International, 2000), 88, did come down emphatically on Schulberg's side: "Brando . . . is inaccurate, as an examination of the shooting script will reveal. At the beginning, during rehearsals, Brando began to improvise and Rod followed suit—until Kazan yelled, 'Stop the shit, Buddy,' which was what Brando's friends called him. After that, they both stuck to the words Budd Schulberg had written." In fact, on the day the taxi scene was shot, Kazan let Brando leave the set early; and Kazan then read Brando's lines to Steiger when it was time to film Steiger's close-ups. To this day, according to Hutchinson, Steiger is still "childishly" angry over Brando's departure.

21. Fax, Schulberg to Larry King, October 6, 1994.

22. Donald Chase, *Filmmaking: The Collaborative Art* (Boston: Little, Brown, 1975), 45, 58–59.

23. Harvey Breit, "In and Out of Books: Waterfront," *New York Times Book Review* (7 August 1955), 8.

24. "Why Write It When You Can't Sell It to the Pictures," *Saturday Review* (3 September 1955), 6.

25. In 1956 the novel won a prestigious Christopher Book Award.

26. Father Corridan's zeal for justice on the docks had earned him reassignment to a small parish in upstate New York.

27. *Playbill* (31 May 1995), 10, 14.

28. *Variety* reported on November 14, 1994, that both David Caruso and Matt Dillon had turned down the role of Terry Malloy, but that Danny Aiello was then under consideration for the part of Father Barry. Sean Penn was among several others believed to have been approached about playing Terry Malloy.

29. "Going Back to the Waterfront before the Curtain Rises." *New York Times* (March 16, 1995), D22.

30. Vincent Canby, "A Classic Film Is Transposed to 3 Dimensions." *New York Times* (2 May 1995), B1.

14

HARRY COHN AND
ANDY GRIFFITH

In 1956, Schulberg undertook what should have been one of his most satisfying projects—a film at Columbia, starring Steiger and Humphrey Bogart—of his 1947 novel, *The Harder They Fall.* Instead, it proved one of the more contentious chapters in the writer's life. Budd's old friend (and alleged "Sammy Glick") Jerry Wald, who was now vice president in charge of production at the studio, had agreed that Budd could write the screenplay at his New Hope, Pennsylvania, farm. But when the notorious studio head Harry Cohn, who had hated B.P. Schulberg and never cared much for Budd, thundered, "My writers work *at* my studio," Schulberg withdrew from the project.[1] Phil Yordan, the producer, wound up writing the screenplay, with Mark Robson directing. Fight aficionado Schulberg, who had written the novel as a period piece about boxing in its corrupt early-1930s Dark Ages, was outraged when the picture turned out to be a savage attack on the sport, ending with newspaperman Bogart (in his last film) typing a story that begins: "Boxing must be abolished in America."

In his capacity as boxing editor of *Sports Illustrated,* Schulberg charged the film with being "guilty on at least a dozen counts of presenting an inaccurate and overstated picture of boxing evils as they exist today." He was incensed by the character played by former heavyweight champion Max Baer ("a leering psychopath") who wants to be known as the "real" killer of a fighter who has died from a ring injury; and by documentary footage of a demented ex-fighter and wino who was actually "interviewed" on a Hollywood street. Schulberg, stating that boxing "can no more be abolished than booze, sex, religion and other hungers," threatened to have his name taken off the film unless Yordan and the studio changed the sentence Bogart is writing to, "The boxing business must rid itself of . . . evil influence—even if it takes an act of Congress to do so." The studio complied.[2]

The next year, Kazan and Schulberg teamed again, this time at Warner Bros., on *A Face in the Crowd,* based on Budd's story "Your Arkansas Traveler," which had been part of his 1953 short story collection, *Some Faces in the Crowd.* The film marked the motion picture debuts of Andy Griffith and Lee Remick and also starred Patricia Neal, Walter Matthau, and Tony Franciosa. Schulberg's old friend Marshall Neilan had a small part, and a number of celebrities appeared as themselves, including Walter Winchell, Mike Wallace, Burl Ives, Betty Furness, Faye Emerson, and Bennett Cerf. The story tells of the rise and fall of "Lonesome Rhodes," a hobo-turned radio and television demagogue, reminiscent of entertainment celebrities who are seen by enormous audiences and who gain extraordinary influence over their viewers. The film was a harbinger of *Network* (1976) in its warnings about television's power to manipulate opinion. In his autobiography, Kazan wrote that the story was ahead of its time and that Schulberg had "anticipated Ronald Reagan."[3] Said Schulberg, "Lonesome Rhodes occurred to me one day when I was talking to Will Rogers Jr., a friend, about our fathers; Will suddenly said, 'It was just a myth about my old man, being with the common people; what he really wanted to do was play polo and hang out with the big shots.' And I began to see the sense of power that we confer on certain entertainment world figures."[4]

Griffith, until then known only as the dim-witted country hick Will Stockdale in the 1955 television production of "No Time for Sergeants," was bullied and cajoled by Kazan into a superb performance, almost certainly the best of his career. After the final scene was shot, the exhausted actor looked at Kazan and Schulberg and said, "You S.O.B.s, you're never going to do this to me again." The film won the German Film Critics Award as best picture of the year.[5]

NOTES

1. Cohn's dislike of B.P. and Budd was such that in 1943, when agent Ad Schulberg visited the Columbia set of her ex-husband's final film, *City without Men* (bringing a twenty-year-old Shelley Winters and some other valuable talent to the studio),

Cohn personally shouted over the loudspeaker system he had installed on all the stages, "Here's Ad Schulberg, the lady with all the movie brains in the Schulberg family." (Budd Schulberg, "Family's Cohn Connections," *Variety,* 25 January 1999.)

2. But in the 1990s, when the film showed up on cable television, the original "abolish boxing" message had been restored. (Years earlier, former heavyweight champion Primo Carnera had filed a $1.5 million "invasion of privacy" suit against Columbia Pictures claiming, correctly, that the film was based on or inspired by his own career. In August 1956, Superior Court Judge Stanley Mosk dismissed the suit, stating, "One who becomes a celebrity or public figure waives his right of privacy, and cannot change that waiver at his whim.") See "No Privacy for Primo, Court Says," *Los Angeles Examiner,* 8 August 1956.

3. Elia Kazan, *A Life* (New York: Knopf, 1988), 566. Schulberg first revised the script in 1986 for a remake to star Richard Gere. *Variety* reported on August 30, 1988, that Don Johnson was then being considered for the part; on July 20, 1992, it published an item that said Warner Bros. had brought in Eric Bogoshian to "polish" Schulberg's script and "give it more edge," a move that must have perplexed Schulberg. Finally, in 1996, Schulberg did another rewrite for a version that would have starred Whoopi Goldberg as a down-at-the-heels city dweller named Sunny Skye; nothing came of that project, despite much initial enthusiasm by Goldberg, who then kept Schulberg waiting in a West Los Angeles hotel (and never saw him) after he came from New York for a conference. Writing of the 1957 film, Kazan said Jack Warner's reaction to the original script was, "It's a piece of shit, and you two (Kazan and Schulberg) don't know anything about politics." More than forty years later, however, *Los Angeles Times* television critic Howard Rosenberg said the film "never got the credit it deserved for its commentary on media that in some ways was as visionary as *Network* about what lay ahead for broadcasting." (See "'Face in Crowd' Saw the Danger," *L.A. Times,* 14 August 2000, F1, 14).

4. Donald Chase, *Filmmaking: The Collaborative Art* (Boston: Little, Brown, 1975), 32. Like Sammy Glick, who ultimately is betrayed by the one person he trusts, Lonesome Rhodes is also betrayed—but by himself—when he accidentally speaks into a "live" microphone and reveals himself all too accurately.

5. Spike Lee dedicated his 2000 film *Bamboozled,* a harsh satire of the film and television industries, to Budd Schulberg, explaining it had been inspired partly by *A Face in the Crowd.* In the summer of 2000, Lee, Schulberg, and *Fight Game* boxing magazine publisher Bert Sugar announced that they would produce a feature film dealing with the two (1936 and 1938) heavyweight championship matches between Joe Louis and Germany's Max Schmeling. Schulberg's working title was "The War to Come."

15

FLORIDA AND THE EVERGLADES

Schulberg's life took a sharp turn in 1949 when, on assignment in Florida for *Holiday* magazine, he became intrigued with Collier County and the Chokolosee Bay area, about 150 miles south of Sarasota. In the mid-1950s, he sold his Pennsylvania farm and bought a tropical, one-story home on an island (Siesta Key) off Sarasota, adjacent to the home of novelist McKinley Kantor (1904–1977), who before long (and probably to his astonishment) would appear in Schulberg's next motion picture.[1] Budd's sojourn in the state fueled a deep interest in preserving the Everglades and its wildlife, and he soon expressed his convictions in an unusual screenplay he called *Across the Everglades*.

Renamed *Wind across the Everglades* at the request of Warner Bros., it was one of the first cinematic pleas for animal conservation, the story of a turn-of-the-century Audubon warden and his efforts to prevent the slaughter of Florida egrets for their plumage. It turned out to be a trying project for Schulberg and brother Stuart, who were also producing, and who were determined to give the film authenticity. They had decided to shoot in difficult conditions in the Everglades National Wildlife Refuge, and they made their headquarters in Everglade City in December 1957. There, they were joined by their stars: Burl Ives (the chief poacher), Christopher Plummer in his second film (as the warden), and Gypsy Rose Lee (as "Mrs. Bradford," proprietor of a Miami casino and brothel). Peter Falk was making his film debut as "Writer," and the amused Kantor was, of course, making his, as "Judge Tippins." But disaster struck when, almost before shooting began, director Nicholas Ray (*They Live by Night, Rebel without a Cause*), the socially conscious former colleague of Elia Kazan, suffered a severe breakdown and was hospitalized. With virtually no hope of obtaining a top substitute at such a late hour, the

Schulbergs called on all their Hollywood experience and finished the film themselves.[2] Budd actually did the directing, with help from Kazan's assistant director, Charlie Maguire.[3]

NOTES

1. Later in that decade, Schulberg, wife Vicki, and their two sons lived in Princeton, N.J. In the summer of 1960, they moved to Mexico City, purchasing an apartment just off the Paseo de la Reforma. Although Schulberg lived in Beverly Hills in the mid-1960s to facilitate third wife Geraldine Brooks' film career, he owned and regularly used the Mexico City flat until it was destroyed in the massive earthquakes of September 19–20, 1985. Schulberg and Brooks later moved to Westhampton Beach on New York's Long Island, where Budd lives today with his fourth wife.

2. Stuart Schulberg produced Marshall Plan films for the U.S. government after World War II, then coproduced two feature films, *No Way Back* (named best West German film in 1954) and *Special Delivery*, with Joseph Cotten and Eva Bartok, in 1955. In October 1956, he and Budd formed Schulberg Productions, Inc., which produced *Wind across the Everglades* in 1958. Stuart joined NBC Television in 1961 as coproducer of "David Brinkley's Journal" and in 1965 was named producer of NBC's "Sports in Action." After a period as an independent documentary film producer (*The Angry Voices of Watts*, 1966, and *The New Voices of Watts*, 1968), he rejoined NBC and was producer of "The Today Show" until 1976. Both Stuart and Budd were nominated for Emmys for *Angry Voices*. Stuart died in 1979. (Sonya Schulberg, who in 1937 had her novel *They Cried a Little* published by Scribner's—with fabled Max Perkins as her editor—has in recent years served as her brother's almost daily confidant and adviser. *They Cried a Little* received a good review from Margaret Wallace in the *New York Times Book Review* on October 3, 1937. Ms. Schulberg was married for fifty-six years to noted New York attorney Benjamin C. O'Sullivan, who died in 1998.)

3. When Random House published the screenplay (as *Across the Everglades*) after the film's release in mid-1958, Schulberg dedicated it to Bennett Cerf.

16

SAMMY: ON TV, ON BROADWAY

In 1959, with Stuart's collaboration, Budd wrote the television play for a two-part dramatization of *What Makes Sammy Run?* It was shown live on September 27 and October 4 on NBC's Sunday Showcase, sponsored by Crest Toothpaste (which interrupted the show repeatedly for an ongoing fluoride toothpaste test of 600 Minnesota boys and girls). Larry Blyden starred as Sammy, with John Forsythe as Al. When critics, who liked the show, said they detected a "more human" Sammy Glick as played by Blyden, Schulberg agreed, adding, "I never saw Sammy as a monster. I saw him like many of my friends. I saw him as one to whom you'd say, 'Hi,' and you'd be glad to see him." *Variety* (September 30, 1959) praised the show as "a fast-moving, persuasive slice of what has been, what is and what'll always be all too real."[1]

In 1960, Dartmouth College made peace with Schulberg by awarding him an honorary Doctor of Laws degree. The citation read: "Recalling the enthrallment of your undergraduate editorship and the disenchantment that ensued from returning pen in hand to a halcyon winter Hanover, would you not enjoy coming to us today under a flag of literary truce?" Smiling, and clearly delighted, Schulberg replied that he had "always been welcome on returns here . . . it shows the liberal and generous spirit of the college."[2]

That same year, television lyricist and composer Ervin Drake approached Schulberg and proposed that they adapt *Sammy* to the musical stage. When the writer agreed, Drake—who had never done a Broadway show but who had written dozens of hit songs, including "I Believe," "Good Morning Heartache," and "It Was a Very Good Year"—set to work composing a score that included eight very good vocal selections; Schulberg, again with his brother's collaboration, wrote the book. Abe

Burrows (*Can-Can, Silk Stockings,* and *How to Succeed in Business without Really Trying*) directed, with Joseph Cates (*Spoon River*) producing, and the show opened on February 27, 1964 at the Fifty-fourth Street Theatre. It starred Steve Lawrence (in his Broadway debut) as Sammy, Robert Alda as Al, and Sally Ann Howes as Kit.

The production ran 540 performances, breaking the record for the longest run in the history of the Fifty-fourth Street Theatre; and two of Drake's songs, "A Room without Windows" and "The Friendliest Thing Two People Can Do," became standards. Drake's score also won him a Grammy nomination.

Schulberg's twenty-year marriage to Victoria Anderson also came to an end in early 1964. On July 12 of that year, at the Beverly Hills home of producer Collier Young (Schulberg's one-time agent), he was married to stage and screen actress Geraldine Brooks (*Possessed, The Reckless Moment*).[3]

Not long after the wedding, Budd and "Gerry" sailed their ninety-foot schooner *Double Eagle* into Puerto Vallarta, only to find actor John Wayne piloting his own yacht alongside and shouting at Schulberg that he was spoiling for a fight. Wayne had apparently believed for years that *What Makes Sammy Run?* was not only an attack on Hollywood but an assault on America itself; at more than one Hollywood party, he had accused the shy and gentle Schulberg of being "un-American." Despite Schulberg's best efforts to avoid a fight, the mismatched men squared off that night on the beach in front of their hotel. By then, fortunately, both were well stocked with tequila, and as they scuffled clumsily to the point of exhaustion, the five-foot Gerry got in the middle and somehow ended it. Schulberg said he was more than satisfied to call it a "no-decision" bout.

NOTES

1. The reviewer, however, thought Barbara Rush, as Kit, was "out of character with the glibness and sophistication required."

2. Schulberg would also by awarded a Doctor of Letters degree by Long Island University (1983) and a Doctor of Humane Letters degree by Hofstra College (1987). He would win the *Prix Literaire* at the Deauville (France) Festival of Ameri-

can Film in 1989. His many other honors would include the B'nai B'rith's Susie Humanitarian Award, the NAACP Image Award, and the Amistad Award for this work with African American writers, presented by Howard University.

3. Ms. Brooks took the photographs used in Swan Watch, the 1975 book she and Budd wrote about two swans, Loh and Grin, living on the Aspatuck Inlet in front of their Westampton Beach home.

17

WATTS AND AFTER

In the first days after the so-called Watts Riots[1] of August 1965, Schulberg (then living temporarily in Beverly Hills) and a friend bravely ventured into the burned-out South-Central Los Angeles neighborhood intent on finding out what really had happened. They came upon a battered two-story building operated by the Westminster Neighborhood Association (a social services agency affiliated with the Presbyterian Church) where, after some awkward conversation, Schulberg asked a young social worker what one person could do to help. The guide replied, "You said you were a writer—maybe you could start a writers' class."[2]

Although not a single volunteer would show up for three weeks— and in the face of the lingering hostility he encountered in the neighborhood—Schulberg resolved to remain for three months, or longer, if that's what it took to create a writing program. Finally, a nineteen-year-old arrived one night and asked Schulberg his purpose in setting up a class for writers. "Nothing up my sleeve," Schulberg answered. "It's just that I'm sick of people talking about the problem—The Negro Problem, as the whites call it, The White Problem as *Ebony* calls it—and not doing something personal about it. I'm not the anti-poverty program. I'm not the NAACP. I'm just me, a writer, here to see if I can find other writers."[3]

Schulberg eventually enlisted the aid of writers Irving Stone and Irving Wallace, who in turn urged others in their own literary circles to support the workshop.[4] The South-Central writers soon were able to move to a nine-room structure that became the Frederick Douglass House (named after the runaway slave who taught himself to read and write), "where indigent young writers could board." The class (known popularly as the "Watts Writers' Workshop") began to pick up new members at almost every meeting.

By 1967, the program was humming and Schulberg was able to gather some of the best of its work and present it (with his own detailed introduction) in anthology form as *From the Ashes: Voices of Watts*. It was a solid collection of poetry, fiction, and nonfiction by eighteen of the writers, so uniformly impressive that a number of the writers obtained jobs in film and television, in academia, and in educational publishing. The book also became a standard resource in African American Studies programs and a model for creative writing workshops in other cities.

When Schulberg moved east at the end of the decade, leadership in the workshop passed to the talented Harry Dolan, whose television play *Losers Weepers* (produced by Stuart Schulberg) had been shown on NBC in 1967. Budd Schulberg went on to cofound (with Fred Hudson, director of a Douglass House program in San Francisco) the enormously successful Frederick Douglass Creative Arts Center in New York, which thirty years later was enrolling 250 students each semester in eighteen workshops covering every writing discipline from poetry and the novel to screenwriting.[5] Sadly, after Dolan's death, the Watts workshop slowly withered. It was revived briefly in 1987, but a similar attempt in 1991 was unsuccessful.

Sanctuary V, Schulberg's first novel in fourteen years, was published in 1969 to good reviews, although sales were only moderate. The book tells the story of a sympathetic and idealistic Latin American politician, Justo Moreno Suarez, whose high hopes for revolutionary reform have been dashed and who must now seek refuge from the leader he had loved but now fears. It was called "fine, powerful, well-crafted, revealing" by *Saturday Review,* which added, "The passage of time has sharpened Schulberg's understanding and deepened his perceptions." The title derives from an article in the Pan American Convention governing diplomatic asylum.

After the death of Geraldine Brooks in 1977, Schulberg slowly began work on *Everything That Moves,* a novel about a Jimmy Hoffa-like power-seeker out to control the International Brotherhood of Truckers and Haulers.[6] It tells the story of Jerry Hopper, an honest trade unionist who is corrupted by a growing lust for power. The book, which Schulberg described as a "documentary novel," explores the connections among organized crime, labor unions, and big business. It is unusual in that it is told in the present tense, is divided into fifty-six short chapters, and reads much like a screenplay.

In 1981, Schulberg delivered one of his great successes, *Motion Pictures: Memories of a Hollywood Prince,* the account of his privileged life in the film capital until 1931, when he left for Deerfield Academy and Dartmouth. Said Garson Kanin, "Perhaps the outstanding second generation movie man is Budd Schulberg, who from the very beginning of his life was able to observe movies and moviemakers from a preferred and favored vantage point."[7] Schulberg adapted the autobiography into a six-part miniseries that was announced in 1991 as a selection for the Public Broadcasting System's American Playhouse, but the project stalled and then was placed on indefinite hold.

In 1990, Random House published a fiftieth anniversary edition of *What Makes Sammy Run?* with an author's note and afterword, along with the two *Liberty* Sammy Glick stories.[8] Also published that year by Random House was Schulberg's second collection of short stories, *Love, Action, Laughter and Other Sad Tales.* The selections were written over a sixty-year period and include pieces from *Esquire, Collier's, The Dartmouth, Liberty, Playboy, Redbook, Story,* and the *Ellery Queen Mystery Magazine.*

Just a month after the disappointing May 1995 early closing of the play *On the Waterfront,* Schulberg's collection of his nonfiction boxing writing, *Sparring with Hemingway: And Other Legends of the Fight Game,* was published to generally good notices but to modest sales.[9] Undeterred, Schulberg began making plans for two other books: a second volume of nonfiction boxing (working title *The Hardest Game*), and a book about his friendship and unhappy collaboration with F. Scott Fitzgerald. At the same time, the news from Hollywood was encouraging. Warner Bros. wanted to make *What Makes Sammy Run?* and needed only a director and an actor to play Sammy Glick. And perhaps, studio executives said, about $13 million in financing.

NOTES

1. To this day, Schulberg and the surviving workshop writers refer to the events of the hot summer of 1965 not as "riots" but as an "uprising" or "a rebellion."

2. Budd Schulberg, ed., introduction to *From the Ashes: Voices of Watts* (New York: New American Library, 1967), 5–6.

3. Schulberg, *From the Ashes,* 8–9.

4. Schulberg reported that checks arrived from James Baldwin, Irwin Shaw, the Richard Burtons, Steve Allen, Ira Gershwin, Herbert Gold, Robert F. Kennedy, Art Buchwald, Richard Rodgers, Ann Petry, Dore Schary, Paddy Chayefsky, Frank Loesser, Harry Golden, Hodding Carter, Elia Kazan, and John Steinbeck.

5. The center is located at 275 W. 43rd Street. Among its greatest successes (four books published, three plays produced, and three American Film Institute fellowships won) are Kevin Arkadie, who wrote scripts for *Law & Order* and *Dr. Quinn, Medicine Woman,* and then became executive producer of the TV series *Soul Food;* and Phil Bertelsen, who wrote, produced, and directed the prizewinning short films *Around the Time* (1997) and *The Sunshine* (2000). In 2000, the center received a $40,000 Department of Commerce matching grant to assist its after-school program in computer technology for inner-city kids.

6. Schulberg was married for a fourth time, on June 9, 1978, to Betsy Ann Langman, the daughter of conservationist and author Anne Simon and niece of historian Barbara Tuchman *(The Guns of August).* The ceremony was held at the home of Elia Kazan in Montauk, at the eastern tip of Long Island. The Schulbergs and their two children, Benn Stuart (born in 1979), and Jessica Adeline (born in 1981), live in Schulberg's Westhampton Beach home, close by the houses of Kurt Vonnegut and Wilfred Sheed.

7. Schulberg has hinted that a second volume is in preparation.

8. The story "Romance Comes to Sammy Glick," from the *Liberty* issue of July 16, 1938, is mistitled "Love Comes to Sammy Glick."

9. The book displayed a handsome dust jacket showing George Foreman and Michael Moorer in their November 1994 heavyweight title match, but the publisher inexplicably decided not to use photographs in the book itself.

18

GETTING *SAMMY* TO
THE BIG SCREEN. ALMOST.

The more than fifty-year effort to bring *What Makes Sammy Run?* to the big screen began, rather unexpectedly, in 1950. Louis B. Mayer, who less than a decade earlier had called for Budd Schulberg's "deportation," surprised Hollywood by asking Budd to adapt *What Makes Sammy Run?* for a major production at MGM. Schulberg, however (dooming perhaps his best-ever chance to get the film made), both balked at a deal *and* hinted that he didn't trust the studio to be true to the story. In retaliation, an angry Mayer set MGM to work on its own "ruthless producer" story, *The Bad and the Beautiful*. Released in 1952, starring Kirk Douglas and directed by Vincente Minelli, it was a huge success and it captured five Oscars. "I always felt it was kind of a rip-off," said Schulberg, "an effective film; but I felt the MGM powers got together and said, 'Well, screw him if he doesn't want to do it, we'll do our own *Sammy*.'"[1]

In 1955, writer-producer Fred F. Finklehoffe (1911–1977), who had written the blockbuster *Meet Me in St. Louis* (1944), bought the film rights to *Sammy*, and speculation began about who would play Sammy Glick, the favorites being Frank Sinatra, Tony Curtis, Nick Adams, and Mickey Rooney. Absolutely nothing came of the talk, however; in fact, the project showed no pulse at all for the next thirty-odd years, during which time another generation of "ideal" *Sammys*—Dustin Hoffman, Harvey Keitel, even Jane Fonda (Samantha Glick?)—matured and grew too old for the part.[2] Schulberg and producer/friend Gene Kirkwood (*Ironweed,* and executive producer on *Rocky*) got it back on board in 1987 at Warner Bros., with an unexpected assist from Billy Gerber, the studio's vice-president for theatrical production. Schulberg had dropped by the studio one day to discuss a remake of *A Face in the Crowd* when Gerber casually asked who owned the rights to *Sammy*. Schulberg raised his hand, and

Gerber set about persuading the studio to take an option. Schulberg went to work on the screenplay and in 1990, Gerber announced that Sidney Lumet (*12 Angry Men, The Pawnbroker, Network*) would direct; better still, Lumet was saying privately that he thought he could get Tom Cruise to star. Lumet already had two films in the pipeline, *Family Business* (1989) and *Q&A* (1990), however; when both motion pictures foundered, critically as well as at the box office, the shaken Lumet (in January 1991) quietly took himself out of the running for *Sammy*.[3] Shocked and disappointed, Schulberg and Kirkwood began casting around for another director. Their first thoughts, not surprisingly, were of Kazan.

But the eighty-two-year-old Kazan was already determined to retire from filmmaking (to write novels) and made his decision public in 1993. Several other veterans whom both Budd and Gene admired, including Billy Wilder and Robert Wise, were by then too old to obtain insurance bonding. Desperate, they agreed to consider an unlikely volunteer, the thirty-three-year-old Scotsman Michael Caton-Jones (*Scandal, Memphis Belle, Doc Hollywood*). At first apprehensive about Caton-Jones' suitability for a subject as American as Sammy Glick, Schulberg soon found that he liked Caton-Jones; and he was pleased when the Scotsman said he thought he could convince Michael J. Fox (who had just starred in Caton-Jones' *Doc Hollywood)* to play Sammy. Then, within a few weeks, the high spirits vanished when Schulberg and Kirkwood read in the trades that Caton-Jones was busy on another project, one that would derail *Sammy* indefinitely.

Enter Ben Stiller, the thirtyish son of comedians Jerry Stiller and Anne Meara, future star of *There's Something about Mary* (1998) and director of Jim Carrey in *The Cable Guy* (1996). Stiller had just read the novel, said he loved it, and wanted to direct the film *and* to play Sammy. If he couldn't do both, he said, he was willing to direct the movie and get Carrey to star. Stiller's only stipulation was that he be allowed to scrap Schulberg's screenplay and write his own, in collaboration with friend Jerry Stahl (whose book *Permanent Midnight* had received high marks from the critics). Schulberg was not thrilled that his script would be thrown out, but Stiller pleaded that this was the only way he was able to work. Stiller and Stahl did two drafts in 1997, neither of which pleased Schulberg; but a third, in April 1998, seemed more acceptable. What did he have to lose, thought Schulberg.

"So far," a resigned and generally agreeable Schulberg wrote to a friend, "it's taken me one year to write the novel and 57 years to try to get it to the screen. Waiting for Lefty, waiting for Godot, and now waiting for . . ."

Not long after Stiller's name surfaced as the project's director, superstar Julia Roberts called Warner Bros., asking to speak to Stiller. A surprised Gerber took the call and learned that Roberts wanted to play Kit and also thought she could get either Alec Baldwin or Tim Robbins to play Al Manheim. Once again, though, nothing developed; Schulberg wrote to the same friend, "I'm getting ready to call Ben Stiller again to find out if there's life after Julia Roberts and Tim Robbins. I think my tombstone inscription should say, 'I'm waiting to hear from Stiller.'"

Gerber, meanwhile, had become an independent producer at Warner Bros. and, when Stiller and Schulberg threatened to take the film to Paramount, Gerber pleaded that a deal was all but made. In fact, he, Schulberg, and Kirkwood had believed all along that Stiller's status as a hot property in Hollywood (he had been paid $3 million merely to act in the popular but sophomoric *There's Something about Mary*) would make it easy to raise the money needed to film *Sammy*.

Still, there was almost no movement, and Stiller suddenly was no longer returning Schulberg's calls. In May 1999, to his loyal correspondent, Budd wrote: "I fear the rollercoaster has come to rest. Out of touch with Busy Ben. I've lost my boyish laughter." And a month later: "On the *Sammy* front, it's all quiet. It's become an absurdist play: 'Waiting for Stiller.' Billy Gerber says he hasn't given up, but with Ben on the lam, I'd be surprised if we could put it back together." And in August: "Looks as if *Sammy* the movie is finito, kaput, Ben-Stillerized."

After a year had passed, Schulberg reflected on his disappointment with Stiller. "Somewhere along the line he stopped returning phone calls," Schulberg wrote in October 2000. "Too busy making those raunchy teenaged movies. Every once in a while he announces that he plans to do *Sammy*, but I no longer hold my breath. Mickey Gerber says there is a producer 'very interested' in the project. It really shoulda been done but there are an awful lot of shouldas in Hollywood."

Stiller, meanwhile, said he hadn't given up on making *Sammy*. Interviewed for the November 2000 issue of *Playboy*, he explained, "I think it's been in every conceivable state of almost-happening but just hasn't come together. Sammy is a tough character for people to embrace, because he's a guy who will do anything to get to the top. He represents the underbelly of show business that people in show business don't really care to explore. This is probably why I can't get the movie made, why no one's been able to get it made since the book came out. I'm not the first to try. I would love to see the movie made in my lifetime. I want to play Sammy . . . but nobody will put up the $20 million—which is cheap by today's standards."[4]

NOTES

1. Douglas, who played the tormented producer, Jonathan Shields, later starred in Irwin Shaw's (and Minelli's) *Two Weeks in Another Town* (1962), in some ways a sequel to *The Bad and the Beautiful*.

2. In recent years, the list has included Tom Cruise, Matthew Broderick, Sean Penn, Robert Downey Jr., and Leonardo DiCaprio.

3. Kirkwood later told the *Los Angeles Times* that "Sidney let another film project take precedence."

4. Stiller was reported to have turned down a $2 million offer from HBO to do *Sammy* as a made-for-TV movie.

19

BACK TO WORK

Schulberg's life was virtually derailed in early May 2000 when he re-turned home from an appearance at Vassar. He was troubled by his asthma, and his wife noticed that he looked "very, very tired" and ap-peared to have lost weight. She wisely got him to the family doctor, who just as quickly sent him to a cardiologist. On May 11, at St. Francis Hos-pital in Rosslyn, N.Y., eighty-six-year-old Schulberg underwent a suc-cessful quadruple heart bypass. The surgeon told Betsy Schulberg that without the operation, Budd would not have lived six months. Three weeks later, he was moved to St. Charles Hospital, in New York's Suffolk County, for a cardiac rehabilitation program of exercise and nutrition ed-ucation. He went home on June 20.[1]

Like one of the proud standup fighters he so admires, Schulberg im-mediately resumed work on the Joe Louis–Max Schmeling script for Spike Lee, on his book of recollections about F. Scott Fitzgerald, and on *The Hardest Game,* the collection of his own nonfiction boxing articles. Actually, his wife said, he had started working on all three projects while he was still in St. Francis Hospital.

"It must be that work ethic my mother instilled in me," Schulberg later explained. "I feel almost obligated to do something useful every day."

Asked in 1998 to characterize his unique and varied lifetime of writing, Schulberg said,

> My writing pattern, moving from fiction to dramatic writing to re-portage, was clearly established at Dartmouth, where I edited the daily, wrote short stories for *The Dart,* light verse and humor for the *Jack O'Lantern*, and my series on the marbleworkers strike, that caught the eye of Bennett Cerf and led to my Random House contract for *Sammy.*

I have a feeling that being able to play all the positions has somewhat weakened my standing in one particular one. I continue to swing back and forth from the novel to film writing, to theater to non-fiction. The problem is, I'm good at all of them (a frustrated lyricist as well) and enjoy doing all of them. God help me, I even enjoy writing for television when things go smoothly, though they rarely do in that producer-controlled medium. But if there were a literary decathlon, I'd have a shot.

Schulberg deplores the fact that *Sammy*, his first and best-known fictional creation, has over the years gone from pariah to an object of emulation and admiration.

"The Sammy I thought I was describing as viciously anti-social turned out to be a role model for the Yuppies of the 90s," he said, "from Malibu to Marathon on the keys of Florida."

He is not bitter about his inability to get *What Makes Sammy Run?* made, although he sometimes quips that his father used to make fifty-two pictures a year at Paramount but today he can't seem to get just one made at Warner Bros.

And he has no illusions or particular disappointments about his old hometown, Hollywood. He is reminded of his own characterization of the "film capital": "There is no moral separation between Hollywood and the rest of America. Hollywood *is* America, only speeded up, more brightly colored and lit."

NOTES

1. Schulberg's health, and his work schedule, quickly returned to normal; then in August 2000, possibly because of an ill-advised increase in the dosage of an asthma medicine, he suffered a spontaneous burst Achilles tendon and wound up with a heavy cast on his right leg. In October, a cast had to be placed on his left leg. Confined to a wheelchair, he did the only thing Budd Schulberg could. He went back to work.

Adeline "Ad" Jaffe Schulberg and Benjamin Percival "B.P."
Schulberg with little Budd, 1914. *Sonya Schulberg O'Sullivan*

B.P. Schulberg in 1931. He was head of West Coast production (at a peak salary of $10,000 per week) at Paramount Pictures from 1925 to 1932. *Sonya Schulberg O'Sullivan*

The Schulberg home at 525 South Lorraine Boulevard at Windsor Square in Hancock Park, Los Angeles, about 1928.

Urban military classmates Budd Schulberg (left) and Chuck Isaacs showing off their uniforms on one of the Paramount Pictures stages, 1926. Isaacs was later married to Eva Gabor. *Sonya Schulberg O'Sullivan*

The Schulbergs: Stuart, Sonya, Ad, Budd, and B.P., about 1930.
Sonya Schulberg O'Sullivan

Virginia "Jigee" Ray
and Budd Schulberg,
after announcing
their engagement
in 1936.
*University of
Southern California
Library Special
Collections*

Budd Schulberg about the time *What Makes Sammy Run?* was published in 1941.

Novelist F. Scott Fitzgerald at his peak in the 1920s, long before his disastrous collaboration with Schulberg on *Winter Carnival.*

Writer John O'Hara, one of many literary friends of Schulberg in Hollywood.

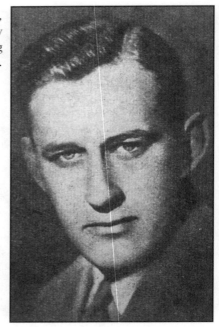

The offspring of some of Hollywood's top players met at the Midwick Country Club in Pasadena in 1940. Among them were future super agent Henry Wilson (extreme left); Jack Warner Jr. (the tallest in the back row); Julian Bud Lesser (center, arms folded), son of producer Sol Lesser; and Budd Schulberg (extreme right). *The Julian Lesser Collection*

For their work in the Elia Kazan-Budd Schulberg film *On the Waterfront* in 1954, Eva Marie Saint won an Oscar as Best Supporting Actress and Marlon Brando won Best Actor.

Nick Beck introduces Budd Schulberg at the Doheny Library at
the University of Southern California during a 1991 celebration
of the 50th anniversary of the publication of *What Makes
Sammy Run?* A hoped-for appearance by Sammy Glick did not
materialize. *University of Southern California Library Special
Collections*

Appendix A

HCUA TESTIMONY, MAY 23, 1951

Budd Schulberg appeared before the House Committee on Un-American Activities on May 23, 1951 in Room 226 of the Old House Office Building, Washington, D.C. His second wife, Virginia Anderson Schulberg, was present. He was accompanied by his counsel, Gerard D. Reilly and Charles Edward Rhetts of the firm of Reilly, Rhetts & Ruckelshaus. He was questioned by Staff Counsel Frank S. Tavenner Jr., and by committee members Harold H. Velde (Illinois), Francis E. Walter (Pennsylvania), Donald L. Jackson (California), Clyde Doyle (California), and staff investigator William A. Wheeler. Chairman John S. Wood (Georgia) was the presiding officer.

MORNING SESSION

Mr. Tavenner: When and where were you born, Mr. Schulberg?

Mr. Schulberg: I was born March 27, 1914, in the city of New York.

Mr. Tavenner: Where do you live?

Mr. Schulberg: I now live in New Hope, Pennsylvania.

Mr. Tavenner: What is your occupation?

Mr. Schulberg: I am a writer.

Mr. Tavenner: Will you state for the committee briefly your educational training?

Mr. Schulberg: I went through the public-school system of the city of Los Angeles, graduated from Los Angeles High School, went to Deerfield Academy, and to Dartmouth College.

Mr. Tavenner: When were you at Dartmouth College?

Mr. Schulberg: I was graduated in June of 1936.

Mr. Tavenner: Did you take additional educational training after that, or not?

Mr. Schulberg: No, sir, I didn't. I received no other degrees except my B.A.

Mr. Wheeler: Mr. Schulberg, have you ever served in the Armed Forces of the United States?

Mr. Schulberg: Yes, I have.

Mr. Tavenner: What branch of the military service?

Mr. Schulberg: Naval Reserve.

Mr. Tavenner: When did you become active in the United States Navy?

Mr. Schulberg: March 10, 1943.

Mr. Tavenner: Did you enlist?

Mr. Schulberg: Yes, I enlisted.

Mr. Tavenner: Were you an officer?

Mr. Schulberg: I became a lieutenant in the Navy.

Mr. Tavenner: How long did you serve in the United States Navy?

Mr. Schulberg: Until March 17, 1946.

Mr. Tavenner: Did you have any foreign service?

Mr. Schulberg: Yes, I did. I received one battle star in the European Theater of Operations. I received commendation from the War Department for directing a security Nazi film to be used as evidence in the Nuremberg trial of major war criminals. I also received a commendation from Secretary (James) Forrestal.

Mr. Tavenner: When were you discharged from the United States Navy?

Mr. Schulberg: I was released to inactive status on March 17, 1946.

Mr. Tavenner: You still retain your commission in the United States Naval Reserve?

Mr. Schulberg: Yes.

Mr. Tavenner: When did you enter upon your profession?

Mr. Schulberg: It is a difficult question to answer, sir. I have been writing since about the age of 11 or 12, I would say.

Mr. Tavenner: Will you outline to the committee what your professional experience has been since you graduated from Dartmouth in 1936?

Mr. Schulberg: I will try to do it, sir, as briefly as I can. In the summer of 1936 I returned to Hollywood, California. During that summer

I wrote short stories. In the fall I went to work at a film studio called the Selznick International, as a reader, and from that time, to I would say, 1939, on and off, I was what is known as a junior writer for the screen, although my main interest was in short-story writing and fiction. And from 1936 until the present I have been publishing almost constantly in international magazines, as well as writing some novels.

Mr. Tavenner: What novels have you written?

Mr. Schulberg: I have written three, sir. The titles of them are: *What Makes Sammy Run?*, *The Harder They Fall*, and *The Disenchanted*.

Mr. Tavenner: Did you write them in the order in which you named them?

Mr. Schulberg: Yes, sir, I did.

Mr. Tavenner: Mr. Schulberg, there has been testimony before the committee by Mr. Richard Collins, who appeared here on April 12, 1951, that you had been a member of the Communist Party in Hollywood in the late thirties, and that he had understood that you had withdrawn from the Communist Party as the result of a difficulty over the book *What Makes Sammy Run?*

Mr. Schulberg: I guess some others run too, sir.

Mr. Tavenner: And shortly after that testimony—in fact, on April 14—this telegram was received by the chairman of this committee:

I have noted the public statement of your committee inviting those named in recent testimony to appear before your committee. My recollection of Communist affiliation is that it was approximately from 1937 to 1940. My opposition to Communists and Soviet dictatorship is a matter of record. I will cooperate with you in any way I can.

Budd Schulberg,
New Hope, Pa.

Now, as a result of the receipt of that telegram, you were asked to appear at a time that the committee could hear you.

Mr. Schulberg: Yes, sir.

Mr. Tavenner: Had you at any time voluntarily made known to an investigative agency of the Federal Government, prior to the testimony of Richard Collins, that you had been a member of the Communist Party?

Mr. Schulberg: Yes, sir, I had.

Mr. Tavenner: I would like to refer back for a moment to your educational training. You state that you completed your college course at Dartmouth in 1936. While at Dartmouth, did you become acquainted with William Remington?

Mr. Schulberg: I believe when I was a senior at Dartmouth College that he was a junior—no; I am sorry. I mean a freshman; and that when I was the editor of the college newspaper that he was one of the heelers, freshman heelers, for the paper. A heeler is someone bucking for a job on a newspaper. I did meet him at that time, yes, sir.

Mr. Tavenner: You had left Dartmouth College prior to his return to that institution after having been with the TVA in Tennessee?

Mr. Schulberg: I am not sure of the dates of his return to college. I am more sure of mine. I left Dartmouth College in June 1936, and in May 1939 I didn't return to the college, but there is a town very close by where I took up residence while I was writing my first book.

Mr. Tavenner: The testimony of Mr. Remington before this committee was that he returned to Dartmouth in September 1937. That would have been after you had left the institution?

Mr. Schulberg: Yes, sir; it would; I would say about a year and 2 or 3 months after I had left the institution.

Mr. Tavenner: Were you a member of the Communist Party at the time you attended Dartmouth College?

Mr. Schulberg: No, sir.

Mr. Tavenner: Mr. Schulberg, there has been testimony before this committee of efforts made by the Communist Party in Hollywood to influence the work of writers in Hollywood, such as the Albert Maltz incident, with which I am certain you are familiar.

Mr. Schulberg: Yes, sir.

Mr. Tavenner: The screenplay written by Richard Collins, which you may recall from the testimony of Mr. Collins, and the adaptation of a book to the screen, I believe the title of which was "Cornered," or possibly the title of which was "Crossfire"; do you recall which of the two it was, with which Mr. Dmytryk was concerned in his testimony?

Mr. Schulberg: I think he made them both.

Mr. Tavenner: The point is that Mr. Dmytryk testified at length regarding efforts made to influence the production of that picture, that is, efforts by the Communist Party.

Mr. Schulberg: Yes, sir; I am aware of that, and that did strike a bell with me. I remember a somewhat similar incident in my life at a much earlier date.

Mr. Tavenner: I would like for you to tell the committee in detail what your experience was while a member of the Communist Party with the efforts of the Communist Party to influence you in your writings.

Mr. Schulberg: I will try to do that, sir. From about 1937, as I say, I was first in a study group, a Marxist study group, which, without any formality that I remember, became a Young Communist League group and then, I believe became a youth group, still more or less the same group, some changes here or there, a youth group of the Communist Party, as I say, in each step without much formality that I remember. I joined because at the time I felt that the political issues that they seemed to be in favor of, mostly I recall the opposition to the Nazis and to Mussolini and a feeling that something should be done about it, those things attracted me, and there were some others, too. At the same time I was very much interested in my own writing, as I say. In 1937, while a member of the group, and in 1938 also, I began to write short stories. These stories were published in many, many different magazines. I believe the feeling of the group was that these stories were not exactly what would be expected of someone writing as a Communist. Long before any difficulty that I got into for writing *What Makes Sammy Run?* I was told these stories were too realistic, they were too depressing, decadent, and there were many other words. Having some soft sides in my nature, and on some sides a little stronger, I decided that as a writer I had to go ahead and write as well as I could what I felt like writing. During these years, I would say through 1938, while there was a growing tension about this dispute, I must say I was, on the political side, still in favor of the immediate issues as the Communists seemed to be following them. I don't remember having any arguments then about trying to arouse people against the Nazis, and so forth, but I do remember many arguments about my writings. Though I had been somewhat of a zealot in 1936, I think I was much more of a zealot before I was in any organization. It is much easier before you are subjected to any discipline. By early 1939 I was definitely backsliding. I was trying to avoid as many meetings as I could and as many responsibilities as I could. I wasn't seeing the right people. Most of the people I was seeing were writers. Some of these writers might have been strongly opposed to the Party. Some perhaps had not even heard of the Party, I don't know, but they were not interested in the party as a group. The subject was brought up at the meetings that I was attending, and I told them that I was then interested in—

Mr. Tavenner: What type of meetings are you referring to now?

Mr. Schulberg: I would say by 1939 that these were meetings of the youth group of the Communist Party. Whether it was a Young Communist League in early 1939 or a youth group of the Communist Party in the party, I honestly cannot say. I haven't been able to check. To my mind it was more or less a technicality. I think anytime around 1938 if they had asked me, "Do you mind if it is changed?" I don't think I would have said "No," but I don't remember its being discussed. At these meetings I do remember my writing was discussed, and my attitude toward my work was discussed, and it was suggested that I correct my errors, I suppose you would say. At that time I told them I had decided to write a book. The feeling of the group was: "That is fine. Writing is very important, books are very important, provided that they are useful weapons. What kind of a book do you intend to write?"—since I had used my book as an excuse for dropping out and not going to meetings. I said I had written a short story published in *Liberty* magazine in 1937 which was entitled "What Makes Sammy Run?" and that I had been thinking seriously of developing that into a novel. In fact, I had begun to write a series of short stories about a central character which were published in *Liberty* and other magazines and which later became a part of the book that I was to write. The reaction to my idea for this book was not favorable, I would say. The feeling was that this was a destructive idea; that, again, it was much too individualistic; that it didn't begin to show what were called the progressive forces in Hollywood; and that it was something they thought should either be abandoned or discussed with some higher authority than the youth group before I began to work on it.

Mr. Tavenner: Let me interrupt you at that point. Who in the Communist Party group made suggestions of that type to you?

Mr. Schulberg: Well, sir, in the youth group many people felt strongly about it. I believe the one who either felt most strongly or was most responsible at that time was Richard Collins. He disapproved strongly of my attitude toward writing and toward the Communists. When no agreement could be reached, and when both sides were adamant about this, it was suggested by Collins, as I recall, that I speak to

John Howard Lawson and that possibly he could advise me on the changes of the approach or in some way direct my work so that it would not have the destructive and individualistic approach that the group felt I was taking, one which was in opposition to the program of the Party, I believe.

Mr. Tavenner: Well, as a result of that advice, did you confer with John Howard Lawson?

Mr. Schulberg: Yes, sir, I did. I went to see Lawson. I believe it was suggested—I can't remember any longer if it was the group or Lawson that suggested that I submit an outline and discuss the whole matter further, and if it was considered a project that was useful—there was a lot of talk at that time about proletarian novels. That is a museum piece now, but at the time there was a great deal of talk about the proletarian novel and how writers could be useful.

Mr. Tavenner: Describe to the committee the proletarian novel to which you refer.

Mr. Schulberg: That is a difficult assignment. I will try. It was a kind of stock writing formula in that day. The writers were trying to write books about factories, about strikes, about opposition to capitalists, and so forth. This would be hindsight. I don't pretend any wisdom on the subject. But now that I look back, after having studied it more fully, I think it was very similar to what the writers in the Soviet Union were being told at the same time. They were being told that anything that helped the 5-year plan, that made the workers happier in their role, was a good book; if it did not, it was not a good book. Looking back now, it seems that most of the best writers in the Soviet Union were silenced because they were not willing to take that command. But I don't pretend to have known that at the time I was having my squabbles and arguments with Richard Collins, John Howard Lawson, and other people in the Party.

Mr. Tavenner: All right. I interrupted you in your narrative of what occurred with reference to the pressure brought to bear upon you by Lawson and others.

Mr. Schulberg: I believe it was decided that this was not a worthy project unless I submitted to much more discipline. It is always called self-discipline, though I didn't find much self-discipline in it, but it was called self-discipline and it was suggested you submit to it. Many people have submitted to this self-discipline, which, from what I can see, is imposed from without and does not have much to do with self. I decided I would have to get away from this if I was ever to be a writer. I decided to leave the group, cut myself off, pay no more dues, listen to no more advice, indulge in no more political literary discussions, and to go away from the Party, from Hollywood, and try to write a book, which is what I did. I went to Vermont in May of 1939. I settled there and I began to write. I stayed there all through 1939 and into 1940. I believe I spent a month or two at Mount Kisco in a hotel doing my final revisions—not final revisions, I guess a book is never finally revised, but doing some revisions. After that I returned to Hollywood again, after I had submitted my book to the publishers.

Mr. Tavenner: When did you return to Hollywood?

Mr. Schulberg: I believe in February or March 1940.

Mr. Tavenner: Well, had your book been published by that time?

Mr. Schulberg: No, sir; it had not been published. It was at that time being prepared for publication. It was not to be published for another year. There is a long period of work, doing the manuscript cutting, going over the galleys, and so forth, before a book is published. The book finally was published on March 27, 1941.

Mr. Tavenner: Did you have any further difficulty, or did you receive any further advice from the Communist Party, before the publication of the book?

Mr. Schulberg: Yes, sir, I did. When I returned, Richard Collins came to me—I am not absolutely sure, but I believe by this time he seems to have grown somewhat in importance in party groups. I think he had been treasurer of the group when I left. He seemed now to be in some position of greater authority. He came to me and said that they felt that my whole attitude had been sharply in opposition to the Party. I had gone away without announcement. In those days—I suppose it is the same today—I am sure it is—you were not supposed to go away without saying where you were going and getting what was called a transfer. You were supposed to transfer, so that they could pick up your dues, and so forth, at the next place you went. I hadn't done this. I had simply broken off and gone away. They didn't think this was a very good idea. They didn't think finishing my book and turning it in to my publisher without further consultation was a very good idea.

Mr. Tavenner: Right there, let me ask you: You were requested to furnish to Lawson an outline of your book?

Mr. Schulberg: Yes, I was.

Mr. Tavenner: Did you do that?

Mr. Schulberg: No, sir, I did not. I think it was also suggested that I show him the book itself, which, also, I did not do. I feel very, very strongly that every writer has to choose his own guidance in these matters.

Mr. Tavenner: Are you of the opinion that the lack of freedom of that description would destroy you as a writer?

Mr. Schulberg: I am not sure how consciously I knew it at that time. At the time I felt I had to get away from any control in order to be able to write at all; and, as I say, though Mr. Collins, I think, suggested that I get out because of the adverse criticism of the party to my book, actually, as I am sure he would remember, this had a very long history. It had begun with my very first short story and had increased as I continued writing. What was your question?

Mr. Tavenner: I interrupted you to ask whether or not you had furnished to Lawson a copy of the book or outline.

Mr. Schulberg: Never; never; I never did.

Mr. Tavenner: Then you were describing to us what had occurred prior to the publication and release of your book.

Mr. Schulberg: Yes, sir. Collins came to me and told me all the criticisms that had been made against me. By this time there was another problem. I didn't seem to be too much in favor of the Nazi-Soviet pact.

Mr. Tavenner: Let us go into that subject a little later. Let us confine ourselves for the moment to this pressure and influence brought to bear upon you as a writer.

Mr. Schulberg: He said he thought I should come back to the group and not just go away and talk against them, as he had heard I had talked; not to be undisciplined, as he felt I had been for many years; and if I had these objections which he had heard I had told to others that I should come and at least present them and do it clean. I believe he said, "Are you in or out of this thing?" and that I said, "As far as I am concerned, since I left in May I am out." I had these discussions with the group, which were lengthy, both sides presenting their views, which continued to clash, and it was then suggested that I talk to John Howard Lawson, and that since they couldn't settle it, that maybe he could. And I did have a talk again with John Howard Lawson about the book. He felt that they should see it and felt that it was not the sort of thing I should do, and in a sense indicated that I was not functioning as a Communist writer. This also was inconclusive. I think both positions were maintained just as they had been in the group. Finally it was suggested that I talk with a man by the name of V. J. Jerome, who was in Hollywood at that time. I went to see him. Looking back, it may be hard to understand why, after all these wrangles and arguments, I should go ahead and see V. J. Jerome. But maybe every writer has an insatiable curiosity about these things; I don't know. Anyway, I went. It was on Hollywood Boulevard in an apartment. I didn't do much talking. I listened to V. J. Jerome. I am not sure what his position was, but I remember being told that my entire attitude was wrong; that I was wrong about writing; wrong about this book; wrong about the Party; wrong about the so-called peace movement at that particular time. I don't remember saying much. I remember it more as a kind of harangue. When I came away I felt maybe, almost for the first time, that this was to me the real face of the Party. I didn't feel I had talked to just a comrade. I felt I had talked to someone rigid and dictatorial who was trying to tell me how to live my life, and as far as I remember, I didn't want to have anything more to do with them.

Mr. Tavenner: You have spoken several times of your conferences with a group, and you named Richard Collins as a member of that group. Will you identify that group more fully at this time as to whom they were who were talking to you, endeavoring to persuade you to desist in your plan of writing? I am not asking to state at this time the names of all the members of the Communist Party with whom you came in contact. I want to limit it at this point to those who took part in these discussions to which you have referred.

Mr. Schulberg: This will be the tone of the group in general. Some would feel more strongly about it and others less so. We think of the Communists as a monolithic block. The individuals varied. There were some stronger and some weaker. But I believe it was also the view of Paul Jarrico, and not to the same extent that of Ring Lardner, Jr.

Mr. Tavenner: Who?

Mr. Schulberg: Ring Lardner, Jr., who I felt always to be more tolerant in these matters than the others. Those are the principal members in the group itself that I remember discussing this with.

Mr. Tavenner: You were telling us what occurred after you returned to Hollywood in 1940 and prior to the release of your book in 1941.

Mr. Schulberg: Yes, sir. Well, in the fall of 1940 I returned to New York to correct my galleys, and stayed there doing that and making last-minute changes until sometime early in 1941. It seems to me I returned to Hollywood again shortly before my book was actually supposed to appear. I was only there a short time then, but I gathered that the feeling of the Communist Party against the book had been mounting. I think by that time there were advance copies of the book out. A book is in a sense out sometimes three months before it actually appears. I think advance copies had been read before it was out, and the feeling was that all the storm warnings that had been raised against me had been disregarded, and that the work that was about to come out was even worse than anyone could imagine. I was told at that time that a meeting would take place. Well, no, I am not sure I was right then; I am not sure. I was a little bit excited because it was my first novel and I was very curious as to what people would think of it, and I felt some people were not going to like it very well, and I decided to go down to a quiet spot and sit around on the beach, and maybe drop in at de Houslaus' Bar or something, and wait until this whole thing blew over. I did. I went to Ensenada, and I thought I was waiting for it to blow over. I guess it hasn't quite blown over yet. As I say, I had been told that there was going to be a meeting against the book. When I returned to Hollywood after the book had been published, I ran into various people. It turned out to be rather a controversial book inside the Communist Party, apparently, and outside. People took rather violent sides on this. Some people disliked it intensely, and others were more favorable to it. I heard that a meeting was to take place. No, it wasn't quite like that. There was a review in the *Daily Worker* about that time. I think it was early April sometime before I returned from Ensenada.

Mr. Tavenner: How long was that before the release of the book, do you recall?

Mr. Schulberg: As I recall, it was shortly after. It would be about the time any other book review would come out.

Mr. Tavenner: What was the date of the release of your book?

Mr. Schulberg: March 27, 1941. So I would say that was about a week later. The book review was a very favorable book review.

Mr. Tavenner: From the *Daily Worker?*

Mr. Schulberg: Yes, sir. It said that this was "the Hollywood novel." It said that most of the novels before that treated with Hollywood had resorted to filth, and that this book was hearteningly free from all of this, that it dealt realistically with the Hollywood scene. I think I was called a realist; I think I was called an important comer; and, in general, it was a pretty good review. Apparently, the review was a mistake. I heard there was consternation about the review and that somehow the reviewer had missed a signal.

Mr. Tavenner: Were there any meetings held in Communist Party circles before the so-called mistake had been discovered?

Mr. Schulberg: What meetings there were in Communist circles before, I honestly couldn't say, because I wouldn't have been a part of them, but I was told there was going to be a public meeting engineered by, but I don't believe confined to, Communists, at which the reviewer would be called to account and the real Party line on the book would be laid down. I was asked if I wanted to come to this meeting, and I said that I didn't believe any writer should defend his book in public. I hope I am not doing it here, because it is something I don't believe in. A book is defended by the writer when he writes it, and after that everybody has a right to like or dislike it if he wishes.

Mr. Tavenner: That is, in the United States?

Mr. Schulberg: Exactly; in the United States and I would say generally in the Western World.

Mr. Jackson: Who extended this invitation or told you of this indignation meeting that was to be held?

Mr. Schulberg: That I can't remember. I can't remember exactly who it was who asked me to the meeting. It may have been one of any number of people, and I don't recall. I simply remember I was asked, and I remember what I said and that I refused to go.

Mr. Tavenner: Then, after the meeting, I understand various mistakes were discovered. What were you referring to?

Mr. Schulberg: Well, I understand that it was pointed out at the meeting that this review was entirely opposite to what it should have been; that the book was not an honest book; that it was a dishonest book. I have copies of the two reviews. It would be too lengthy to describe them point by point.

Mr. Tavenner: I have them here. I will introduce them.

Mr. Schulberg: In that case I will try to remember it as well as I can. The feeling was that I had slandered the progressive forces. I believe they said it was not a Hollywood novel at all. All the things brought out in the meeting which I am reporting, I neglected to say, appeared in a new review shortly after the meeting. A new review, by the same reviewer. It is the only time I have been reviewed good and bad by the same reviewer. It is the only time I ever remember one book reviewer reviewing the same book twice, ten days apart, and in almost every instance one review was completely at variance with the other, point by point. The book which was "not filthy" was "filthy"; the book which was realistic was reactionary; the book which was healthy was diseased.

Mr. Velde: Was it reviewed by the same man in both instances?

Mr. Schulberg: Yes. I remember his name. It was Charles Glenn.

Mr. Tavenner: Where was Charles Glenn then employed?

Mr. Schulberg: I imagine both by the *Daily Worker* and the *People's World*. I believe those reviews appeared simultaneously in both newspapers.

Mr. Tavenner: Had you known Charles Glenn prior to that time?

Mr. Schulberg: I may have met him once in Hollywood browsing around in a bookshop one day. I knew him, I think I was introduced to him once before that, and that is all, simply as somebody who wrote on that paper.

Mr. Walter: May I ask you a question at this point? What was there in the book *What Makes Sammy Run?* that would cause the Communists to attack the book?

Mr. Schulberg: Well, sir; they could answer that much better than I could. As I recall the attack and the reviews, the objection was to what I believe they called the whole approach to literature. I think they feel that you have to have a propagandistic point of view. They felt that I simply had not shown the things that they thought ought to be shown; that I had just written an individual story about one person. I never intended it to be typical of Hollywood. I didn't intend it to be typical of all the Hollywood producers. It was the story of one person as I saw him, characteristic, that I thought could happen, but didn't happen in Hollywood all the time. It was at variance with what they thought a book about Hollywood should be.

Mr. Walter: In other words, they objected to the fact you had overlooked a chance to slant a story?

Mr. Schulberg: I would say so, yes, sir.

Mr. Tavenner: In fact, one of the criticisms was that you had not dealt strongly enough with the work that had been done in the reorganization of the Screen Writers Guild?

Mr. Schulberg: That was one of their many objections. They felt I had almost—I am not sure if the word "slandered" was used, but they felt I had completely overlooked the real work that had been done to build up the guild, and not placed enough emphasis on the little people of Hollywood, and so on. I was not attempting to prove or disprove anything. I was just trying to tell my story.

Mr. Tavenner: Did you become acquainted with a person by the name of Elizabeth Leech Glenn?

Mr. Schulberg: No, sir. I don't remember ever being acquainted with her.

Mr. Tavenner: Mr. Chairman, I desire to introduce in evidence the book reviews referred to. The first is taken from *People's World* of April 2, 1941, page 5, the heading of which is "Novel—the story of a Hollywood heel," by Charles Glenn. I desire to offer it in evidence as Schulberg exhibit No. 1. The second is the issue of the *Daily Worker* of April 7, 1941 (p. 7), the heading of which is "What Makes Sammy Run?—story of a Hollywood heel," by Charles Glenn. I offer it in evidence as Schulberg exhibit No. 2. The third is the issue of the *Daily Worker* of April 8, 1941 (p. 7), and appears under the heading "News in the world of stage and screen," by Charles Glenn. I desire to offer it in evidence as Schulberg exhibit No. 3. The next is the April 24, 1941, issue of the *People's World* (p. 5), under the heading "Hollywood Vine," by Charles Glenn. I offer it in evidence as Schulberg exhibit No. 4. And finally, the issue of April 23, 1941 (p. 7), of the *Daily Worker,* an article entitled "Hollywood Can Be Won to the Side of the American People—Actors and Directors Respond to Criticism of Film Audiences," by Charles Glenn. I desire to offer it in evidence as Schulberg exhibit No. 5.

Mr. Wood: Let them be received.

Mr. Tavenner: Mr. Schulberg, I referred a moment ago to the review by Charles Glenn in which he made a favorable review, and the only criticism was that which I mentioned, that the battle to organize the Screen

Writers Guild was sketched too lightly in the novel. And you have described in a general way the favorable comment that was made by the representative of the *Daily Worker.*

Mr. Schulberg: Yes, sir, I tried to.

Mr. Tavenner: There was also an additional review by Charles Glenn on April 8, 1941, page 7, which has been introduced in evidence as Schulberg exhibit No. 3. Were you familiar with that second review which was also a favorable review?

Mr. Schulberg: No, sir, that I don't know about. I was aware of two reviews, one favorable and another that was not.

Mr. Tavenner: In the course of this second review, exhibit 3, this statement is made:

> Originally we passed on second-hand word about Budd Schulberg's new book, *What Makes Sammy Run?* Having finished it now, may we pass on word that while it doesn't qualify as the great American novel, it's still the best work done on Hollywood?

Showing that there had been a rather deliberate and painstaking review of your book by the reviewer of the *Daily Worker* which extended over a period of days. I would like to read into the record that portion of exhibits 4 and 5 in which Glenn explains the reasons for his change. In the *Daily People's World* of April 24, 1941, Mr. Glenn explained his about-face by this statement, and I quote:

> Since writing the review, I have received several criticisms on it. On the basis of these criticisms, I've done a reevaluation of my work. It's rather important that this reevaluation be done, not in the light of breast beating, but in the light of constructive self-criticism, by which anyone who writes for this paper must work. Understanding your own mistakes is the first requirement of criticism. If you don't understand your own, how can you be expected to consistently understand the weaknesses and mistakes of those on the other side of the fence?

I also want to read into the record the explanation which appeared in the *Daily Worker* of April 23, 1941, which is exhibit 5. It is in this language, and I quote:

> On the basis of quite lengthy discussion on the book, I've done a little reevaluation, and this helps me emphasize the points I've tried to make

here. . . . To say I felt more than a trifle silly when these weaknesses (in the Schulberg novel) were called to my attention is putting it a bit mildly. It is precisely the superficial subjective attitude shown in this review which reflects the dangers of an "anti-Hollywood" approach, conscious or unconscious. This isn't breast beating. It's necessary criticism, because until the attitude reflected is cleaned up, Hollywood will not and cannot be considered the force for peace and progress it is and can be.

Those were the explanations given after the meeting which you have referred to, in which your book had been criticized and Glenn had been called on the carpet about his first favorable report on your novel.

Mr. Schulberg: I had not realized there were two different reviews, but that does check with my memory of the one review I recall.

Mr. Tavenner: To emphasize clearly the way in which the Communist Party changed and followed the dictates of some directing authority, I want to read into the record some of those outstanding points which you mentioned in the course of your testimony. What I am going to read now is from the *Daily Worker* of April 7, 1941, and also from the *People's World* of April 2, 1941, being the favorable review of Charles Glenn. This is his language:

> For slightly fewer years than they have awaited the great American novel, whatever that may be, American bibliophiles and critics have been awaiting the Hollywood novel. While they may argue its merits and demerits I've a feeling that all critics, no matter their carping standards, will have to admit they've found the Hollywood novel in Budd Schulberg's *What Makes Sammy Run?*

Now, in the retractive statement of Charles Glenn published in the *People's World* of April 24, 1941, this is what he says, and I quote:

> The first error I made was in calling the book the Hollywood novel.

And I quote again, from the *Daily Worker* of April 23, 1941:

> Recently I wrote a review on Budd Schulberg's book, *What Makes Sammy Run?* I said it was the story of a Hollywood heel and could be regarded as the Hollywood novel. On the basis of quite lengthy discussion on the book, I've done a little re-evaluation, and this helps me emphasize the points I've tried to make here.

He then makes various criticisms, and adds:

> Can it then be termed "the Hollywood novel"?

I want the record to also show one or two other points, so that it may be plain. I quote from the *Daily Worker* of April 7, 1941, and the *People's World* of April 2, 1941, which was the favorable review:

> Former works on the film city have been filthy with four-letter words, spoken and implied . . . None of these things hold true for Schulberg's novel.
>
> There is nothing vulgar in what he says, nothing superficially vulgar, that is. . . . Writing in the first person, Schulberg tells of the good as well as the bad.

Then, after the meeting, from the *Daily Worker* of April 23, 1941, appears this statement:

> We do not intend to go into all the aspects of the conscience of a writer, a conscience which allows him (with full knowledge of the facts) to show only the dirt and filth.

And from the *People's World* again, of April 24, 1941, after the meeting, I quote:

> In a full-drawn portraiture of either Sammy Glick or Hollywood, the people must be seen in action, living the lives they lead. Even more effective would the filth of Sammy Glick become when counterposed to the cleanliness of the people.

> Mr. Velde: Mr. Counsel, may I make a comment at this point?
>
> Mr. Tavenner: Yes, sir.
>
> Mr. Velde: I feel very definitely that this illustrates the degree of control the Communist Party had over the *People's World* and the New York *Daily Worker* and all writers in their jurisdiction.
>
> Mr. Tavenner: I call attention to one other point which I desire to be shown in the record. In the *Daily Worker* of April 7, 1941, and the *People's World* of April 2, 1941, which are the favorable reviews, this language appears:

> Characters [referring to former books on Hollywood] have been drawn black and white, most Hollywood denizens turning out to be unadulterated heels. . . . None of these things hold true for Schulberg's novel.

Then, after the meeting, from the *People's World* of April 24, 1941, appears this language:

> Some day that story of the Guild will be thoroughly told, well drama-
> tized, and done in all the shades of gray which entered the picture, not
> on the plain black and white drawn in the Schulberg book.

You mentioned a moment ago that you have never known of a more complete reversal in a review than there was in this case.

Mr. Schulberg: I have never seen anything like that; no, sir. I have seen some reviews of my work that I myself might like to change a little bit, but I believe very deeply that in this country every man must act on the basis of his own individual conscience, and that that is one of our privileges and that no one should ever have to change his mind because of dictation from above or outside.

Mr. Tavenner: Has your attention been drawn to another criticism of your book from Communist sources?

Mr. Schulberg: Well, sir, I could not identify it as officially a Communist source, but there was a magazine review which I believe was more or less in line with this general attack on me and my work; yes, sir.

Mr. Tavenner: Is that the article written by W. L. River, appearing in the *Clipper* publication?

Mr. Schulberg: Yes, sir; it is.

Mr. Tavenner: The issue of June 21, 1941, at page 20. I will ask you to look at that review and state if it is the one to which you refer?

Mr. Schulberg: Thank you. [After examining document] Yes, it is.

Mr. Tavenner: I desire merely to file this. I will not introduce it as an exhibit.

Mr. Schulberg: May I say, sir, that I do remember that review quite well, and that I felt he had a right to write it. If it was his own individual opinion, I would have no objection. If it was part of, in a sense, a mass effort, I would then object very strongly.

Mr. Tavenner: Do you know the writer, W. L. River?

Mr. Schulberg: I knew him slightly; yes, sir.

Mr. Tavenner: Do you know whether or not he was a member of the Communist Party at that time?

Mr. Schulberg: I could not say definitely that he was; no sir.

Mr. Walter: Do you know whether or not Charles Glenn was a member of the Communist Party?

Mr. Schulberg: Only by assuming that anyone writing for those publications would be.

Mr. Walter: By that you mean nobody would have a job with the *Daily Worker* or this other publication unless he was a Communist?

Mr. Schulberg: That would be my hunch. I have never tried to get a job with them, but that would be my hunch.

Mr. Tavenner: A pretty good hunch.

Mr. Schulberg: Pretty good; yes.

Mr. Velde: As a matter of fact, I think testimony before this committee was to the effect that all writers for the *Daily Worker, People's World,* and *New Masses* had to be Communist Party members.

Mr. Tavenner: Mr. Schulberg, is this effort within the Communist Party of the United States to control the work of writers, which you have so graphically described in your own case, consistent with what is occurring in Russia, from any information that is available to you?

Mr. Schulberg: I believe it is; yes, sir; I do. I believe that writing has been very tightly controlled there, and that those who refused to follow the party line were not able to write, or sometimes ceased to exist. On the other hand, those who did, received all kinds of emoluments and were the most privileged people there. I think that has been the history of writing in the Soviet Union, with perhaps one exception.

Mr. Tavenner: Have you been in the Soviet Union?

Mr. Schulberg: Yes; I was.

Mr. Tavenner: When was that?

Mr. Schulberg: In 1934, during the summer. May I say that I don't want to sound too sure of the subject, but two or three months ago I did begin to write an article on the subject of what has happened to writing in the Soviet Union between my first visit in 1934, when I must say I was very impressed, and 1951, which is a relatively short period. I have done a great deal of research on the subject.

Mr. Tavenner: Will you give the committee the benefit of your research and your views at this time, briefly? I think it fits in exactly with the pattern that you have described in matters that have affected you, and it is particularly pertinent that you contrast the experience which you have gone through with what you have discovered from your studies are the conditions in the other country.

Mr. Schulberg: In the late twenties and early thirties writing was controlled by a proletarian group. I have forgotten the name of the organization. It was an organization that controlled all writing, and unless you were satisfactory to the head of this group you just didn't write. I am talking about the Soviet Union. This is Russia. Those writers who didn't conform to that were silenced. I think the very best writers, Isaac Babel and many others, felt they could not write under those circumstances. They had slogans for writing. One slogan was "All novels must make workers feel happier under the five-year plan." If the book suggested it was not altogether true, or only 99.9 percent true, there was a good chance it would not be published. If it suggested it was only 50 percent true, there was a good chance the writer would not be around any more. One day, according to my research, Stalin looked around and said, "Our writing is pretty dull." They said, "Let's find the man who is making it dull." They got the man, who had been silenced and under cover. The reason for that was that Gorki, head of the writing organization, believed there should be a more lenient attitude. I was on the platform at that writers' congress, and that is what did impress me. I remember Gorki speaking, and a man named Bukharin spoke, and Isaac Babel spoke, and many of the great poets, Pasternak, and so forth. This is hindsight. I think it is a striking fact that every man who appeared on the platform and called for greater leniency—I think it was called a new silver age of literature—every one of these men by 1938 had either been shot or been silenced, and after that none of these writers, who were trying to follow their individual line, were able to function any more. Some were silenced. Some committed suicide. Some disappeared. Some decided to conform and wrote in the approved style and made a lot of money and did very well. I believe that is much the situation today. I really believe that you have to conform or in some way you get out or they put you out. I don't know if I should say it in connection with this, but there is an organization called Friends for Intellectual Freedom.

Mr. Tavenner: I was just going to ask you about that.

Mr. Schulberg: The organization is interested in helping those writers who have suffered under those conditions and who are able to get out and to try to rehabilitate them and to help them write as they please.

For that reason, a number of writers, novelists—Arthur Koestler, Aldous Huxley, Graham Greene, John Dos Passos, James T. Farrell, Richard Rovere, Stephen Spender, and myself, among others; I believe there are others—have decided to try to raise funds if they can, to help these people. I am in a sense sorry to have to mention it, because it has not been an organization that has been seeking any publicity at all. It is supposed to be just a direct contribution from writer to writer and has discouraged any wide publicity. The thought was that those who were able to write as they pleased would turn over a percentage of their own royalties to those people who haven't been able to do that.

Mr. Walter: Where are the beneficiaries of that program located?

Mr. Schulberg: In Western Germany, I believe, and in France, and here, any writers who are deemed worthy and who are refugees from the system.

Mr. Rhetts: Mr. Tavenner, we have here simply a statement what this organization is, its purposes, and something about it, and if the committee would like to have it I would be glad to make it available.

Mr. Tavenner: Yes; we shall be glad to have it.

Mr. Rhetts: Would you care to introduce it as an exhibit?

Mr. Tavenner: We will file it with his testimony.

Mr. Schulberg: I believe through these people we will have an opportunity to get firsthand information on what has actually been happening. For instance, I have heard a number of stories. One is that a very distinguished Soviet critic, Corvely Zelinsky, decided he would try to write the history of the Soviet literature. He began with high hopes after the writers' congress I have described, but so many changes had to be made—for instance, one chapter would have to be thrown out because it was written about a writer who was just arrested, and so forth, that he decided after three years that if was impossible to write a history of literature in the Soviet Union that would be honest.

Mr. Tavenner: In other words, the changes were probably for the same reason that John Howard Lawson was required to change his history that he was writing, if you are familiar with that testimony?

Mr. Schulberg: I believe it does have exactly the same effect; yes, sir. I was very interested in finding out that meetings are held and writers are denounced and from that time on their works are no longer in publication. I feel that the only difference with me is that we have many different forms of publications. There is not a single one where, if you fall out with a group, you are finished.

Mr. Tavenner: Have there been any instances where you have obtained direct information from a person who has been subjected to that type of treatment in Russia?

Mr. Schulberg: Yes, sir. In the preparation of this article which I began, as I said, three months ago, I wrote to someone who was somewhat of an authority in this field, who had come out of Russia only in the last two or three years, and I told him of my experience in 1934, when I had been impressed. I told him I had met Gorki and a playwright by the name of Afinogenoff, and many others, and it had begun to strike me that all the people who told me how hopeful they were, in 1934, weren't around any more. I said I didn't know any more about it than that writers' congress I had attended. I asked if he could fill me in on what happened after that time, and he did write me a letter which I found extremely enlightening, and I will read some parts of it.

Mr. Tavenner: I will not ask you to disclose at this time the name of the person who wrote you the letter.

Mr. Schulberg: Thank you, sir. It is a rather long letter. I don't want to read it all.

Mr. Tavenner: I would like for you to read the parts that are pertinent to the inquiry, whether short or long.

Mr. Schulberg (reading):

You were very fortunate to be in Moscow in 1934. The period from April 1932 (decree abolishing the special proletarian groups in literature and art) to 1935 was a time of good and new hopes. During that period the Soviet literature was under the strong and friendly leadership and protection of Maxim Gorki. The apogee of that short "silver age" was the first convention of Soviet writers in September 1934. The principal speakers at the first convention were Gorki (*Soviet Literature and Socialistic Realism*) and Nicholai Bukharin (*The Problems of Soviet Poetry*). The last name certainly shows what a tolerant atmosphere was present at the convention. Among the many speakers was Isaac Babel. This gifted novelist was silenced since 1927 (or 1928) and I still remember how surprised and pleased I was to see him on the podium speaking a brilliant speech in his usual sharp-witted manner.

"All the materials of the first convention seemed to be unorthodox, doubtful, and unreliable for Stalin. This is very important for clear understanding what had happened in 1936 and 1937. It is easy to remark that all repressions and liquidations in the literature and in the literary circles which took place during the Yernov era—"

I don't know what that is—

were tightly connected with the first convention, its most important speakers and organizers. Gorki was poisoned (1936), Bukharin was dismissed from his office as editor in chief of *Izvestia,* arrested (1937) and shot (1938) . . .

Then there were a bunch of Russian names (continuing reading):

and many other novelists were arrested—the same as poets Pavel Vassiliyev, Boris Kornilov, Zaholotsky, Smelyakoff, and others. Some of their colleagues—prominent Soviet writers and poets completely stopped their creative activity—among them, Selvinsky, Pasternak, Sholokhov, Fedin, and Leonov.

After 1937 Soviet literature was like a big army retreating after unsuccessful decisive battle. Some generals were missing, some retreated in silence, trying not to show their fear and doubts. Others tried to make a gay look and impression that nothing of importance was happening. This group did not stop their activity during Yernov era and produced some bad plays and novels . . .

Some of the writers who belonged to the silent group later (in 1939 or 1940) broke the silence and started to write in the new orthodox way. It was a great creative degradation for them. So did Tolstoy, Sholokhov, Fedin, poet Antokolsky. Some of the writers never tried again—like Boris Pasternak—the finest poet of contemporary Russian and an extremely noble and honest person. So far as I know he only translates from English and French. During the war he translated *Hamlet.* But I have never heard that any of them did some active "anti" like Meyerhold.

I might say when I went to the Soviet Union in 1934 one of the things that had impressed me most was that I had an opportunity to meet Meyerhold, who was the foremost stage director in the Soviet Union and probably one of the outstanding ones in the world, and he showed me through his theater (continuing reading):

The case of Meyerhold was a unique one. It certainly was a very rare combination of the big mistakes of Government . . .

I think I should explain he is writing something that is known to me. Meyerhold had been a director until 1937. At that time his technique fell into disrepute and he was under a very strong cloud. I don't think he was allowed to produce anything at all in 1937. In 1939 there was a meeting of the stage directors in Russia, and Meyerhold, who had been silenced for a long time, asked for an opportunity to speak. He got up and spoke on June 14, 1939, and I honestly believe that his speech will go down as one of the great speeches in defense of individual conscience in the field of art. He told them he had always done the best that he could in his own way; that he couldn't follow anybody else's line or point of view; but that if he was a formalist, and if all the plays he saw on the stage at that time were Socialist realism, he was glad to be a formalist, and so forth. The day after that speech Meyerhold disappeared, and when the yearbook came out at the end of the year, giving all the speeches of the directors at this convention, Meyerhold's speech was conspicuous by its absence. I think in another twenty or thirty years probably nobody in that country will have ever heard of Meyerhold. I think he will be completely removed and will be what is called a nonperson. Shall I continue this letter, sir?

Mr. Tavenner: If there is anything else there pertinent to our discussion.

Mr. Schulberg: I don't believe so, except for one last word about Afinogenoff. He had been one of my hosts. I had gone to his home when I was in the Soviet Union in 1934. I went to see one of his plays. I asked what had happened to Afinogenoff, and he said in 1937 or 1938 they decided Afinogenoff's plays were not good, not following the line, and they were removed from the repertoire of the Soviet Union.

Mr. Tavenner: And do I understand it was the same general type of disagreement with regard to a writer's freedom to write that caused your original disaffection with the Communist Party?

Mr. Schulberg: I now believe it was. I didn't relate it that way at that time, but it was something which the Communists call a social command. A writer in a sense was looked upon as a soldier, and he was given certain social commands, and if he didn't follow those social commands he was no longer permitted to function in that system. I think at that time I was being given a social command. I didn't know it at the time by that name, neither did they, but I think in a mild way that is what it was.

Mr. Wood: The committee will stand in recess until 2:30.

AFTERNOON SESSION

Mr. Tavenner: Mr. Schulberg, in the course of your testimony this morning you told us of your trip in 1934 to the Soviet Union. Were you a member of the Communist Party at that time?

Mr. Schulberg: No, sir.

Mr. Tavenner: I wish you would now tell the committee the circumstances under which you became a member of the Communist Party, fixing the date as nearly as you can.

Mr. Schulberg: In the summer of 1936 I returned to Hollywood and in the fall of that year I went to work as a reader in a studio as what they call a junior writer. I was disturbed by the unemployment problem and what seemed to me the rising tide of aggression in Europe. It was during that period that somebody came to me by the name of Stanley Lawrence.

Mr. Tavenner: Stanley Lawrence?

Mr. Schulberg: Yes, sir. I have been trying to fix the place where we met, and I can't. I have the impression of his just coming up to me somewhere, either at home—I am just not sure any more—and saying that he heard that I was interested in this problem, that I was concerned about the growth of nazism and so forth, and that I might be interested in joining a Marxist study group. I said that I thought I would be interested in joining it.

Mr. Tavenner: Do you know or did you know at that time whether or not Lawrence held a high position within the Communist Party in Hollywood?

Mr. Schulberg: No, sir, at the time I had no idea who he was. He said that he had done a good deal of teaching of Marxism and had a job during the day and was interested in teaching this class at night. As far as I know, at that time that was the only way I could identify him.

Mr. Tavenner: Did you subsequently discover how high his position was in the Communist Party?

Mr. Schulberg: I would say in the next year and a half I definitely did, sir, yes. By degrees, I would say.

Mr. Tavenner: Will you describe what his function was in the Communist Party as far as you are able to do so?

Mr. Schulberg: We began this study group—it seems to me it was somewhere in 1937. I think that the teaching of Marx was fairly elementary, and I honestly don't think I ever mastered it. After the study group was going for some time, Lawrence dropped out of it and only would come once in a while. It was only later on that I did find out that he had started, I suppose, many groups like this one group that I was in and that he had become the head of the Communist movement in Hollywood at that time. I believe that would be around 1938.

Mr. Tavenner: Did other individuals confer with you either before Stanley Lawrence spoke to you or soon thereafter about your joining the Communist Party?

Mr. Schulberg: There were two people about the same time late in 1936 or early in 1937 who talked to me about the Communist Party in general and told me that they felt that it was sort of leading the way in trying to work up as much feeling as possible against the Nazis and against aggression in Europe and so on. They talked to me in pretty general terms, but they did talk to me about the Communist Party. They didn't ask me to join it directly, no. I should say that this first study group was not part of the party. When Stanley Lawrence came to me he simply said, do you want to join this study group, and I said "Yes," not conscious that this was actually a part of the Community Party. In fact, I suppose in some ways it wasn't.

Mr. Tavenner: When did the conversation with the two other persons take place in relation to the first approach by Stanley Lawrence?

Mr. Schulberg: In my mind it is just about the same period, either late in 1936 or somewhere early in 1937. I think it preceded—I think it preceded Lawrence's coming to me and asking me about the study group.

Mr. Tavenner: Who were the individuals who approached you?

Mr. Schulberg: Their names were Robert Tasker and John Bright.

Mr. Tavenner: Bright? How do you spell the last name?

Mr. Schulberg: B–r–i–g–h–t.

Mr. Tavenner: How do you spell the first person you mentioned?

Mr. Schulberg: T–a–s–k–e–r.

Mr. Tavenner: Tasker is now deceased, I believe.

Mr. Schulberg: Yes, I think he is.

Mr. Tavenner: Can you give us any information as to the present occupation of John Bright?

Mr. Schulberg: He was a screenwriter at the time. I haven't seen him in many years, and I don't know where he is.

Mr. Tavenner: Now will you proceed to tell us further about your recruitment into the Party?

Mr. Schulberg: The group was studying Marx, and Lawrence at that early time would relate these things to current events. At some point, which I can't identify exactly, there was a change—I think one reason I can't is that it wasn't a formal change and was pretty much the same group, as I remember, and I remember them mostly because these were the people who went on with me as being the ones I mentioned this morning, Richard Collins and Paul Jarrico, and Ring Lardner. At some point it was suggested by Lawrence that these things that we were talking about and all believed in, which at that time were very, very general issues because the feeling in those days seemed to be extremely broad, they said that any man of good will, anybody opposed to Fascism, really could join the Party. I believe it was even said that you didn't have to believe in all of the points of the program. You could even disagree with some. I am pretty sure that was said to me at that time. It was also said that this was not a revolutionary organization and that it supported the Constitution and so forth. That was also said. Anyway, somewhere in 1937, I believe, the group changed from a study group to a Young Communist League group. As I said, without any formality that I can recall, they all came back and sat down the same way as before and sat around and talked the same way as before, pretty much the same people as before, but simply implemented their studies now with more actual activity. The stress began to be more in the field of activity than in any kind of study.

Mr. Walter: Then what actually happened was that Stanley Lawrence set up this organization and after giving the members some fundamental instructions he moved on to continue the same sort of work elsewhere.

Mr. Schulberg: That is exactly the way it seemed to me, sir. At first he spent most of his time, all of his time, and then less and less, and the group continued by its own momentum.

Mr. Walter: Who took over after he abandoned it?

Mr. Schulberg: There was no real director of it. There was a leader. I think at the very first I was probably as much of a leader as anybody was. I would say about 1937. As I became more interested in writing I became less interested in being active in the political activities. Lawrence would drop in from time—he would come in often, as a matter of fact, not just from time to time. He would come in, say, every two or three times, and sometimes even at the end of such a gathering he would come in for 15 minutes or half an hour. So in a sense I would say he kept tabs on it probably in the same line, I am not sure, also he kept tabs on it probably in the same way.

Mr. Tavenner: He joined the Abraham Lincoln Brigade and was killed in overseas fighting, was he not?

Mr. Schulberg: I heard that he did, yes, sir. I don't remember exactly. It seems to me it was in 1938 sometime.

Mr. Jackson: How many members were there in this group that was established by Mr. Lawrence.

Mr. Schulberg: About eight—six to eight. It would vary somewhat because things were much more informal in those days. Young men would be asked in or invited or just drop in, who were not actually members of the group and could sit in and see if they liked it. People would bring friends, and so forth, so it would vary. That is why I think more of the people who went on, but others did come in and go out. I would say an average would be seven or eight.

Mr. Jackson: How many meetings would you say you attended over the period of time in which you were associated with the group?

Mr. Schulberg: I have never tried to figure that out, sir. I believe the group met about once every two weeks. My attendance was quite consistent at the beginning, and then from 1938 on began to drop off. In other words, there would be meetings that I would not attend.

Mr. Jackson: But your attendance commenced when?

Mr. Schulberg: My attendance—let's see. The study group began early in 1937. Just when we made the change to the Young Communist League, I am not sure.

Mr. Jackson: It was a period of about a year, then, that your attendance was more or less regular.

Mr. Schulberg: I would say more or less regular. I think from 1937 it was probably most regular, at which time it was a study group, and I would say that somewhere along the end of that year is when the change was made to the Young Communist League, although I am not sure of the actual date of transition.

Mr. Jackson: This was not by any chance the same study group that gave Mr. Lawrence headaches, was it? He testified that dialectics gave him headaches. Was Marc Lawrence in that group?

Mr. Schulberg: I think not.

Mr. Tavenner: Your testimony has related to Stanley Lawrence, an entirely different individual?

Mr. Schulberg: Yes.

Mr. Jackson: Not Marc Lawrence, but Stanley Lawrence. I can understand how the dialectics would give people headaches over many things which are difficult to understand.

Mr. Velde: I am not quite sure on the name of the organization which you first joined. Was it the Young Communist League or was the name changed?

Mr. Schulberg: No sir. The first organization had no name at all. It was like any informal class at night.

Mr. Velde: Then later it did, in 1938, change into the Young Communist League?

Mr. Schulberg: That is right, sir.

Mr. Velde: And you had membership then in what you knew as the Young Communist League?

Mr. Schulberg: Yes, sir; I did.

Mr. Velde: I believe this morning you testified that later it changed into something else. Was that the American Youth for Democracy—the AYD, as it is commonly known?

Mr. Schulberg: I don't remember that at all. This is my impression of the transition. It seems that it went through three or possibly four stages. First, a study group which had, as far as I knew, no organizational connection. It was just a study group. Then it became a Young Communist League group.

Mr. Tavenner: Was it in the nature of an indoctrinational group for prospective Communist recruits?

Mr. Schulberg: The Young Communist League?

Mr. Tavenner: The first group.

Mr. Schulberg: I am sure that that is what it was, though I didn't think of it that way at the time. That is what it turned out to be because at a time when we were far enough along and when Lawrence said, we are really doing the same things, and these were the things which seemed to me right at the time, we were concerned with this problem and it did seem to me—and we were also being told at the same time that the Communists seemed to be taking the lead in breaking down the feeling of isolationism and so forth, building up and participating in the Anti-Nazi League, and that sort of thing. At one point Lawrence said, "Well, this is really the same thing. You feel this way and think this way," which I did. "And the Young Communist League has the same principles, except that they do more about it than simply sit around and study," and at that time I agreed.

Mr. Velde: You mentioned the Young Communist League again. I wonder if counsel recalls when the Young Communist League was changed to the American Youth for Democracy.

Mr. Schulberg: I didn't know that it had been.

Mr. Tavenner: I will give you the exact date in a moment. It was October 1943.

Mr. Velde: Then as far as you are concerned, Mr. Schulberg, you never participated in any of the activities of the American Youth for Democracy?

Mr. Schulberg: No, sir; I don't think I know much about it, for that matter.

Mr. Doyle: May I ask this question. I notice, Mr. Schulberg, the group about which you testified organized in 1937? You said that in 1939, at the age of 25, you broke with the Communists because of their efforts to dictate. You just stated that Mr. Lawrence made certain statements to you, and you replied "I agree." Did he make those statements to you alone or were you in a group which he was trying to convert? In other words, was it an argument? Was it a speech? How did he present these comparative ideas showing that the Communist idea was the same as that which the group already held? Was it to you individually or to the group?

Mr. Schulberg: This would be to the group, sir; to a group. He would say that this is really an extension of democracy; that these things needed to be done. He would talk about the current events of the time to the group, not to me alone. I don't recall after the first meeting any— I can't recall, at least, any talks with him alone.

Mr. Doyle: Was he an invited speaker? Was he a program speaker? How did it come about that he attended the meetings?

Mr. Schulberg: He formed it. He set up the group in the beginning.

Mr. Doyle: Was he the sole speaker or did you have other speakers—this group which he organized?

Mr. Schulberg: It wouldn't really be as formal as that. It was a study group which he would lead.

Mr. Doyle: He was the sole leader?

Mr. Schulberg: Yes, sir; he was the sole leader.

Mr. Walter: Proceed, Mr. Tavenner.

Mr. Tavenner: I would like to ask you whether the individual whose name was John Bright was a member of this group.

Mr. Schulberg: No, sir; he was not in that group. One reason might have been that these were all very young people, all about from the age of, I would say, almost 18 or 19 to 21 or 22. It was set up specifically as a group of young people.

Mr. Tavenner: Do you know of any of the work which Bright did later in the moving-picture industry?

Mr. Schulberg: He was for a long time—he has written many screenplays over the years. I am not sure specifically of any one. I connect him chiefly with gangster films in those days, around 1936 or 1937. I think he wrote a number of gangster films.

Mr. Tavenner: Will you give us names of other persons who from time to time became affiliated with that group—that is, the group in the Communist Party to which you belonged?

Mr. Schulberg: Besides the ones I remember definitely in 1937, there was Waldo Salt.

Mr. Tavenner: Waldo Salt?

Mr. Schulberg: Yes. I don't believe he was in the original group, but came in at some later time. I couldn't place the time. It seems to me early in 1938, but I am not too clear on these dates.

Mr. Tavenner: In whose homes were meetings held?

Mr. Schulberg: They would be held at the various homes of the people in the group. As far as I recall, it would rotate. Once in a while, mine, sometimes at Jarrico's or Collins' apartment, at the house of Ring Lardner.

Mr. Tavenner: Ring Lardner?

Mr. Schulberg: Yes.

Mr. Tavenner: Ring Lardner, Jr.?

Mr. Schulberg: Yes, sir.

Mr. Jackson: Who assumed the initiative in calling these meetings?

Mr. Schulberg: It went on under a kind of momentum, I would say. They would be at set periods, I think, every two weeks. It might have been every week. I think there was a time when it varied—sometimes every two weeks and sometimes every week. At the end we would just say "Next time we will see you over at such-and-such a place."

Mr. Tavenner: Did you meet at the home of Waldo Salt?

Mr. Schulberg: I believe so. I can't say for sure, but I believe so.

Mr. Tavenner: I interrupted you in the course of your statement of the names of persons who became affiliated with this group. You named Waldo Salt.

Mr. Schulberg: Yes; I did.

Mr. Tavenner: Now, are there others?

Mr. Schulberg: Meta Reis was in this group.

Mr. Tavenner: Meta Reis Rosenberg? Is that the same person?

Mr. Schulberg: Meta Reis Rosenberg; yes, that is right. At that time her name was Meta Reis. She was in it. It seemed to me that at some point, as I remember, she was there for not very long and then went to some other group.

Mr. Tavenner: Are there others?

Mr. Schulberg: The others that I remember are Mrs. Tuttle, Tania Tuttle, who was also in this group. She may have replaced Meta Reis in it. That is my impression. I believe that she did. Then after I left and came back—after I left the group—

Mr. Tavenner: Excuse me. Go ahead.

Mr. Schulberg: In 1939 when I began these—not began, but when the argument culminated about my writing which I had begun about the end of 1937, which had been going on in short stories, and I had begun to think about novel writing, when I came back in 1940 and talked to Collins and told him I didn't want to come back at all and he urged me at least to present my point of view, at that time I also had written out my reasons for being against the Nazi-Soviet pact. I told him all these different reasons why I didn't want to go back. Much of what I went into this morning was the gist of what I told him, although by this time I had also many political differences which frankly I hadn't had before. I had felt all through the thirties that this was a good thing and that this was really a leading force against Fascism and that it should be supported. After that pact I didn't feel the same way about it and I told him. He asked me to at least come back and in a sense make a clean break, to present my various reasons, and so at that time I attended some meetings. I don't believe that I paid any dues at that time. I think I simply came back and was presenting my point of view. At that time I had the distinct impression that the group had changed in about the year or nine or ten months that I had been away in Vermont; that the group had changed its character; in other words, that it was no longer a youth group. All through that time it had been a study group and then a Young Communist League group of young people, and now it was a mixture more or less of people of varying ages. The youth nature of it had been dissolved. I believe that somewhere in here the young Communist group—the Young Communist League—came into the Communist Party. I don't want to say it was while I was away because that might look as though I am trying to be only in the Young Communist League and not in the Communist Party. I am not trying to do that because I think it well might have come before I left to go to Vermont. But I don't remember any discussion about the Young Communist League group becoming a youth group of the Communist Party. However, when I came back the nature of the group had changed. There were still a few of the people I had seen before, but now two or three or four older persons as well.

Mr. Tavenner: Who were they?

Mr. Schulberg: I believe Herbert Biberman was in that group. I say "believe" because he had come to meetings before, of the Young Communist League group, and he might have come to this group especially because of me. Lester Cole was in that group and somebody by the name of Kelly. Kelly, I don't remember having seen before I left California. Incidentally—no, sir, it was not Gene Kelly.

Mr. Tavenner: I didn't mean to indicate that it was. I wanted you to make certain that it was not.

Mr. Schulberg: No, sir; it was not.

Mr. Tavenner: You meant that it was not.

Mr. Schulberg: I meant that it was not Gene Kelly. Someone called Kelly who, with Collins seemed to be the most active or the most responsible in the group. Beyond that I thought that Kelly was a person of some authority on some administrative level beyond that group. But I don't remember his actual position in the industry or ever having been introduced to him before.

Mr. Tavenner: There is no way by which you can give any further identification of him as to where he lived, his approximate age?

Mr. Schulberg: I could give a vague description and that is all. He seemed to be in his early thirties.

Mr. Tavenner: A vague description would not be of any value.

Mr. Schulberg: That is all I could do, sir. I didn't know where he lived or exactly what he did. I gathered he had some job in the film business, but I had never seen him before.

Mr. Jackson: May I ask a question, Mr. Chairman? Mr. Schulberg, during this period of time did you know an individual by the name of Wirsig?

Mr. Schulberg: No, sir: I did not.

Mr. Jackson: Von Blatt?

Mr. Schulberg: No, sir; I never heard that name.

Mr. Jackson: That is all.

Mr. Schulberg: Was that all one name?

Mr. Jackson: No; those are two names.

Mr. Tavenner: Are you acquainted with Albert Maltz?

Mr. Schulberg: Yes, sir, I knew Albert Maltz, and my one distinct memory of him is during the time of the attack on my book by the Party. I couldn't definitely identify him in the Party, as he was never in a meeting with me, but he called me one day at a time when I was telling everybody how I felt about what was happening. He asked me to drop over and see him if I was ever going by. Mr. Maltz said he heard that I felt very strongly about the attack that had been made on my book by Lawson and by all these people, and that he felt rather sympathetic, that he felt there was too tight a control of writing by the Communists and that I was somewhat on the right track but much too impulsive and wanting to solve the whole thing overnight. He gave me the impression that he agreed with me, but felt that it could be done possibly in a more gradual way. That is why, very frankly, I was extremely interested when I heard about the testimony of Mr. Dmytryk, because when Mr. Dmytryk was under the same sort of attack six or seven years later and strangely enough by much the same people, I believe, I forget now, but I think John Lawson and Richard Collins were also involved in that. I believe he said it was Albert Maltz who was more or less the voice of reason there who tried to get them to ease off. That did interest me very much because that was much the same kind of conversation that I remembered having with him that day.

Mr. Tavenner: Were there outside speakers who attended your group meetings?

Mr. Schulberg: In the Young Communist League days the two that I definitely remembered were Herbert Biberman and Lester Cole, but they did come in and speak—also John Howard Lawson—on various issues, such as world events. Mostly in the case of Biberman he seemed to specialize in that, or the Screen Writers' Guild and since local issues seemed to be more Lester Cole's province, just the general approach, the over-all approach seemed to fall to John Howard Lawson.

Mr. Tavenner: You spoke this morning of the great proletarian novel. You used that term.

Mr. Schulberg: Yes, so I did.

Mr. Tavenner: Was there any individual within the Communist Party whom you can identify with reference to the so-called great proletarian novel?

Mr. Schulberg: I think as far back as 1937 when I was still—at that time I felt split. On the political side I was completely in agreement with the other members. I don't remember having any differences there. But I always had differences on the literary side. Even for a short story as early as 1937 I was criticized very severely along the lines that I stated this morning. About this time a writer known to me as a Communist by the name of Harry Carlisle just called on me at my home and talked to me about the Communist approach and told me that there was a young Communist writer living in Santa Monica who had just written some very effective labor stories for one of the Communist periodicals at the time. He said he thought if I talked more with her and got a better understanding of what a Communist writer's responsibilities were, I might be able to strengthen my own work. I had several meetings with her.

Mr. Tavenner: With whom?

Mr. Schulberg: With a young writer by the name of Tillie Lerner. She was then writing a proletarian novel, I think an extension of a series of short stories that she had written. I think at that time I had the feeling that maybe I could learn how this proletarian novel was done. I have yet to see one that really pulled the trick. I feel the so-called proletarian novel is a kind of museum piece myself.

Mr. Tavenner: Can you further identify Harry Carlisle—that is, as to his position?

Mr. Schulberg: No, sir, I can't. The only time I saw him was this one time, and I don't know what position he had. I don't know if he was told to come and see me about my deviations and the rest. He must have heard about it, of course, so I gather he was.

Mr. Tavenner: Can you give us the names of any other persons who became associated with your group from time to time, particularly after your return in 1940?

Mr. Schulberg: Besides those I have tried to tell you, there was Kelly, Biberman, Cole, I believe—I am almost sure that Gordon Kahn was there. When I say almost sure, it may seem strange at times you can't remember exactly who was in a group, but I think he was there also. Then I believe I did tell you about my final talk with Jerome, at which time— I hadn't known exactly what his position was, but from what everybody said I gathered very much that he was—

Mr. Tavenner: I will ask you to repeat your experience with Jerome. You did tell us this morning that in connection with your difficulties with the Communist Party relating to its efforts to bridle you in your work, you also came into disagreement with the party on political grounds and that the two things combined to result in your disaffection with the party. So now will you tell us more in detail just how you became disaffected with the party and how you left the party, if you did.

Mr. Schulberg: I definitely did, sir, and I will try to tell you how, though it does repeat much of what I said.

Mr. Tavenner: Try not to repeat what you have already said. Just make reference to it in a general way.

Mr. Schulberg: In a way not to repeat it is to say that when I returned in 1940 after the completion of my book, my first book, and had these sharp disagreements first with Collins, then the group, then with Lawson and finally with Jerome, that parallel with the talk about the book went my disagreements on these other things. In fact, I brought to the meeting my actual points, which I do still have in my files, for objecting strenuously to the Nazi-Soviet pact. I also objected—I think I had just finished at that time or it was shortly after that—to the invasion of

Finland. It does become repetitious because all of these things together were treated as simply the final result that I refused to accept any of the discipline that you are expected to assume as a member of the party.

Mr. Tavenner: As a result you broke with the party?

Mr. Schulberg: Yes, sir; I did.

Mr. Tavenner: Notwithstanding this break with the Party which you have described, you did continue from time to time, did you not, to make contributions of writings to the Communist press, such as *New Masses?* I think I am aware of several contributions you made to that publication after the time of your break.

Mr. Schulberg: Well, sir, I suppose you would call them writings. I would hardly dignify them as such. They weren't articles or anything. But on two specific occasions I was asked specifically by the *New Masses* to make some comment on a particular event. I believe the first time was when Germany invaded Russia. They said that they were canvassing opinion of various people, various points of view. I did send them a statement in which I believe I said that in a sense by force—I can't remember the actual wording of it by now, but my feeling was that by German force in the invasion the collective security policies which England and France at first and then Russia had ducked out on finally had come to pass. I don't remember the actual wording of it, but I do remember sending it to them. The other one was about a year later, some sort of controversy between a Republican Congressman, I think it was, and Mrs. Roosevelt over the appointment of Melvyn Douglas. I believe the particular objection had been that Melvyn Douglas had changed his name. This was used as a reason for feeling he shouldn't have some sort of civilian office. It was some sort of civilian office. I was queried directly by them, and I answered them in a short statement, saying that I felt, especially in the film business, that many people changed their names, that it was almost a common practice. That Robert Taylor had changed his name, that Cary Grant had changed his name, and so forth, and that I didn't feel that the changing of a name was really a reason for criticizing any man as long as he acted honestly, and so forth. I believe that Senator Downey also made some comment on the same thing at that time. I didn't feel in either case that I was endorsing the *New Masses* as a magazine.

Mr. Tavenner: The committee is in possession of information indicating that you either joined or continued your affiliation with several organizations which have been referred to generally as Communist-front organizations. Is that correct?

Mr. Schulberg: I believe I have joined—in most cases not joined but lent my name to specific issues in which these organizations were canvassing. I remember lending my name to a kind of circular letter put out by the Council of Arts, Sciences, and Professions in favor of the candidacy of Henry Wallace. I was in favor of Henry Wallace.

Mr. Velde: Do you remember the approximate date of that, Mr. Schulberg?

Mr. Schulberg: It must have been sometime, just before; it must have been sometime early in the campaign.

Mr. Velde: 1948?

Mr. Schulberg: 1948. At that time I felt I was doing this as an independent liberal. I wasn't unaware of the ways that the Communists had used Mr. Wallace. As the campaign went on, I became increasingly sure that this was being done. I spoke about it to people, not that I didn't feel that Mr. Wallace was an honorable and also an independent man, and a pretty good American. Finally after the campaign, however, I did write to Mr. Wallace and tell him I thought that he might have had some chance to win some support from the American people if he hadn't lent himself completely to the line of the Communist Party, which seemed to increase as the campaign went on. Since we are on this particular subject, at the time of the final break between Mr. Wallace and the Progressive Party I think over the issues of Korea when he couldn't quite convince himself that the South Koreans had invaded the North Koreans, I wrote the Progressive Party that I wasn't sure if I was still on their rolls as I had told them that I wanted to have no further part after the campaign was over, but if I was I wanted to have my name removed and I have this letter with me if you wish to hear it.

Mr. Tavenner: I ask that it be introduced in the record, Mr. Chairman. Let's refer, first of all, to your letter addressed to Mr. Wallace. Do you know the date of that letter and do you have it?

Mr. Schulberg: No, sir; I don't, but they were just about the same time. This letter to the Progressive Party is dated October 1, 1950, and I believe that the other was some time before that, approximately the same time.

Mr. Tavenner: I will offer the letter in evidence and have it marked Schulberg Exhibit No. 6.

Mr. Walter: That will be received. Read any part that you feel is relevant.

Mr. Schulberg (reading):

> Since I have not been active in Progressive or any other political circles since the 1948 campaign, I do not know whether my name is still carried on the rolls of the Progressive Party. But if it is, I must ask that it be removed for I find that my own political convictions are no longer adequately represented by the policies of your party.
>
> My feelings in this matter reached a crisis in the Wallace controversy of some months back. It seemed to me that Henry Wallace was right in pointing out that aggression of any kind, in these precarious days, is a more immediate threat to world peace than the potential use of the atom bomb. The Progressive Party stand struck me as ambiguous and on the basic issue of aggression suspiciously skittish.
>
> Therefore, while continuing to believe in the constitutional right of all minority parties to remain free from political persecution, I myself can no longer lend my name or my activities to the Progressive Party.

Mr. Tavenner: I believe you were associated with certain activities of the Council of Arts, Sciences, and Professions, such as the signing of a letter requesting the abolition of the Committee on Un-American Activities. I am not asking you about your views as to this committee, but I would like to know the manner in which your endorsement of the letter was secured and what you know about the formation of the plan to abolish this committee.

Mr. Schulberg: Letters like this do pour in every day, and I suppose you sign one for ten that you either say "No" or toss in the wastebasket. This one I did sign, and I remember doing so. I think it was late in 1948, although the date might have 1949. As far as I recall, it simply came to my desk in the general mail and I signed it. If you are interested in knowing why I should sign it, I will be glad to tell you.

Mr. Walter: We will be glad to hear anything you have to say about it.

Mr. Schulberg: Unless you are extremely interested—I did sign it, I remember signing it, and I will tell you why if you wish.

Mr. Tavenner: That is satisfactory as far as I am concerned.

Mr. Walter: No; it isn't satisfactory. Please state your reason.

Mr. Schulberg: I will be glad to, sir. When you see a name on a letter or on any petition, it is really a question of yes or no. I feel that these things are much like a vote. When you vote, you vote "yes" or "no." I feel that you must sometimes say you are 55 or 60 percent in favor or 40 or 45 percent against, and you vote "yes" and the 40 or 45 percent doesn't show. I felt somewhat that way that day. I felt that there was to my mind a definite concern that had nothing to do with my love for the Communist Party and the fact that people should be called in and their political views should be inquired into. I honestly felt that there was a great danger in that. I didn't feel it was 100 to nothing. I felt that there was also on the other side information, say, about the Communist Party and the Communist operation that could be of no value (of value?) to the American people. I tried to decide which is the greater danger. To me it was like a balance, like this. That was my reason in principle. I also had a kind of personal reason which I have never told anybody to this moment anywhere, but if you are curious I will also tell you that.

Mr. Walter: Please do.

Mr. Schulberg: In 1940 this committee under a different leadership came to Hollywood at just about the time I believe I had broken with the Communist Party. I believe it was under the chairmanship then of Martin Dies. On the day he arrived an announcement was made in the paper that there were six leading Communists in Hollywood, I think it was, and I was named as one of the six. The statement also said that anybody who didn't feel that he was being treated quite fairly was invited to come down to the committee room, which was at the Hotel Biltmore, and present himself. I just hopped in the car and drove down to the Hotel Biltmore. I telephoned upstairs to the investigator. I told him, "My name is Budd Schulberg. I am downstairs. I saw the note in the paper. I feel that there is something that isn't quite just about making an announcement in the paper about people before they have had a chance to come down and at least talk with you." I said, "I can't prove it, but I just have a strong hunch that that list is a faulty list."

Mr. Walter: At that time you were no longer a member of the Communist Party, is that the fact?

Mr. Schulberg: That is right, sir. I was told, "Well, we are very busy now, but call back in half an hour or so and we will see." I did. I called back in half an hour. I remember the date very well. I don't know why these things end up with my going to a bar, but I went to a bar in the Hotel Biltmore and listened to a speech by Wendell Willkie. In about thirty-five or forty minutes I called back again, and I was told, "We can't see you again, but call back in another half hour." At five o'clock, at the end of the day, I called again and I was told, "We are going to San Francisco on the next train. We have to leave and we are sorry we can't see you." Frankly, that didn't give me the most favorable impression. Maybe I should have been more reasonable later. But, as I say, it was on one side a matter of principle and on the other side a sense of personal pique that induced me to sign that letter in 1949.

Mr. Walter: If your expressed views at that time had been followed, there wouldn't be in existence today a vehicle to give to the American people and to the world the valuable information you have given concerning the insidious attempts that are made to control the thought and writing.

Mr. Schulberg: Thank you, sir.

Mr. Walter: As a matter of fact, Mr. Schulberg, wasn't most of this agitation to eliminate this committee started by Communist groups that realized that sooner or later this committee would expose some of their machinations?

Mr. Schulberg: Undoubtedly Communists would join for that reason; yes. I do think that others joined for other reasons.

Mr. Tavenner: Did you in 1941 become a sponsor of the American Peace Mobilization?

Mr. Schulberg: Not to my knowledge, sir. That seems to conflict with what I was doing and saying at that time. I remember very distinctly lending both my name and my presence to, I believe it was, the William Allen White Committee to Defend the Allies. I know I talked to innumerable people about the fact that I did not believe in this kind of neutrality; that I didn't think that would be any kind of peace that I find it very hard to believe that I would sponsor such a meeting. Could I ask, sir, is there any index of that, a general index that would carry my name as being a member of that, not as a sponsor of that meeting but as a member of that organization?

Mr. Tavenner: I hand you a photostatic copy of a flyer under date of April 5, 1941, of the American People's Meeting held at Randalls Island, N.Y., and I notice at the bottom of the page that your name is used as a sponsor of the American Peace Mobilization. Will you examine it, please [handed to the witness]. Your name appears at the bottom of the second page.

Mr. Rhetts: May I inquire, Mr. Tavenner, whether you have the—is this all there is to this document, or is this merely an excerpt from it?

Mr. Tavenner: That is an excerpt from the document.

Mr. Rhetts: I wonder if you have the—

Mr. Tavenner: I hand you now one of the original pamphlets [hands pamphlet to the witness].

Mr. Rhetts: Thank you.

Mr. Schulberg (after examining the document): I don't remember this meeting, and also I don't remember lending my name to it. I think I was out of the country at the time. I feel sure I was opposed to the policies that this represented. All I can say is that I strongly doubt that I authorized this. Anything that has been brought up I would be glad to admit, no matter how objectionable it might seem, if I am sure I did it.

Mr. Walter: This is the first knowledge you have of this?

Mr. Schulberg: I have never seen this before I came down here, sir.

Mr. Rhetts: May I say, Mr. Chairman, that I note that this photostatic excerpt lists Mr. Schulberg's name on one page, which would indicate he is one of nine sponsors, a rather small group. I note from the original that that is simply one of a large number of pages here which finally run over on to the back page. There seem to be well over a couple of hundred names listed here as including sponsors, for whatever value that may be.

Mr. Schulberg: That particular mention seems to me absolutely inconsistent with my position at the time. I remember quite well—I think it was just about then or shortly before—attending and buying tables for the committee to aid the Allies. I remember signing petitions to aid the Allies and talking with many people about it. It also happens to be almost exactly the date of the attack of the Communist meeting on me and my book. This meeting at Randalls Island was April 5, 1941. As I say, I have no memory of that meeting. I have no memory of anybody having asked me to do that. This particular thing I feel unauthorized and it seems inconsistent with everything I was doing and saying there.

Mr. Velde: Mr. Schulberg, prior to June 22, 1941, were you aware of the nature of the organization, American Peace Mobilization?

Mr. Schulberg: I have some recollection, sir, on the West Coast, of saying that I did not wish to join that organization.

Mr. Velde: Were you also aware that after the attack by Hitler on Russia the name of that organization was changed to American People's Mobilization?

Mr. Schulberg: No, sir; I wasn't aware of that, but it sounds familiar.

Mr. Velde: What were you aware of about the American Peace Mobilization, the one prior to June 22, 1941?

Mr. Schulberg: I was aware that the American Peace Mobilization was isolationist and doing everything it could to keep us from aiding the Allies against the Nazis, and I felt that in that way it was actually aiding the Nazis.

Mr. Velde: You were opposed to their position regarding the peace pact between Russia and Germany at the time, as I understand it.

Mr. Schulberg: Yes, sir; I was. Also this meeting seems to have taken place almost exactly the time, as I say, that my first book was published, and at a time when I was, to the best of my knowledge, in Mexico. I doubt very, very strongly that I lent my name to this particular organization at that time.

Mr. Tavenner: Mr. Schulberg, excuse me. Were you going to say anything else?

Mr. Schulberg: No. It just seems that I can't conceive of having done that.

Mr. Tavenner: Mr. Schulberg, your name appears as one of the signers of a brief *amicus curiae* which was filed in the Supreme Court of the United States in the case against John Howard Lawson and also in the case against Dalton Trumbo. You recall that, I suppose?

Mr. Schulberg: I do, sir.

Mr. Tavenner: What were the circumstances under which your signature was obtained to that brief?

Mr. Schulberg: It was sent to me in the mail at my farm; I believe from the office of the principal signer. I think it was Max Radin. I wouldn't want to say whose office, but it came there. I read it, I suppose, not too carefully. I have been told by some lawyers that this was not very good legally, but I did sign it. I believe I signed it for somewhat the same reasons as I signed the others, although in this case I had an additional feeling at the time that possibly this was something that should be tested in the courts, and once it was that also affected my attitude that this was a law and that we should abide by it.

Mr. Tavenner: Is there anything further you desire to say in regard to the subject of our inquiry?

Mr. Schulberg: Just one or two brief things. I do feel the questioning has been very fair and that possibly there isn't time always in gathering material to gather it on all sides. In other words, every one of these things that you mentioned, except for one of these things that you have mentioned, except for one which I don't think I did, of course I did and believed in for some reason at the time. I honestly feel that certain other activities that people do take part in should also be part of these files so that you are able to get a clear and balanced picture.

Mr. Tavenner: Let me suggest in that connection, if you have any information of a documentary character which you desire to be considered along with your testimony here, that you send it to us.

Mr. Rhetts: All right.

Mr. Schulberg: Yes; I will.

Mr. Tavenner: If there is anything further, proceed.

Mr. Schulberg: Anything further?

Mr. Tavenner: Yes, anything further you desire to say. I don't know whether that completed what you were about to say or not.

Mr. Schulberg: Yes, sir; it did.

Mr. Tavenner: That is all, Mr. Chairman.

Mr. Doyle: Mr. Schulberg, you stated that you withdrew from the group against the urging of Mr. Lawrence, I think. Did any member of the group themselves other than he try to get you to stay in the Communist group? In other words, was it a one-man affair so far as trying to keep you in, or did other members come to you and try to urge you to stay in with them?

Mr. Schulberg: It wasn't Lawrence, sir. It wasn't one man. It was rather a somewhat extended process. It was first Mr. Collins. It was secondly the group that Mr. Collins represented. It was then John Howard Lawson, and it was finally V. J. Jerome. This covered some period of time.

Mr. Doyle: In other words, I am to understand, then, that the group itself actively, other than just its leaders, the membership of the group itself, 7 or 10 or a dozen, you were aware of the fact that the group did not want you to retire from it; is that correct?

Mr. Schulberg: I believe that some thought that I should be argued back in and some thought that I should be kicked out.

Mr. Doyle: What I am trying to get at, Mr. Schulberg, is this: As you look back in retrospect, was it the conviction of the rank and file of the group that their Communist activities were good and important for them, or was it just the leadership of the group, two or three? In other words, was the group itself imbued with the communistic principles to the extent that they tried to get you to stick to them?

Mr. Schulberg: Sir, I feel they were or they would also have left the group in this way. I might add that in a sense I feel it is a hopeful sign. Sometimes you think of a Communist group as being very rigid, once you get into it you can never get out of it. I think there is a certain fear of that. I think it is interesting to find ways to help people to get out of it. People can and do get out of it all the time. I feel one of the hopeful things is that there are so many people who have come into the thinking that it is something idealistic, leave it for the same reason. Once they leave it, there are, of course, efforts to bring them back, but they can get out and can stay out. I do think that it is interesting in this investigation, lest people think, which I am sure you wouldn't want the American people to believe, either, that Hollywood is just teeming with Communists. Of course as some people have been able to tell you better than I, who have been in it in the forties, they can reach positions of real power. Yet the turnover I feel is constant, and people are getting out of it all the time. Sometimes I honestly expect to see a meeting in the Gilmore Stadium in Hollywood of all the ex-Communists. It can be done, in other words, it can be done.

Mr. Doyle: You mentioned the word "fear." Do I understand that there is anything done directly or indirectly in these young Communist groups to instill in the members a fear of something happening to them if they withdraw, or is there fear of some discipline that might harm them, that it would be bad for them if they withdrew from the Communist group? Is that the sense in which used the term "fear"?

Mr. Schulberg: Not exactly, sir; no. I have heard of that, and I think in groups which are really revolutionary groups, which these at that time really didn't consider themselves, there obviously was some fear of physical violence. In my case I can't say that that was so. There are two kinds of fears, I think. Once before the step is taken, you don't know quite how to make it. I know that is true. You sit there for a long time wanting to get out and you can't find the words to say it. One day you are sitting there— many people seem to have the same fears. You go on maybe for a year in which you think about how to get out and not really agreeing with it, but still in it. One day you say what am I doing here, I am not a Communist and finally you go. I happened to read an interesting book the other day by the editor of the British Daily Worker. It is called *I Believed* [by Douglas Hyde]. He said for two years he edited the *Daily Worker* of England and was one of the top men in the Communist Party of England and at the same time he was taking instructions, planning to join the Catholic Church. Every day in a sense he was doing both. This might seem the behavior of a very dishonest man, of a hypocrite, but I don't think it really was in that case. I think sometimes these things break slowly. That is all.

Mr. Doyle: Did I understand you just now to say "I can think of some revolutionary groups?"

Mr. Schulberg: I have read about revolutionary groups.

Mr. Doyle: I see. You have read about them?

Mr. Schulberg: Yes, sir.

Mr. Doyle: You are not personally acquainted with any of them?

Mr. Schulberg: I can't say that I am. I honestly cannot.

Mr. Doyle: I misunderstood the words you used.

Mr. Schulberg: No, sir.

Mr. Doyle: One more question. I just assume that you haven't had an opportunity to read Public Law 601, the part of it under which this committee operates, which refers to the Committee on Un-American Activities. I wish just to read to you three or four lines and call your attention to the last line and ask you if you have anything you can suggest to us that would be helpful. It provides that this committee shall investigate "the extent, character, and objects of un-American propaganda activities in the United States," and "the diffusion within the United States of subversive and un-American propaganda. . . ." Let me call your attention to this line expressly—

> that is instigated from foreign countries or of a domestic origin and attacks the principle of the form of government as guaranteed by the Constitution, and . . . all other questions in relation thereto that would aid Congress in any necessary remedial legislation.

I am sure that I, as a member of the committee, would not want to lose the opportunity to give you every opportunity to give us any suggestion you might have, if you have any, any processes or any action, any attitude that we should take with reference to any possible remedial legislation to meet the present subversive misconduct of people.

Mr. Schulberg: Like any other citizen these days I do think a good deal about that. I feel there is no doubt that it has been brought out in the last few years that there has been a very serious phase of the Communist Party work which is devoted to espionage and which is really not in the interest of the American people. I think that the large percentage of the people who join the Communist Party do so without honestly knowing that, that there are people in it today who don't know that, who in some way are deeply misguided. I feel that somehow [they believe] this is going to help peace on earth and good will to men. These people I feel definitely are being used. The problem to me falls into two parts. One is to check in every way the manipulators and conspirators of this, who do use these other people who are, I would call, innocents. I think personally the best way to do that is to tighten up in every way the laws on espionage and sabotage, which probably is being done. If they aren't airtight, they should be improved. On the subject of outlawing the Communist Party, my mind itself is not made up. I think there are some reasons for that. As long as some line can be drawn between simply political action and all this other business that goes on. I feel if the thing is outlawed it will probably spring up under some other name. That part is the problem, which begins to come more in my province frankly than the other, which is how do you get people not to join these other groups, whichever they are, that come out under this name. I feel that that is a question of finding an American organization, American activities which will give American people the ability that they have always had to protest, to talk up for the underdog, to have humanitarian impulses and so forth without falling into the hands of these people who use these causes, and the Civil Rights Congress I am convinced is an example of that. Those are good causes often. Those are people often who really are suffering some injustice and they attract people who don't like injustice and they fall into the hands of the Communists. I simply hope that on one side everything can be done to check sabotage and to cut off and cut out this conspiratorial side, and on the other that these democratic efforts be really taken away from the Communists, that people do them themselves and they will find that they won't need Communism because they can still talk and act on their own.

Mr. Frazier: Mr. Schulberg, did I understand you to say you attended Dartmouth College?

Mr. Schulberg: Yes, sir: I did.

Mr. Frazier: What year did you graduate if you did graduate?

Mr. Schulberg: I was graduated, sir, in 1936.

Mr. Frazier: Then did you go with the TVA?

Mr. Schulberg: Never, sir.

Mr. Frazier: You never did?

Mr. Schulberg: Never did. I don't know what they were doing.

Mr. Frazier: I thought you went from Dartmouth down there.

Mr. Schulberg: I didn't; no, sir. I never had anything to do with it ever.

Mr. Jackson: That was Mr. Remington; was it not?

Mr. Frazier: That is all.

Mr. Walter: Mr. Velde?

Mr. Velde: Mr. Schulberg, have you now given us all the names of the people who were associated with you in the study group which you mentioned, the Marxist study group prior to your entrance into the Young Communist Party or the Young Communist League?

Mr. Schulberg: I believe so, sir. I have given you all the names of those who passed on into the Communist Party; yes, sir.

Mr. Velde: You feel that you do recall all those who were associated with you in that study group? If you should recall at a later date the names of others, would you give this committee or our investigators their names?

Mr. Schulberg: Yes, sir. I would say all except certain things which I have discussed fully with your investigators.

Mr. Velde: Have you also given us all the names of the members of the YCL that were in your particular group?

Mr. Schulberg: To the best of my memory, I have.

Mr. Velde: At any time during that time did you carry a Communist Party card?

Mr. Schulberg: I have wondered about that. I don't remember having one. I think it is possible, but for some reason I don't remember having one. Whether they didn't have them in those days I am not sure, but I just don't remember having a Communist Party card. However, I might have.

Mr. Velde: Do you recall what the amount of the dues was that you paid to the Communist Party, the Young Communist League?

Mr. Schulberg: In the study group I don't think there were any. I believe there might have been just a pittance for the books, the pamphlets, or something. It was very small. In the Young Communist League the dues were very, very minimum because I don't think anybody was making very much money. In this later stage there was a percentage of the dues. If I had been asked I would have had no memory of it. I understand Mr. Collins—I think when I left California he was the treasurer, so I feel I know nothing about—said it was four percent.

Mr. Velde: That was in the nature of a special assessment?

Mr. Schulberg: That struck me as being high. I thought maybe in our time it was lower, two percent or something like that. Possibly it was raised at some later date. I do remember that there was a percentage of your income taken as dues. It seems to me it was one or two then.

Mr. Velde: Would you mind telling the committee what your particular income was at that time?

Mr. Schulberg: It would be somewhat difficult for me to figure it out because I had jobs at short periods. When I worked at that time as a screenwriter I was paid $350 a week. However, in 1938 I wrote the Screen Writers' Guild that I was going to devote the majority of my time to magazine writing, and from that time on it was catch-as-catch-can depending upon the stories I was able to sell. So I don't remember exactly what my income was, but I think around that time I was selling possibly one magazine short story a month.

Mr. Velde: Can you give us an approximation of the amount that you paid in special assessment, just a general figure? I realize it is difficult for you to remember exactly.

Mr. Schulberg: Sir, I honestly don't think I could. I don't remember the special assessment apart from the dues or anything. I just remember that we paid some. I do remember that we paid some percentage of our dues. I thought that is what you meant by the special assessment. I am not quite clear.

Mr. Velde: I am not quite clear, either, on what you mean. I believe Mr. Collins or someone testified here that the Communist Party assessed four percent of your income, of your weekly or monthly income, as a special assessment, other than the regular party dues which went into the Communist Party fund, and on some occasion it was collected by the national committee of the Communist Party directly. That is what I am referring to. Did you make any such payments of special assessments on you income?

Mr. Schulberg: The payment I remember making is more like the one that you described than a regular dues. In other words, I don't remember paying two different kinds, dues and a special assessment; I do remember—

Mr. Velde: I believe, if I am not mistaken—and maybe the investigators or Mr. Nixon knows about this—it seems to me that the YCL charged only very nominal dues, maybe 25 cents a month or something like that. You refer to a larger payment than that, do you not?

Mr. Schulberg: Yes, sir.

Mr. Velde: So it more than likely was a special assessment on your income.

Mr. Schulberg: Yes. That probably came when the Young Communist League evolved in the Communist Party.

Mr. Velde: I see. You have no independent recollection of any amounts that you paid in by check or cash or whom you it to?

Mr. Schulberg: I paid them by cash, and I believe around 1938 into early 1939 I do believe Mr. Collins was the treasurer then. It seems to me I remember giving him certain cash payments, but I don't remember how large.

Mr. Velde: Since you left the party and made a complete break with the Communist Party itself, you testified that you were associated with a few what are now known as Communist-front groups. Have you given the committee all of the Communist-front groups with which you are associated since your break with the Communist Party?

Mr. Schulberg: As far as I know, I have, sir.

Mr. Velde: Are you connected in any way with the Committee to Defend Harry Bridges? Did you have anything to do with that committee?

Mr. Schulberg: In 1940 there was some kind of open letter. I believe to Attorney General Biddle, I think in the latter part of 1942, signed by some 600 people.

Mr. Velde: Were you a signer of that letter?

Mr. Schulberg: I was one of the signers of that letter which asked him at that time not to deport Harry Bridges; yes, sir. I recall no funds being contributed. In fact, in all these cases that I have mentioned I lent my name I agreed at that particular time with the specific issues if not with the organization, and I never attended any of these meetings. As far as I know, I gave no funds.

Mr. Velde: Were you associated with a committee known as the American Committee for the Protection of the Foreign Born?

Mr. Schulberg: Yes, sir; I have been. I believed that was mentioned.

Mr. Velde: I am sorry. There is no other front group of Communist-controlled group that you can think of at the present time with which you have been associated since your break with the Communist Party?

Mr. Schulberg: There may be others that I have signed cards for. I tried my best to remember the ones that I was sure of, yes, sir.

Mr. Velde: Thank you kindly, Mr. Schulberg, for your cooperation with this committee. I think you have given a lot of valuable information which we have not heretofore had.

Mr. Schulberg: Thank you very much, sir.

Mr. Walter: Mr. Jackson?

Mr. Jackson: Mr. Schulberg, I join heartily in the sentiments expressed by Mr. Velde. I feel that you have made a substantial contribution to the knowledge of the committee as to the physical operators of the Communist Party. I have several questions I should like to ask. You testified this morning regarding an organization of writers in the Soviet Union which more or less controlled the output of writers, or [had] more control rather than less of the writers of the Soviet Union.

Mr. Schulberg: Yes.

Mr. Jackson: You could not recall the name of the organization at that time. Was it by any chance the International Union of Revolutionary Writers?

Mr. Schulberg: That is correct.

Mr. Jackson: That is the name of it?

Mr. Schulberg: That is the name of the organization.

Mr. Jackson: Was that an organization that had an American offshoot called the League of American Writers, do you know?

Mr. Schulberg: That I did not know.

Mr. Jackson: You were never associated with any organization by that name?

Mr. Schulberg: I was associated with the League of American Writers from 1937 to I believe 1939.

Mr. Jackson: Was that organization an organization with definite Communist influence?

Mr. Schulberg: In 1939, at that time I didn't think that it was dominated by Communists. I imagine I would think so today, but I didn't think so then.

Mr. Jackson: Have you done any movie scripts?

Mr. Schulberg: I have done a few; yes, sir.

Mr. Jackson: What were they?

Mr. Schulberg: None that I am very proud to talk about.

Mr. Jackson: That is true of some of the movies I have seen, but would you mind mentioning the names of these scripts that you did that were made into pictures?

Mr. Schulberg: One was called *Winter Carnival*. Another was called *City without Men*. Another one was—not that I wrote a script for it, but just wrote a story from which the film was made, called *Week-End for Three*. I can't remember any others.

Mr. Jackson: Who made those pictures respectively?

Mr. Schulberg: One was made by Walter Wanger, one by Columbia Pictures, and one by RKO.

Mr. Jackson: What was the date, the approximate date?

Mr. Schulberg: I will have to try to figure that out, sir.

Mr. Jackson: Just generally, within a year or two.

Mr. Schulberg: Oh, I would say from '38 to '40. I believe they were all pretty much in that period.

Mr. Jackson: Was there any indication at any time that your association in the Communist Party was an assistance to you in selling scripts in Hollywood?

Mr. Schulberg: No, sir.

Mr. Jackson: In association with John Howard Lawson and any others within the industry?

Mr. Schulberg: I honestly can't say, sir, that I ever had much assistance from that source.

Mr. Jackson: You at no time were referred by any member of the group to any specific agent, or was it suggested that any specific person in the studio might be of assistance to you?

Mr. Schulberg: No, sir; it really wasn't. My employment was quite brief at that time, as I say. In 1939 I worked a few months, at which time I wrote a letter to the Guild saying I was leaving. In 1939 I worked for three or four months, and then went to Vermont. So honestly my screen work has been limited to a short time. During that time I don't remember anybody from that source saying that they would help me to get any better job or any assignments, possibly because I wasn't very interested, either, in getting them.

Mr. Jackson: Who was your agent in Hollywood?

Mr. Schulberg: The Myron Selznick Agency.

Mr. Jackson: Who handled your account in the agency, do you know?

Mr. Schulberg: I do know that, of course.

Mr. Jackson: Would you mind, and I should say this has no necessary connotation.

Mr. Schulberg: My only hesitation—at times through no fault of your own, sir, people read things in papers and say, "I saw your name in the paper. You must be in some kind of trouble." That was my only hesitation.

Mr. Jackson: I think with that preface it will be all right.

Mr. Schulberg: My agent at that time was Collier Young, who at no time was ever associated with the Communist Party in any way.

Mr. Jackson: During the time that you were associated with the youth group or the Young Communist League, did you know of any activity on the campus of the University of California at Los Angeles? You are familiar with the university. You know where it is.

Mr. Schulberg: Of course.

Mr. Jackson: You knew of no activities and had no members who came from the campus?

Mr. Schulberg: No, sir.

Mr. Jackson: Generally, in summation, Mr. Schulberg, your testimony has gone directly to the point that there were very definite efforts made by the Communist Party, by individuals within the Communist Party, to direct your writing efforts. In that case they were unsuccessful in that you broke with the party. Further than that, that there were other efforts made in other cases by the Communist Party or by individuals in the Communist Party which achieved a greater measure of success than in your own case. I think that is the thing we are trying to establish beyond any doubt. I am glad that you mentioned the fact that Hollywood is not teeming with Communists. I have a personal interest in that. I see a great many of my constituents sitting right where you are sitting, and I hope if that Gilmore thing ever develops you will move it over to Wrigley Field. Would you suggest in light of your own experience, both as a member of the Communist Party and also as one who has appeared before this committee, that others might be well advised who have sincerely broken with the party and want to make a clean breast of it to come before this committee as you have? Would that be your advice?

Mr. Schulberg: Sir, it would be my own personal advice. May I add one suggestion?

Mr. Jackson: Please do.

Mr. Schulberg: I feel that there are some people who might come forward more readily. I don't know who they are. But just judging some of the experiences I have read about, I think that there is a fear, the fear that I talked about before, the fear of retribution by society, the fear that this is something that you might never be able to live down. I think that since many of these people obviously in a sense are in nowise really subversive, they got into something they really didn't understand and once they are out, they should help in every way. Industries should not be encouraged to crack down on them. I think the people in Hollywood still are frightened about hiring some of these people. I have less fear about it, quite frankly, because I am more self-employed. I wouldn't mind working in Hollywood again some time. If I write a book and they want to make it, I have no objection and I would be rather shocked if they did make it because I have appeared here. However, I feel I will get by if they did do that. I think everything must be done to help those particular people. I did read a headline last week which said something like, "Wait and see attitude on ex-Reds," I think it said. I think it is that sort of thing, this reluctance or hesitation which naturally will make people think twice, because if you say, "Come up and make a full disclosure," and then they are hurt for it, they are going to be more reluctant. So I hope you will be able to do everything that you can to help those people.

Mr. Jackson: You have expressed yourself so far as those people are concerned who voluntarily come forward or who come forward under subpoena and disclose the nature of their activities in the party. What is your feeling with respect to those who come forward and refuse to co-operate with the committee? Do you think that that same amnesty should be extended to them by industry or by the American people at the box office?

Mr. Schulberg: Frankly, I haven't quite decided that problem myself. I don't feel it is the same as the other. I do feel there is some difference, but I haven't quite made up my own mind. I can understand certain hesitance on the part of the industry and the American people. It is something I would like to think more about.

Mr. Jackson: Would you mind giving the committee your personal reaction upon reading that such and such an individual has come forward or a number of individuals have come forward and refused to testify and have taken refuge behind the first or fifth amendments? Several of the witnesses, notably Mr. Dmytryk, said that they draw the conclusion that they are not sincerely devoted to the Constitution but are rather taking that refuge because it is either take that or possibly conceivably be cited. What is your feeling? What reaction do you obtain when you read of noncooperative witnesses taking their undoubted right to retire under the umbrella of the Constitution? What is your reaction? What is your feeling?

Mr. Schulberg: My reaction is somewhat along the line of Mr. Dmytryk. I would say that the majority of those were not completely sincere. However, I might entertain the thought that in a case here and there are people who without being Communists might possibly for some matter of principle do that.

Mr. Jackson: You mean out of deep conviction?

Mr. Schulberg: Out of some deep conviction.

Mr. Jackson: Thought control, and so forth?

Mr. Schulberg: I do think it is possible.

Mr. Jackson: I assume you have read of those who have deep convictions which do not extend to the Silver Shirts or the Ku Klux Klan, but who have very deep conviction when questioned on the Communist Party.

Mr. Schulberg: If I had the same conviction, obviously, I wouldn't have broken with the Party.

Mr. Jackson: Do you believe that a member of the Communist Party can at the same time be dedicated to a free America as we understand it and to the dignity of the individual?

Mr. Schulberg: Not if he knows the whole story of what Communism and the Communist Party is. I think there are innocents in there that might fit that category, yes.

Mr. Jackson: You mean at the present time there are Communists who could be Communists and at the same time loyal Americans?

Mr. Schulberg: I think there might be some who are not presently in the process of getting out who might become loyal Americans. I do, yes, although I wouldn't make a strong point of that. It is something I haven't really thought through. I would think by this time every member would see exactly how it was run and who it was run for. I would think that.

Mr. Jackson: You have terminated, of course, your association with the various fronts to which you lent your name on occasion or do you still retain membership in any of them—not membership, but do you still attend any of the meetings of those groups?

Mr. Schulberg: I have never attended any of the meetings, ever. I don't think I ever attended any of the meetings of any of these organizations that have been named. I don't think one. I don't believe I am a member of any of them now.

Mr. Jackson: Mr. Chairman, may I ask one more question just in conclusion? Knowing the Communist Party line, what would your reaction be to a set of principles which I will enumerate here? "Washington is a very unhealthy place." These are from minutes. "The Un-American Committee is a modern inquisition. The committee members are self-centered tyrants. Parks, Hayden, and Collins are mentally ill—"

Mr. Velde: I think there is something added to that one line which modesty forbids your reading.

Mr. Jackson: It says—

The Committee members are self-centered tyrants, especially a man named Jackson. Pressure of people for peace is greatly retarding the war. ... We demand immediate peace negotiations with People's China in the United Nations.... Our goal is to work for peace.... We have never deviated from the aim of working forces.... The present task is to cooper-

ate with the Marine Cooks and Stewards in the fund-raising campaigns.
. . . Our duty is to enlighten people who read the Washington investigations and liken the investigations to the inquisition. . . . The newspapers
all slant to testimony of the witnesses, and people are losing their sense of
direction . . . we must assume the leadership.

Does that strike a familiar chord?

Mr. Schulberg: That does, yes.

Mr. Jackson: What is the song? What is the music?

Mr. Schulberg: That sounds like a very familiar line.

Mr. Jackson: The Communist Party line.

Mr. Schulberg: It sounds like the Communist line.

Mr. Jackson: This is a report of the membership committee of the
Council of Arts, Sciences, and Professions in Los Angeles, April 12, 1951,
and I insert it in the record so people may know the words and the music. Thank you again for your testimony.

Mr. Walter: Mr. Schulberg, this committee is indebted to you for
making one of the most constructive statements that I have heard since
I have been a member of this committee. It can only come through the
lips of people who have had the experiences that you have had, the information that the American people should have, so as to bring home to
everybody in every community of America an awareness of the menace
of this world-wide conspiracy, and in our efforts to enlighten our people
you have made a very fine contribution. We thank you.

Mr. Schulberg: Thank you, sir.

Mr. Walter: The committee will stand adjourned, to meet at 10
o'clock tomorrow morning.

Appendix B

PEOPLE'S WORLD, APRIL 2, 1941

NOVEL: THE STORY OF A HOLLYWOOD HEEL

What Makes Sammy Run? A novel by Budd Schulberg; publisher, Random House. $2.50. [by Charles Glenn]

For slightly fewer years than they have awaited the great American novel, whatever that may be, American bibliophiles and critics have been awaiting the Hollywood novel. While they may argue its merits and demerits I've a feeling that all critics, no matter their carping standards, will have to admit they've found the Hollywood novel in Budd Schulberg's "What Makes Sammy Run?"

Former works on the film city have been filthy with four-letter words, spoken and implied. Characters have been drawn black and white, most Hollywood denizens turning out to be unadulterated heels. Former Hollywood stories have been superficial, skipping social implication as a flat stone skips the surface of a lake.

None of these things hold true for Schulberg's novel, the first of this 27-year-old author, a boy with much to offer.

Hollywood Heel

This is the story of Sammy Glick, who starts as a copy boy on a New York paper and "works" his way up to Hollywood fame and fortune as a leading writer and producer. Glick is the "genius" who uses the lives of all those who surround him as the rungs on his ladder to the top.

He is all the heels the world has known or will know. As a matter of fact, he is so many heels and is so well drawn as such, Hollywood folk find diversion in fitting the character of Sammy Glick to any and all the "leading people" of the village.

Schulberg might have placed his "hero" anywhere in the world. He chose Hollywood because Hollywood is the author's more familiar world. Writing in the first person, Schulberg tells of the good as well as the bad. The hectic tale of the writers' battle to organize the Screen Writers Guild is sketched lightly, somehow, one feels, too lightly.

But even here, Sammy Glick plays the role of fink, placing himself with what comes very close to a picture of the company union Screen Playwrights. That picture and the men therein will be a bit of reportage several of Hollywood's better strikebreakers won't forget for a long time.

The distinguishing characteristic of Schulberg's novel, however, is the insight and understanding which allowed him to penetrate a disgraceful social system which fosters the Sammy Glicks. His chapter defining the reasons for Sammy's compulsion to run back to New York's lower East Side and what it has been to so many thousands, degrading, criminal, lustful. This is the society which formed Sammy. The "nether" Hollywood finished the job.

Read this book and when you have read it, consider this: The Sammy Glicks (and this character is plentiful) have been given the job in Hollywood of propagandizing for America's entry into the war. They have been given high government positions. They are in the saddle, a fitting commentary on "our order" of things.

Novelist with a Future

Schulberg has written a bold and daring work. He has demolished the fine superstructure of godliness which publicity departments and ego have raised about Hollywood's Sammy Glicks. There is much more to be said and it can be told as entertainingly as Schulberg has told this story.

Schulberg must be considered an important "comer." That he has taken a real person from a real society, that he has invested him only with the trappings which that society has given him, these are the big things in Schulberg. He is a realist and a materialist. There is nothing vulgar in what he says, nothing superficially vulgar that is. The vulgar thing is the society responsible for Sammy Glick.

The fact that Schulberg sees this is enough to recommend him for your list of Authors to Be Watched.

Appendix C

PEOPLE'S WORLD, APRIL 24, 1941

HOLLYWOOD VINE

By Charles Glenn

Recently I wrote a series of articles on Hollywood, its people and its masters by proxy. It was pointed out in the series that the people of Hollywood do matter, that they work like the very devil for a better America and that they are in the majority here just as they are in any American city.

This seemed to be in direct contradiction with a book review I dashed off a few weeks previously, a review on Budd Schulberg's "What Makes Sammy Run?"

Since writing the review, I have received several criticisms on it. On the basis of these criticisms, I've done a re-evaluation of my work. It's rather important that this re-evaluation be done, not in the light of breast beating, but in the light of constructive self-criticism, by which anyone who writes for this paper must work.

Understanding your own mistakes is the first requirement of criticism. If you don't understand your own, how can you be expected to consistently understand the weaknesses and mistakes of those on the other side of the fence?

The first error I made was in calling the book "The Hollywood Novel." Well, "What Makes Sammy Run?" is the story of a Hollywood heel and insofar as Sammy Glick is concerned, that's all right. But all Hollywood people are not Sammy Glicks and the Hollywood people are not shown at all clearly. As a matter of fact, they are not seen at all, and being the people, they're the ones who make the wheels go 'round.

In a full-drawn portraiture of either Sammy Glick or Hollywood, the people must be seen in action, living the lives they lead. Even more effective would the filth of Sammy Glick become when counterposed to the cleanliness of the people. In its effect, "What Makes Sammy Run?" says to the people, "This is Hollywood." And this isn't Hollywood, it's only a very small part of the film city.

Second Error

Then, the review said, "The hectic tale of the writers' battle to unionize the Screen Writers Guild is sketched lightly, somehow, one feels, too lightly." This puts me in the market for an award as Master of Understatement.

Since Sammy Glick was a fink of the Screen Playwriters and since "protagonist" Al Mannheim *[sic]* was a member of the Screenwriters Guild, it was necessary to bring in the fight between the Screen Writers Guild and the Hollywood producers and their little strikebreaking tools.

However, Mannheim and the female protagonist of the book, are brought in as the outstanding members of the Guild, by virtue of their ubiquitous presence at Guild meetings. And their main interest is not organization, but sex. One gets no picture of the brave and (if we may use the word) heroic battle put up by the scripters for the right to guarantee their pay checks. Mannheim and his girl friend are weaklings; the leaders of the Guild were not, and are not.

Someday the story of the Guild will be thoroughly told, well dramatized and done in all the shades of gray which entered the picture, not in the plain black and whites drawn in the Schulberg book.

Third Error

Finally, the criticism has been broached that the book was anti-Semitic. I was inclined to balk at this suggestion at first, but more and more thought leaves me with the conclusion that the criticism is correct. Not that Budd Schulberg meant to be anti-Semitic in his writing, nor that he is anti-Semitic himself. Far from it.

His protagonist, Al Mannheim, is a Jew as is his "hero," Sammy Glick, and other Jewish characters are portrayed sympathetically throughout the book.

One of my critics told me, "You might not think the book is anti-Semitic, because for Sammy Glick there is Al Mannheim and Sammy's mother and brother and so on. But because the book is so predominantly about Sammy Glick it is so on the bad side, because of all these things, Fascist critics of Hollywood will be able to say, 'See? That's Hollywood, and the Jew who runs it.'"

No Hits, No Runs

I don't have to go here into all the rotten anti-Semitic stuff that has been printed and spoken about the film town. Probably everyone has read it and heard it. The Sammy Glicks of Hollywood are of all nationalities and if this book allows the enemies of the people more of their filthy propaganda weapons, and it does by omission and commission, then this criticism must be agreed with.

All in all, "What Makes Sammy Run?" is an anti-Hollywood book. It paints a familiar picture of gin and sex over again . . . and adds another coat of shellac to brighten it up a bit, that's all.

It's time a pro-Hollywood book was written, a book about the Hollywood that matters, the Hollywood of trade union struggles, of struggles to keep democracy alive and to bring peace to the world. There's still plenty of drama in the lives of the day-to-day writers and actors and painters and carpenters and white-collar workers.

These are the main reasons my review of "Sammy" stank. There are other and less important reasons. To say of Schulberg's book, "This is Hollywood," is to turn the people away from a fair-sized industrial center as a center of evil, a sink of iniquity, not worth the time and trouble. That's the important thing to remember.

Appendix D

LETTER TO *VARIETY*—
PUBLISHED MAY 23, 1973

In the recent International Film Edition there was a commentary on the continuing predicament of the German woman film documentarian, Leni Riefenstahl. She has been much interviewed by film buffs and in one recent extended taping spoke of those who opposed her. It was she who described Budd Schulberg as a leader of the "Hate Leni" cult. That was quoted in *Variety* and has evoked this letter from Schulberg, which is quoted in part as follows:

Westhampton, N.Y.
Editor, Variety:

I would like to add that Leni Riefenstahl gives me far too much credit when she attributes to me the leadership for the "persisting 'Hate Leni' cult." When I took her into custody, in accordance with my orders, she not only assured me that she had many enemies among the Nazis, but also that she had many friends in Hollywood. She saw me, of course, only as an American officer, and it did not occur to her that I might also be a member of the American film community. She told me of the wonderful party that Hal Roach had given her during her visit to Hollywood in the middle '30s. I remembered, but did not feel it necessary to tell her that the "wonderful party" had been bitterly resented by Hollywood's anti-Nazi community, and that a widespread boycott led by anti-Nazi stars and directors involved an overwhelming majority of the leading Hollywood personalities. They set up a telephone campaign, urging other celebrated invitees not to attend the reception for Riefenstahl. As a result, her reception was a fiasco.

I was only a young Hollywood writer at that time. I would like to think that I was the leader of the "Hate Leni" movement, but, in all modesty, several hundred of Hollywood's best known artists led the demonstration against Riefenstahl. Few of them ever forgave her cine-

141

matic glorification of "Mein Kampf."

It should also be remembered that while Leni Riefenstahl was enjoying unlimited film budgets, due to the generosity of her friend and protector, Adolf Hitler, a long list of distinguished film-makers as gifted as she, if not more so, were running for their lives—and sometimes not making it. These German film-making contemporaries who were either martyred or driven into exile are still the most telling witnesses to the pictorial crimes that Leni Riefenstahl committed through her allegiance to Adolf Hitler.

Incidentally, even Riefenstahl's celebrated documentary on the 1936 Olympics, while photographically stunning, is clearly biased in favor of Der Fuhrer and his doctrine of Aryan racial supremacy. The highlight of those Games was the triple gold-medal performance of our great Jesse Owens, with Hitler making a hurried exit from his box with his fellow Nazi leaders rather than have to stand in honor of an American black man. You will not find this in the beautifully-photographed-and-edited but Nazi-oriented Riefenstahl version of the Games in Berlin. "Strength Through Joy," the Hitlerian call to physical prowess, was glorified in the Riefenstahl film. But not if that strength was demonstrated by athletes racially unacceptable to Adolf Hitler and his cinematic eye-and-mouthpiece Leni Riefenstahl.

Budd Schulberg

Schulberg was awarded both the Army and Navy Commendation Ribbons for his supervision of the gathering of photographic evidence of Crimes against Humanity at the Nuremberg Trials.

REFERENCES

Alexander, Franz. *Our Age of Unreason.* New York: J. B. Lippincott Co., 1942. Pioneering psychologist Alexander analyzes what later would be called "retribalization," the phenomenon that afflicts the sons of immigrant minority families when the old-fashioned father becomes an object of ridicule and the family must pin its hopes on the eldest son, who in turn believes he must succeed at all cost. Alexander: "I am impressed by the accuracy with which Schulberg has described this type."

Baer, William, ed. *Elia Kazan Interviews.* Oxford: University Press of Mississippi, 2000. An interesting collection of interviews, conducted by twenty different writers between 1951 and 1988. Included is Michel Ciment's instructive 1974 *Sight and Sound* interview, "Working with Schulberg: *On the Waterfront.*"

Baxter, Peter. *Just Watch!: Sternberg, Paramount and America.* London: British Film Institute, 1993. The breakup of B.P. Schulberg's marriage and his removal as production head of Paramount Pictures in 1932 are an important part of this detailed chronicle of director Josef Von Sternberg's Great Depression difficulties in getting *Blonde Venus* (with Marlene Dietrich) made at Paramount.

Behlmer, Rudy. *Memo from Darryl F. Zanuck: The Golden Years at Twentieth Century-Fox.* New York: Grove Press, 1993. Behlmer's "sequel" to his hit book on David O. Selznick (*Memo from Selznick*) includes many of the best and most interesting of Zanuck's memos to directors, writers, actors, and studio executives during the years (1935–1956) he ran Twentieth Century-Fox. Among them are the memos to Elia Kazan and Budd Schulberg in 1953, when it appeared that Zanuck and his studio would make *On the Waterfront.*

Bentley, Eric, ed. *Thirty Years of Treason: Excerpts from the Hearings before the House Committee on Un-American Activities, 1938–68.* New York: Viking Press, 1971. In this nearly 1,000-page record, English-born historian, drama critic, and playwright *(Are You Now or Have You Ever Been. . . ?)* Bentley has transcribed and distilled the testimony of forty-five actors, producers, directors, musicians, lawyers, academics, and theologians (and added the statements of Richard M. Nixon, Upton Sinclair, and

Paul Robeson). It is an impressive and essentially evenhanded work, illuminated by
the author's own views and careful analysis.

Bernstein, Matthew. *Walter Wanger: Hollywood Independent.* Los Angeles: University of
California Press, 1994. A good biography of the neglected producer and Dartmouth alumnus who sent Schulberg and F. Scott Fitzgerald to New Hampshire to
write *Winter Carnival.* Wanger is of particular interest to students of Schulberg because the writer used Wanger, in part at least, as a model for producer Victor Mil-
grim in *The Disenchanted.*

Bernstein, Walter. *Inside Out: A Memoir of the Blacklist.* New York: Knopf, 1996. The
screenwriter who drafted the scripts for *Fail Safe, The Front,* and *The Molly Maguires*
writes insightfully, and sometimes humorously, of the injustices of the Blacklist, and
of his admiration for and ambivalent friendship with Budd Schulberg.

Billingsley, Kenneth Lloyd. *Hollywood Party: How Communism Seduced the American
Film Industry in the 1930s and 1940s.* Rocklin, Calif.: Forum, 1998. In one of the
few right-wing versions of the Blacklist years, the author says the "complete story
finally emerges" as he tells of the "Communist Party's strategic plan for taking control of the movie industry during its golden age."

Bowker-Bowers, Nancy. *The Hollywood Novel and Other Novels about Film,
1912–1982.* New York: Garland Publishing, 1985. This deeply researched anno-
tated bibliography contains synopses of plots, identification of central characters
and evaluations of style and quality. Where novels have been made into motion
pictures, Bowker-Bowers has listed titles, studios, directors, and lead actors.

Brando, Marlon, and Robert Lindsey. *Brando: Songs My Mother Taught Me.* New York:
Random House, 1994. The distinguished actor tells his version of the making of
On the Waterfront, claims he and Rod Steiger "improvised" the famous taxicab
scene, and accuses Elia Kazan and Budd Schulberg of making the film "to justify
finking on their friends."

Breit, Harvey. *The Writer Observed.* New York: World Publishing Co., 1956. This small
book contains brief interviews with fifty-nine writers—including T. S. Eliot,
Ernest Hemingway, William Faulkner, and Budd Schulberg—conducted by Breit
between 1948 and 1955 for his column in the *New York Times Book Review.* He interviewed Schulberg in November 1950, just after the author had published *The
Disenchanted.* In 1958 Breit would collaborate with Schulberg on the script for the
hit (189 performances) Broadway play, *The Disenchanted.*

*Budd Schulberg: An Exhibition in Observance of the 50th Anniversary of the Publication of
What Makes Sammy Run?* Catalogue. Los Angeles: University of Southern California, 1991. In an introductory note, Schulberg tells how, and why, *Mannie* Glick became *Sammy* Glick.

Burgess, Anthony. Introduction to *The Disenchanted.* London: Allison & Busby, 1983.
Burgess confesses to some sixteen readings of *The Disenchanted,* which he praises
for dealing "so authoritatively with the Hollywood of the 1930s." Among many

astute observations, he calls Manley Halliday the permanent symbol of the American writer—"whose greatest enemy is early success."

California Legislature. Senate Fact-Finding Committee on Un-American Activities. *Fifth Report to the 1949 Regular California Legislature: Un-American Activities in California, 1949.* Sacramento: Published by the Senate, 1949. A decade after Budd Schulberg had left the Communist Party, California's own Committee on Un-American Activities was still alarmed over the organizations he allegedly belonged to and the man (former Vice President Henry Wallace) he initially had supported for president in 1948.

Ceplair, Larry, and Steven England. *The Inquisition in Hollywood: Politics in the Film Community, 1930–1960.* Garden City, N.Y.: Anchor Press/Doubleday, 1980. A detailed, well-researched account, from a decidedly left-wing perspective, of the political turmoil in Hollywood before, during, and immediately after the hearings and the creation of the blacklist.

Cerf, Bennett. *At Random: The Reminiscences of Bennett Cerf.* New York: Random House, 1977. Cerf's fond recollections of the care and feeding of Random House and its authors and editors include his meeting with Budd Schulberg (then a "crusading" college newspaper editor) at Dartmouth in 1935 and Schulberg's introduction to Saxe Commins, who would remain his editor and friend.

Chapman, John. *Broadway's Best 1959: The Complete Record of the Theatrical Year.* New York: Doubleday, 1959. Contains a ten-page, scene-by-scene summary of the play *The Disenchanted* by Chapman, drama critic of the *New York Daily News.*

Chase, Donald. *Filmmaking: The Collaborative Art.* Boston: Little, Brown, 1975. A collection of transcripts of seminars (conducted by the American Film Institute) with various categories of filmmakers. Screenwriters quoted include Schulberg, Leonard Spiegelgass, Nunnally Johnson, Alvin Sargent, Ray Bradbury, Lonnie Elder III, W. D. Richter, Donald Ogden Stewart, Howard Estabrook, Milos Forman, and Leigh Brackett.

Ciment, Michel. *Kazan on Kazan.* New York: Viking Press, 1974. Ciment, a French critic and admirer of Kazan, for many years had unequaled access to the director, as this and his other works about the director demonstrate.

———. *Elia Kazan: An American Odyssey.* Translated from the French by Sally Sampson. London: Bloomsbury Publishing, 1987.

Cole, Lester. *Hollywood Red: The Autobiography of Lester Cole.* Palo Alto, Calif.: Ramparts Press, 1981. Screenwriter and playwright Cole, one of the founders of the Screen Writers Guild in 1933, collaborated with Schulberg on the ill-fated *Winter Carnival* in 1939. He was blacklisted in 1947 and jailed in 1950, but survived and wrote the script for *Born Free* in 1966. Named by Schulberg, he was still in the CPUSA at his death in 1985.

Commins, Dorothy. *What Is an Editor? Saxe Commins at Work.* Chicago: University of Chicago Press, 1978. The remarkably talented and good-hearted dentist-turned-editor, who worked with William Faulkner, Eugene O'Neill, and James Michener—as well as with Budd Schulberg and dozens of other prominent writers—is recalled by his wife of thirty years (1927–1958). She describes his working friendship with Schulberg, who brought the little longshoreman "Brownie" to the Commins home in Princeton one day, to stay, and to authenticate the waterfront language.

Fariello, Griffin. *Red Scare: Memories of the American Inquisition. An Oral History.* New York: Norton, 1995. An interesting collection of interviews with people who were caught up in the HCUA hearings and the subsequent blacklist. It includes Ring Lardner, Jr.'s account of his lost friendship with Budd Schulberg.

Gabler, Neal. *An Empire of Their Own: How the Jews Invented Hollywood.* New York: Crown Publishers, 1988. The fascinating history of the Jewish immigrants who built the movie industry and who, although often denied entry into the American mainstream, created the mythological vision of the country and its values that most Americans hold today. The author discusses the 1941 publication of *What Makes Sammy Run?* and the studio heads' fears that its alleged anti-Semitism would unleash new attacks on the industry. Gabler also writes of Schulberg's break with the Communist Party over his right to publish the book.

Gardner, Ralph D. *Writers Talk to Ralph D. Gardner.* Metuchen, N.J.: Scarecrow Press, 1989. Between 1974 and 1987, Gardner was the host of "Ralph Gardner's Bookshelf," a syndicated radio show serving the "tri-state" (New York, New Jersey, Connecticut) area. This collection contains the transcripts of twenty-four interviews. Gardner's interview with Schulberg took place in 1981, when the writer was making personal appearances to promote the recently published *Moving Pictures;* thus, much of the discussion focuses on Schulberg's childhood in Hollywood.

Georgakas, Dan, and Lenny Rubenstein, eds. *The Cineaste Interviews on the Art and Politics of the Cinema.* Chicago: Lake View Press, 1983. Contains historian and editor Georgakas' wide-ranging interview of Schulberg (conducted at the time of the publication of *Moving Pictures).* During the interview (for *Cineaste,* perhaps the most political of the film magazines), Schulberg responds for the first time to what he calls Victor Navasky's *(Naming Names)* "hatchet job, under the guise of fair play."

Glenn, Charles. "Novel—the Story of Hollywood Heel." *People's World,* 2 April 1941, 5.

———. "What Makes Sammy Run? Story of a Hollywood Heel." *Daily Worker,* 7 April 1941, 7.

———. "News in the World of Stage and Screen." *Daily Worker,* 8 April 1941, 7.

———. "Hollywood Can Be Won to the Side of the American People—Actors and Directors Respond to Criticism of Film Audiences." *Daily Worker,* 23 April 1941, 7.

———. "Hollywood Vine." *People's World,* 24 April 1941, 5.

Hemingway, Mary Welsh. *How It Was.* New York: Alfred A. Knopf, 1976. Contains material on Hemingway's sometimes tense friendship with screenwriter/novelist

Peter Viertel and his "flirtation" with Viertel's handsome wife Jigee, the former spouse of Budd Schulberg.

Jaffe, Sam. Interview by Barbara Hall, 1992. Oral History 109, transcript. Academy of Motion Picture Arts and Sciences Oral History Program, Margaret Herrick Library, Center for Motion Picture Study, Los Angeles. Transcripts of thirteen sessions (between 5 February and 19 July 1991) with Schulberg's then ninety-year-old uncle. Contains Jaffe's memories of his mentor, B.P. Schulberg, and some of the child "Buddy" and his first boyhood efforts at writing.

Kanfer, Stefan. *A Journal of the Plague Years: A Devastating Chronicle of the Era of the Blacklist.* New York: Atheneum, 1973. In this first history of the Blacklist, editor, film critic, and biographer Kanfer writes of the shady private investigators, "clearance" specialists, former FBI agents, and hustlers who promoted the hysteria and profited from it. The title derives from Daniel Defoe's novel of the black plague in 1664 London, *A Journal of the Plague Year.* One of the fairest retellings of the witch hunts and their human toll.

Kazan, Elia. *A Life.* New York: Alfred A. Knopf, 1988. A lengthy (848 pages) autobiography by the noted stage and screen director (and veteran of the Group Theatre) includes an account of his friendship and collaboration (*On the Waterfront* and *A Face in the Crowd*) with Schulberg.

Kronenberger, Louis, ed. *The Best Plays of 1958–1959 (The Burns Mantle Yearbook).* New York: Dodd, Mead, 1959. Lists cast and credits, and reprints the text of the play *The Disenchanted.*

Lardner, Ring, Jr. *The Lardners: My Family Remembered.* New York: Harper & Row, 1976. Lardner's affectionate recollection of his famous parents and his three brothers also includes an account of his early studio work with Budd Schulberg, his recruitment by Schulberg into the Communist Party, his fruitless pursuit of Jigee Schulberg, and finally his disappointment and surprise when both Budd and Jigee testified as cooperating witnesses before HCUA in the 1950s.

———. *I'd Hate Myself in the Morning: A Memoir.* New York: Nation Books, 2000. Lardner recalls a privileged childhood, his life-changing 1934 journey to the Soviet Union, his frustrating time as a young Hollywood screenwriter (and Communist), and his confrontation with the House Committee and subsequent federal prison term. He also tells his thoughts about the "friendly" testimony of Elia Kazan and old friend Budd Schulberg. The introduction is by Victor Navasky.

Laurents, Arthur. *Original Story By: A Memoir of Broadway and Hollywood.* New York: Alfred A. Knopf, 2000. Screenwriter, playwright, and director Laurents' "tell all" book also discusses his friendships with two of Budd Schulberg's wives, Virginia "Jigee" Ray and Geraldine Brooks, and his sometimes unpleasant encounters with Schulberg.

Lesser, Julian. Interview by Douglas Bell, 1992. Oral History 107; transcript. Academy of Motion Picture Arts and Sciences Oral History Program. Margaret Herrick

Library, Center for Motion Picture Study, Los Angeles. The son of producer Sol Lesser recalls his childhood in the Hollywood of the 1920s, and his friendships with schoolmates and neighbors Budd Schulberg and Maurice Rapf.

McGilligan, Patrick, and Paul Buhle. *Tender Comrades: A Backstory of the Hollywood Blacklist.* New York: St. Martin''s Press, 1997. Thirty-six survivors of the Blacklist—among them writers, actors, directors, and two members of the Hollywood Ten—tell their life stories. Included is a lengthy interview with Budd Schulberg's boyhood friend Maurice Rapf.

Navasky, Victor. *Naming Names.* New York: Viking Press, 1980. This best-known book on the hearings of the House Committee on Un-American Activities and the subsequent blacklist in Hollywood, by the editor of *The Nation,* is based on eight years of research and interviews with 169 people. Included is considerable material on Schulberg.

Primack, Bret, ed. *The Ben Hecht Show: Impolitic Observations from the Freest Thinker of 1950s Television.* Jefferson, N.C.: McFarland, 1993. Excerpts and transcripts from Hecht's short-lived (September 1958–February 1959) talk show on New York's WABC-TV. Included is the transcript of the December 12, 1958 show in which the irascible Hecht disputes Schulberg on the state of American writing and screenwriting.

Rapf, Maurice. *Back Lot: Growing Up with the Movies.* Lanham, Md.: Scarecrow Press, 1999. Schulberg's almost inseparable boyhood pal remembers the Hollywood of the 1920s, when he and Budd played on the backlots at Paramount, and at MGM (where Rapf's father was a top executive); of his time in the Communist Party; and of the twelve-year estrangement that resulted from Schulberg's 1951 testimony before the House Committee on Un-American Activities.

Raymond, Allen. *Waterfront Priest.* New York: Henry Holt, 1955. The full story of Jesuit priest John M. Corridan, the model for "Father Barry" in *On the Waterfront* and the novel *Waterfront,* who fearlessly battled gangsterism on the New York waterfront and campaigned for honest union representation of longshoremen. The introduction is by Budd Schulberg.

Schulberg, Sonya. *They Cried a Little.* New York: Scribner's, 1937. Four years before Budd Schulberg wrote the novel *What Makes Sammy Run?,* his little sister had one published by Scribner's, where her editor was the famous Max Perkins. Charming story of a girls' finishing school in Paris, by a perceptive nineteen-year-old.

Schwartz, Nancy Lynn. *The Hollywood Writers' Wars.* New York: Alfred A. Knopf, 1982. A superb, ground-breaking work about the formation of the Screen Writers Guild, told by the writers, directors and producers who lived through the political turmoil of the 1930s and the witch-hunts of the Red Scare years. Ms. Schwartz, just twenty-two when she received a grant from the National Endowment for the Humanities, died at age twenty-six after finishing a first draft. The book was completed by her mother, Professor Sheila Schwartz.

Shatzky, Joel, and Michael Taub, eds. *Contemporary Jewish-American Novelists: A Bio-Critical Sourcebook.* Westport, Conn.: Greenwood Press, 1997. Contains, among its sixty-three entries on contemporary writers, an interesting discussion of Schulberg's major works, his critical reception, and a bibliography of primary and secondary sources.

Shorris, Sylvia, and Marion Abbott Bundy. *Talking Pictures: With the People Who Made Them.* New York: New Press, 1994. A collection of revealing interviews with producers, assistant directors, soundmen, film editors, cameramen, publicists, extras, and script girls from Hollywood's Golden Age. Included is a 1985 interview with Budd Schulberg's uncle, superagent Sam Jaffe.

Sperling, Cass Warner, and Cork Millner with Jack Warner Jr. *Hollywood Be Thy Name.* Rocklin, Calif.: Prima Publishing, 1994. Harry Warner's granddaughter and her coauthors tell the rags-to-riches story of the four Warner brothers, who created one of Hollywood's major studios and brought sound to the movies. Sperling's father Milton was one of the alleged models for Sammy Glick.

Turnbull, Andrew. *Scott Fitzgerald.* New York: Scribner's, 1962. Unquestionably one of the better biographies of Fitzgerald, Turnbull's book includes a short but insightful account of the friendship and rivalry between Fitzgerald and Schulberg. Turnbull, whose family rented a house in Maryland to Fitzgerald and his daughter, Scottie, in 1932, knew the famous writer when Andrew was a boy of twelve.

U.S. Congress. House Committee on Un-American Activities. *Annual Report of Committee on Un-American Activities for the Year 1951.* 82nd Cong., 2nd Sess., 17 February 1952. Washington, D.C.: Government Printing Office, 1957. Transcripts of the testimony of Schulberg, as well as that of Larry Parks, Mel Ferrer, Richard Collins, and others.

Vaughn, Robert. *Only Victims: A Study of Show Business Blacklisting.* New York: Putnam's Sons, 1972. The eminent film and television actor's 1970 doctoral dissertation (in political science at the University of Southern California) describes the impact of the House Committee on Un-American Activities on the entire entertainment industry from 1938 to 1958. Readable, and also useful in determining when individuals were named publicly for the first time. The foreword is by former Sen. George McGovern.

Viertel, Peter. *Dangerous Friends: At Large with Huston and Hemingway in the Fifties.* New York: St. Martin's, 1992. The well-known screenwriter and novelist describes his tumultuous marriage to second wife Virginia "Jigee" Schulberg, her relationship with Ernest Hemingway, and her daughter (Victoria) by Schulberg.

Viertel, Salka. *The Kindness of Strangers.* New York: Holt, Rinehart & Winston, 1969. An autobiography by the Polish actress Salka Steuermann Viertel (1889–1978), who was also a screenwriter (for Greta Garbo) and the mother of novelist Peter Viertel and mother-in-law of Schulberg's first wife, Virginia. She also writes of Victoria Schulberg, Budd's daughter by Virginia.

Warfel, Harry R. *American Novelists of Today.* New York: American Book Co., 1951.

Young, Jeff. *Kazan: The Master Director Discusses His Films.* New York: Newmarket Press, 1999. Young, a writer, producer, and director, interviewed Kazan over an eighteen-month period in the early 1970s, but agreed not to publish the results until after Kazan published his own autobiography. When Kazan published *A Life* in 1988, Young went to work editing the old transcripts. The interview about *On the Waterfront* is of special interest.

Zolotow, Maurice. "Don't Call Me Mr. Casablanca." *Los Angeles,* September 1988, 130–138. Zolotow tells the saga of screenwriter Julius Epstein (1909–2000), the model for Julian Blumberg (one of Sammy Glick's principal victims in *What Makes Sammy Run?*), who wanted to be known for *Arsenic and Old Lace, The Man Who Came to Dinner,* and *The Male Animal*—and not *Casablanca,* which he called "a very cornball movie, very sentimental."

BUDD WILSON SCHULBERG
(27 MARCH 1914–)

MOTION PICTURES

A Star Is Born (Selznick International Pictures, released by United Artists, 1937); directed by William A. Wellman and (uncredited) Jack Conway; story by Wellman and Robert Carson; screenplay by Carson, Dorothy Parker, and Alan Campbell; and (uncredited) Ben Hecht, Ring Lardner Jr., John Lee Mahin, Budd Schulberg, and David O. Selznick (listed in *Screen Writers Guild Yearbook*); with Janet Gaynor, Fredric March, Adolphe Menjou, May Robson, Andy Devine, and Lionel Stander; 111 minutes.

Nothing Sacred (Selznick International Pictures, released by United Artists, 1937); directed by William A. Wellman; story by James H. Street; screenplay by Ben Hecht and (uncredited) Budd Schulberg and Ring Lardner Jr. (listed in *SWG Yearbook*); with Carole Lombard, Fredric March, Charles Winninger, Walter Connolly, Sig Ruman, Frank Fay, and Maxie Rosenbloom; 75 minutes.

Little Orphan Annie (a Colonial Pictures production, released by Paramount, 1938); working title *Little Orphan Annie and the Champ;* directed by Ben Holmes; story by Endre Bohem and Samuel Badisch Ornitz; screenplay by Budd Schulberg (as Budd Wilson Schulberg); based on the comic strip by Harold Gray and Al Lowenthal for the Chicago Tribune/New York News Syndicate; inspired by the character in James Whitcomb Riley's *The Little Orphant Annie Book* (1908); with Ann Gillis, Charles Coleman, Robert Kent, June Travis, Ian Maclaren, and J. Farrell MacDonald; 57 Minutes.

Winter Carnival (a Walter Wanger Production, released by United Artists, 1939); directed by Charles Reisner; screenplay by Budd Schulberg, Maurice Rapf, and Lester Cole; story by Schulberg and Cole, based on *Echoes That Old Refrain,* by Corey Ford; musical score and direction by Werner Janssen; with Richard Carlson, Ann Sheridan, Virginia Gilmore, Marsha Hunt, Robert Armstrong, and Helen Parrish; 105 minutes.

Foreign Correspondent (a Walter Wanger Production, released by United Artists, 1940); directed by Alfred Hitchcock; screenplay by Charles Bennett, Joan Harrison, James Hilton, and Robert Benchley; and (uncredited) Harold Clurman, Ben Hecht, John Howard Lawson, John Lee Mahin, Richard Maibaum, and Budd Schulberg; with Joel McCrea, Laraine Day, Herbert Marshall, George Sanders, Albert Bassermann, and Edmund Gwenn; 119 minutes.

Weekend for Three (RKO, 1941); produced by Tay Garnett; directed by Irving Reis; story by Budd Schulberg; screenplay by Dorothy Parker and Alan Campbell; with Dennis O'Keefe, Jane Wyatt, Philip Reed, Edward Everett Horton, Zasu Pitts, and Franklin Pangborn; 66 minutes.

Five Were Chosen (distributed by Clasa-Mohme, Inc., 1942); directed by Herbert Kline; story and screenplay by Budd Schulberg; with Victor Kilian, Howard Da Silva, Leonid Kinskey, Ricardo Montalban, and Rosa Harvan Kline; 82 minutes.

Cinco Fueron Escogidos (Alpha Films [Mexico], 1943), Spanish-language version of *Five Were Chosen,* with Mexican cast; directed by Herbert Kline and Agustin P. Delgado; story by Budd Schulberg; screenplay by Rafael M. Muñoz and Xavier Villaurrutia; with Ricardo Montalban, Maria Elena Marques, Antonio Bravo, Fernando Cortes, Andres Soler, and Julio Villarreal.

City without Men (Samuel Bronston Pictures, Inc.; distributed by Columbia Pictures Corp., 1943); produced by B.P. Schulberg; directed by Sidney Salkow; story by Budd Schulberg and Martin Berkeley; screenplay by Schulberg, Samuel Bronston, Donald Davis, W. L. River and George Sklar; Schulberg's only credit with his father as producer; with Linda Darnell, Edgar Buchanan, Glenda Farrell, Sara Allgood, Margaret Hamilton, and Sheldon Leonard; 75 minutes.

Government Girl (RKO, 1943); produced and directed by Dudley Nichols; story by Dudley Nichols and Adela Rogers St. John, based on her story of the same title in the January 1943 *Ladies Home Journal;* screenplay by Dudley Nichols; adaptation by Budd Schulberg; with Olivia De Havilland, Sonny Tufts, Anne Shirley, James Dunn, Agnes Moorehead, Jess Barker, and Una O'Connor; 94 minutes.

The Nazi Plan (1945); produced and presented as evidence at the Nuremberg War Crimes Tribunal, 11 December 1945; directed by George Stevens; written by Budd Schulberg.

On the Waterfront (Horizon Pictures and Columbia Pictures Corp., 1954); produced by Sam Spiegel; directed by Elia Kazan; based on stories in the *New York Sun* (1948) by Malcolm Johnson; story and screenplay by Budd Schulberg; original music by Leonard Bernstein; with Marlon Brando, Karl Malden, Lee J. Cobb, Rod Steiger, and Eva Marie Saint; 108 minutes.

The Harder They Fall (Columbia, 1956); produced by Philip Yordan; directed by Mark Robson; based on the novel by Budd Schulberg; screenplay by Philip Yordan; with Humphrey Bogart, Rod Steiger, Jan Sterling, Mike Lane, Max Baer, Edward Andrews, and Nehemiah Persoff; 109 minutes.

A Face in the Crowd (Warner Bros., 1957); produced and directed by Elia Kazan; screenplay by Budd Schulberg from his short story, *The Arkansas Traveler*; with Andy Griffith, Patricia Neal, Anthony Franciosa, Walter Matthau, Lee Remick, and Marshall Neilan; and (as themselves) Mike Wallace, Walter Winchell, John Cameron Swayze, Earl Wilson, Sam Levinson, Burl Ives, Faye Emerson, and Bennett Cerf; 125 minutes.

Wind across the Everglades (Warner Bros., 1958); in color; produced by Stuart and Budd Schulberg; directed by Nicholas Ray and (uncredited) Budd Schulberg; story and screenplay by Budd Schulberg; with Burl Ives, Christopher Plummer, Chana Eden, Gypsy Rose Lee, Peter Falk, Emmett Kelly, and MacKinlay Kantor; 93 minutes.

RADIO

Hollywood Doctor (1941); script collected in *The Writer's World Theatre,* ed. Norman Weiser (New York: Harper, 1941).

Tomorrow (NBC Blue Network, 1943), play by Schulberg and Jerome Lawrence, based on a statement by Thomas Mann; for the Free World Theatre; a joint presentation of the Office of War Information, the Hollywood Victory Committee and the Hollywood Writers Mobilization; with John Garfield, Beulah Bondi, Ray Collins, and Frank Martin.

TELEVISION

What Makes Sammy Run? (Philco Playhouse, 10 April 1949); sponsored by Actors Equity Association; produced by Fred Coe; Bert Lytell (former president of Actors Equity), host; episode #1.28; with Jose Ferrer.

The Pharmacist's Mate (Pulitzer Prize Playhouse, 22 December 1950); produced for Schlitz Brewing Co. by Edgar Peterson at KECA-TV [later KABC-TV], Hollywood for ABC Television; filmed by the N. P. Rathvon Company at the Long Beach (Calif.) Naval Yard; based on George Weller's Pulitzer Prize-winning account in the *Chicago Daily News* of the heroism of a U.S. Navy Hospital Corpsman; directed by Irving Pichel; one-hour original teleplay by Budd Schulberg; with Gene Raymond, Brian Donlevy, Philip Shawn, Darryl Hickman, Alan Hale Jr., Frank Jenks, and Harold Lloyd Jr.

Paso Doble (Omnibus, CBS-TV, 17 February 1954); production under the auspices of the Ford Foundation Television-Radio Workshop, William Spier, producer; one-act teleplay by Budd Schulberg; with John Cassavetes, Kim Stanley, Arthur Franz, and Jacques Aubuchon.

What Makes Sammy Run? (NBC Sunday Showcase, 27 September and 4 October 1959); sponsored by Proctor & Gamble; produced and directed by Delbert Mann; executive producer Robert Alan Arthur; music by Erwin Bazelon; teleplay by Budd and Stuart Schulberg, based on the novel by Budd Schulberg; with Larry Blyden, John Forsythe, Sidney Blackmer, Barbara Rush, Dina Merrill, David Opatashu, Sidney Feinman, Horace McMahon, and others.

Memory in White (General Electric Theatre, 8 January 1961); teleplay by Budd Schulberg, based on his short story in *Collier's* (26 September 1942); with Charles Bronson, Bert Freed, and Sammy Davis Jr.

The Legend That Walks Like a Man (General Electric Theatre, 12 February 1961); story and teleplay by Budd Schulberg, based on his short story in *Esquire* (August 1950); with Ernest Borgnine, William Schallert, and Zsa Zsa Gabor.

Everglades (Channel 4, New York); 39 30–minute episodes produced for syndication by ZIV Television Programs; created by Budd Schulberg; original music by Harian Howard; first shown on 9 October 1961; with Ron Hayes and Gordon Casell.

The Meal Ticket (The Bob Hope Chrysler Theatre, 28 February 1964); original teleplay by Budd Schulberg; with Cliff Robertson, Janice Rule, Broderick Crawford, Chris Robinson.

The Angry Voices of Watts: An NBC Inquiry (NBC-TV, 24 August 1966); documentary; on film; 60 minutes; produced by Stuart Schulberg; written by Budd Schulberg and others.

Once Upon a Time Is Now: The Story of Princess Grace (The Big Event, NBC, 22 May 1977); documentary; script by Budd Schulberg.

A Question of Honor (original title: *Internal Affairs*, 1980) (EMI Television Programs, Inc. and CBS, 1982); directed by Jud Taylor; based on *Point Blank* by Sonny Grosso and Philip Rosenberg; story and teleplay by Budd Schulberg with Stan Silverman; with Danny Aiello, Ben Gazzara, Tony Roberts, Carol Rossen, Tom Skerritt, Paul Sorvino, Robert Vaughn, and Anthony Zerbe.

Prisoner without a Name, Cell without a Number (NBC Sunday Night at the Movies, 22 May 1983); produced and directed by Linda Yellen; executive producers Terry Ellis and Richard Dorso; based on the book by Jacobo Timerman; two-hour teleplay by Oliver P. Drexell Jr. (Budd Schulberg), Jonathan Platnick, and Linda Yellen; Schulberg asked that his name be removed from the production, but settled for use of a pseudonym; with Roy Scheider, Liv Ullmann, Zach Galligan, Michael Pearlman, Sam Robards, David Cryer, Terrance O'Quinn, Trini Alvarado.

Joe Louis: For All Time (ABC Video Enterprises, 1984); produced by Peter Tatum, Jack Healy, Budd Schulberg, Jim Jacobs, and Bill Cayton; directed by Peter Tatum; script by Budd Schulberg; narrated by Brock Peters.

A Table at Ciro's (Zenith Productions Ltd., 1987); a production of WNET New York and Zenith (London) in association with KCET Los Angeles, for "Great Performances"; produced by David R. Loxton; directed by Leon Ichaso and Paul Bog-art; teleplay by Budd Schulberg and Stan Silverman, based on Schulberg's *Saturday Evening Post* (18 October 1941) short story, *Somebody Has to Be Nobody*; with Dar-ren McGavin, Lois Chiles, Kenneth McMillan, Stella Stevens, Steven Bauer, Neva Patterson, and Earl Boen.

PLAYS

Banned in Boston (performed by the Dartmouth Players at Dartmouth College, May 1935) by Schulberg, Paul Siskind, and Maurice Harry Rapf.

The Disenchanted (New York, Coronet Theatre, 3 December 1958); presented by William Darrid and Eleanore Saidenberg; directed by David Pressman; sets by Ben Edwards; lighting by Jean Rosenthal; costumes by Ann Roth; by Budd Schulberg and Harvey Breit, based on the novel by Schulberg; with George Grizzard, Jason Robards Jr., Rosemary Harris, Salome Jens, and Whitfield Con-nor; 189 performances.

What Makes Sammy Run? (New York, Fifty-Fourth Street Theatre, 27 February 1964); presented by Joseph Cates; directed by Abe Burrows; a new musical by Budd and Stuart Schulberg, based on the novel by Budd Schulberg; music and lyrics by Ervin Drake; musical staging and choreography by Matt Mattox; vocal arrangements and musical direction by Lehman Engel; orchestrations by Don Walker; with Steve Lawrence, Sally Ann Howes, Robert Alda, Bernice Massi, Barry Newman, Arny Freeman, Richard France, George Coe, Graciella Daniele, Mace Barrett, Ralph Stantley, Edward McNally, and Walter Klavun; 540 performances.

On the Waterfront (New York, Brooks Atkinson Theater, 1 May 1995); (world pre-miere, Cleveland Playhouse, 1988; off-Broadway, Theater Row Theater, 1993); presented by Mitchell Maxwell, Dan Markley, Victoria Maxwell, Pines/Gold-berg, Michael Skipper, Harvey Klaris, David Young, Dina Wein-Reis, James L. Simon, Palmer Video Corporation, and Workin' Man Films, in association with Fred H. Krones, Hugh Hayes, and Alan J. Schuster; directed by Adrian Hall; by Budd Schulberg, with Stan Silverman; based on the novel by Schulberg; with Ron Eldard, David Morse, Penelope Ann Miller, Kevin Conway, Michael Har-ney, Brad Sullivan, and George N. Martin; closed after sixteen previews and eight performances.

The Disenchanted (Paris, Silva Montfort Theater, 29 January to 7 March, 1999); in French; a one-person show, adapted by Jean-Pierre Cassel and Francois Bourgeat; directed by Bourgeat; based on the novel and play by Schulberg; starring Jean-Pierre Cassel as Manley Halliday.

BOOKS

What Makes Sammy Run? (New York: Random House, 1941; London: Jarrolds, 1941).

The Harder They Fall (New York: Random House, 1947; London: Bodley Head, 1948; Sydney: Invincible Press, 1947).

The Disenchanted (New York: Random House, 1950; London: Bodley Head, 1951; Sydney: Invincible Press, 1950).

Some Faces in the Crowd (New York: Random House, 1953; London: Bodley Head, 1954).

Waterfront (New York: Random House, 1955; London: Bodley Head, 1956).

A Face in the Crowd: A Play for the Screen (New York: Random House, 1957).

Across the Everglades: A Play for the Screen (New York: Random House, 1958).

The Disenchanted: A Drama in Three Acts, by Budd Schulberg and Harvey Breit (New York: Random House, 1959).

What Makes Sammy Run? A New Musical, by Budd and Stuart Schulberg; music and lyrics by Ervin Drake (New York: Random House, 1964).

From the Ashes: Voices of Watts, edited and with an introduction by Schulberg (New York: New American Library, 1967).

Sanctuary V (New York: New American Library/World, 1969; London: Allen, 1971).

Loser and Still Champion: Muhammad Ali (Garden City, N.J.: Doubleday, 1972; London: New English Library, 1972).

The Four Seasons of Success (Garden City, N.J.: Doubleday, 1972; London: Robson, 1974).

Swan Watch. (text by Schulberg, with photographs by Geraldine Brooks). (New York: Delacorte, 1975; London: Robson, 1975).

Everything That Moves (Garden City, N.J.: Doubleday, 1980; London: Robson, 1981).

On the Waterfront: A Screenplay (Carbondale: Southern Illinois University Press, 1981; Hollywood and New York: Samuel French, n.d.).

Moving Pictures: Memories of a Hollywood Prince (New York: Stein & Day, 1981; London: Souvenir, 1982).

Writers in America: The Four Seasons of Success. (revised and updated edition of *The Four Seasons of Success,* 1972) (New York: Stein and Day, 1983).

Love, Action, Laughter and Other Sad Tales (New York: Random House, 1990).

Sparring with Hemingway: And Other Legends of the Fight Game. (Chicago, Ill.: Ivan R. Dee, 1995; London: Robson, 1997).

La Forêt Interdite (The Forbidden Forest). (Paris: Rivages, 1997); includes *Across the Everglades,* and *Dialogue in Black and White* (with James Baldwin); French only.

On the Waterfront: The Play. (with Stan Silverman). (Chicago, Ill.: Ivan R. Dee, 2001).

The Hardest Game. (Publisher to be determined, 2001).

INTRODUCTIONS, FOREWORDS, AFTERWORDS, AND EPILOGUES

Waterfront Priest, by Allen Raymond. (New York: Henry Holt, 1955). Introduction.

The Golden Book on Writing, by David Lambuth. (Hanover, N.H.: Dartmouth College, 1923). (Reprint. New York: Viking Press, 1964). Foreword.

File on Spratling: An Autobiography, by William Spratling. (Boston: Little, Brown, 1967). Introduction.

. . .*Sting Like a Bee: The Muhammad Ali Story,* by Jose Torres. (New York: Abelard-Schuman, 1971). Epilogue.

The Fall and Rise of Jimmy Hoffa, by Walter Sheridan. (New York: Saturday Review Press, 1972). Introduction.

Queer People, by Carroll and Garrett Graham. (Carbondale: Southern Illinois University Press, 1976. Reprint). Originally published by Vanguard Press, 1930. Afterword.

Dear Muffo: 35 Years in the Fast Lane, by Harold Conrad. (New York: Stein and Day, 1982). Introduction.

The Jerry Izenberg Collection, by Jerry Izenberg. (Dallas: Taylor Publishing Co., 1989). Introduction.

An Exhibition in Observance of the 50th Anniversary of the Publication of "What Makes Sammy Run?" (Catalogue, Doheny Library, University of Southern California), March 4–29, 1991. Introduction.

Food from My Heart, by Zarela Martinez. (New York: Macmillan Publishing Co., 1992). Foreword.

Muhammad Ali: A Thirty-Year Journey, by Howard L. Bingham. (New York: Simon & Schuster, 1993). Introduction.

Babylon Revisited: The Screenplay, by F. Scott Fitzgerald. (New York: Carroll & Graf, 1993). Introduction.

Punch Lines: Berger on Boxing, by Phil Berger. (New York: Four Walls, Eight Windows, 1993). Foreword.

A Life in the Everglades, by Loren G. Totch Brown. (Gainesville: University Press of Florida, 1993). Foreword.

From the Terrace, by John O'Hara. (New York: Carroll & Graf, 1993. Reprint). Originally published by Random House, 1958. Introduction.

The Prizefighters: An Intimate Look at Champions and Contenders, by Arlene Schulman. (New York: Lyons & Burford, 1994). Introduction.

When Boxing Was a Jewish Sport, by Allen Jay Bodner. (Westport, Conn.: Praeger, 1997). Foreword.

Cracking Up: Nice Day for a Brain Hemorrhage, by Peter Swet. (Center City, Minn.: Hazelden, 1998). Introduction.

ANTHOLOGIES

Post Stories of 1941: A Selection of Twenty-Two Stories from the Saturday Evening Post.
(Boston: Little, Brown, 1941). Contains "Somebody Has to Be Nobody" (from
Saturday Evening Post, 18 October 1941).

New Stories for Men. Edited by Charles Grayson. (New York: Doubleday, 1941). Contains "The Road to Recovery," published as "Hollywood Doctor" (from *Collier's,*
6 August 1938).

The Writer's Radio Theatre. Edited by Norman Weiser. (New York: Harper, 1941).
Contains script for radio play *Hollywood Doctor,* broadcast 1941.

The Best Short Stories of 1942 and the Yearbook of the American Short Story. Edited by
Martha Foley. (Boston: Houghton Mifflin, 1942). Contains "The Real Viennese
Schmaltz" (from *Esquire,* September 1941).

Free World Theatre. Edited by Arch Oboler and Stephen Longstreet. (New York: Random House, 1944). Contains script for radio play *Tomorrow,* by Schulberg and
Jerome Lawrence, broadcast 1943.

Continent's End: A Collection of California Writing. Edited by Joseph Henry Jackson.
(New York: Whittlesey House, 1944). Contains "The Great South Sea Story" (selection from *What Makes Sammy Run?*).

These Your Children. Edited by Harold U. Ribalow. (New York: Beechhurst Press,
1952). Contains "Passport to Nowhere" (from *Story,* May 1938).

The Girls from Esquire. Edited by Frederic A Birmingham (New York: Random
House, 1952; London: Arthur Barker, 1953). Contains "The Breaking Point" (from
Esquire, December 1948).

Holiday Book of Food and Drink. (New York: Hermitage House, 1952). Contains "See
You at Dave's" (from *Holiday,* April 1951).

Best Television Plays 1950–51. Edited by William I. Kauffman. (New York: Merlin
Press, 1952). Contains script for "The Pharmacist's Mate," telecast 1950.

This Week's Short-Short Stories. (New York: Random House, 1953). Contains "All the
Town's Talking" (from *This Week*).

Champs and Bums. Edited by Bucklin Moon. (New York: Lion Books, 1954). Contains "Meal Ticket" (originally published as "Formula Fighter" in *Saturday Evening
Post,* 21 March 1953).

Various Temptations. (New York: Avon, 1955). Contains "The Dare" (from *Some Faces
in the Crowd,* 1953).

Ten Years of Holiday: An Anniversary Collection of 40 Memorable Pieces. Selected by the
editors of *Holiday.* Introduction by Clifton Fadiman. (New York: Simon and
Schuster, 1956). Contains "Florida's Gold Coast" (from *Holiday,* January 1952).

Great Stories about Show Business. Edited by Jerry D. Lewis. (New York: Coward-McCann,
Inc., 1957). Contains "The Real Viennese Schmaltz" (from *Esquire,* September 1941).

Great Stories from the World of Sport, vol. 1. Edited by Peter Schwed and Herbert Warren. (New York: Simon and Schuster, 1958). Contains "Spotlight" (from *Liberty,* 19
November 1938).

A Cavalcade of Collier's. Edited by Kenneth McArdle. (New York: A. S. Barnes, 1959).
Contains "Love, Action, Laughter" (from *Collier's,* 15 January 1938).

Writing in America. Edited by John Fischer and Robert B. Silvers. (New Brunswick,
N.J.: Rutgers University Press, 1960). Contains "The Writer and Hollywood"
(from *Harper's,* October 1959).

The Best of the Diners' Club Magazine. Edited by Matty Simmons and Sam Boal. (New
York: Regents American Publishing Corp., 1962). Contains "Calling Major
Adams' Car" (from *Collier's,* 25 June 1938).

Famous Short Short Stories. (New York: New American Library, 1966). Contains
"Spotlight" (from *Liberty,* 19 November 1938).

Sports Classics: American Writers Choose Their Best. Edited by Howard Siner. (New
York: Coward-McCann, 1983). Contains "The Heavyweight Championship"
(originally published as "Sports' Greatest Event" in *Esquire,* January 1962).

Christmas Tales: Celebrated Authors on the Magic of the Season. (New York: Viking Studio Books, 1992). Contains "My Christmas Carol" (1942).

Hampton Shorts: Short Fiction from the Hamptons and the East End. (Water Mill, N.Y.:
Hampton Shorts, 1996). Contains "Eulogy for Judy Garland." Originally published
as "Who Killed Cock Robin? A Farewell to Judy" in *Life,* 11 July 1969.

F. Scott Fitzgerald at 100. (Rockville, Md.: Quill & Brush, 1996). Contains "Thoughts
on the F. Scott Fitzgerald Centennial."

TRANSLATIONS

Qu'est-ce qui fait courir Sammy? Translated by Georges Belmont. (Paris: Robert Laffont, 1947). Reprinted 1984.

Knock-Out (The Harder They Fall). Translated by Jean Périer. (Paris: Robert Laffont, 1949).

Le désenchanté. Translated by George Belmont. Introduction by Anthony Burgess.
(Paris: Robert Laffont, 1951). Reprinted 1991. Published by Editions Rivages,
1992 pour l'edition de poche.

Un homme dans la foule (Some Faces in the Crowd). Translated by Michele Valencia.
(Paris: Editions Rivages, 1991). Reprinted 1992. Contains "Your Arkansas Trav-
eler," "A Short Digest of a Long Novel" (originally published as "The Downfall
of Innocence"), "A Table at Ciro's," "Memory in White," "The Breaking Point,"
"My Christmas Carol," "The One He Called Winnie," "The Typical Gesture of
Colonel Duggan," and "Our White Deer."

Sur les quais (Waterfront). Translated by Jean Cathelin. (Paris: Robert Laffont, 1956).
Reprinted in a deluxe edition, limited to 4,910 copies, for members of the Club

du Livre du Mois; no date. Also published in La Collection Marabout (Vervier, Belgium: Gerard & Co., no date).

Dix-huit images par seconde: Une enfance doree a Hollywood (Moving Pictures: Memories of a Hollywood Prince). Translated by Michel Lebrun. (Paris: Editions Segheres, 1991).

Le visage de Hollywood (Some Faces in the Crowd). Translated by Michele Valencia. (Paris: Editions Payot & Rivages, 1993). Contains "The Pride of Tony Colucci," "The Face of Hollywood," "A Foxhole in Washington," "A Note on the Literary Life," "Ensign Weasel," "The Dare," "Enough," "The Legend That Walks Like a Man," "Meal Ticket," and "Third Night-cap," with historical footnotes.

Amour, action, rire et autres contes tristes (Love, Action, Laughter and Other Sad Tales). Preface by Kurt Vonnegut; introduction by Schulberg. Translated by Michele Valencia. (Paris: Editions Payot & Rivages, 1995). Contains "Say Goodnight to Owl," "The Real Viennese Schmaltz," "Senor Discretion Himself," "Passport to Nowhere," "The Funny Part Is ...," "The Howling Dogs of Taxco," "Letter to MacFadden," "Hollywood versus Chris Samuels, Age Nine," "The Docks of New York," "A Second Father," "The Reluctant Pilgrim," "Counterintelligence in Mexico City," "The Barracudas," "The Pettibone Plan: A Fable," "Mother of Them All," and "Love, Action, Laughter."

La forêt interdite (Across the Everglades), published with *The Watts Workshop* and *Dialogue in Black and White* (with James Baldwin). Translated by Daniele and Pierre Bondil. (Paris: Editions Payot & Rivages, 1997). Only book publication of *Dialogue in Black and White.*

I disincantati (The Disenchanted). Translated by Vincenzo Mantovani; introduction by Oreste Del Buono. (Turin: Giulio Einaudi, 1960). Reprinted 1990.

Por que corre Samuelillo? (What Makes Sammy Run?) Translated by Santos Merino. (Argentina: Compañia General Fabril Editora, 1961).

Más dura será la caída (The Harder They Fall). Translated into Castilian by Guillermo Lopez Hipkiss. (Barcelona: Libros Plaza, n.d.).

Derecho de Asilo (Sanctuary V). Translated by Eduardo Mallorqui. (Barcelona: Plaza & Janes, April 1973).

Die Faust im Nacken (The Harder They Fall). Translated by Werner Balusch. (Konstanz and Stuttgart: Diana Press, 1959).

Gesichter in der Menge (Some Faces in the Crowd). Translated by Rudolf Rocholl. (Munich: Wilhelm Goldmann, 1982).

UNPUBLISHED OR UNPRODUCED
PLAYS, SCREENPLAYS, AND BOOKS

Company House (written for one-act play contest at Dartmouth College, 1935).

Heartbreak Town. (screenplay by Budd Schulberg and Marshall Neilan). For Selznick International Pictures, 21 April 1938.

The Merry, Merry Maidens. (treatment for a film project). For Selznick International Pictures, 20 June 1938.

The Thinking Reed. (uncompleted screenplay by Budd Schulberg). For RKO; George Haight, producer, August 1938.

A Mexican Story. (screenplay by Robert Tasker, based on *The Mexican* by Jack London. A new adaptation by Budd Schulberg and Robert Tasker. Prepared in Mexico City with the collaboration of Herbert Klein and Agustin Delgado. The Orsatti Agency, Hollywood), 1942.

It Happens in Hollywood. (screenplay by Budd Schulberg). For B.P. Schulberg, c. 1946. Combination of several of Schulberg's "Hollywood" short stories. Copy of script in Baker Library, Dartmouth College.

Champions for Sale: The Mike Jacobs Story. (serialized in five-parts in *Collier's,* 15 April–13 May 1950); intended by Schulberg for book publication; original title: Machiavelli on Eighth Avenue.

Prize Fight. (manuscript in Saxe Commins papers, Princeton University, Princeton, N.J.), no date.

The Enemy Within. (a motion picture based on the book by Robert F. Kennedy, 1960; for Jerry Wald Productions), 1961.

Hide and Seek. (screenplay based on Schulberg's novel, *Sanctuary V*), 1970.

In the Streets. (based on *Down These Mean Streets*, by Piri Thomas; original research by Budd Schulberg and Elia Kazan; screenplay by Schulberg; producer Sam Spiegel; for Warner Bros.), 1972.

On the Waterfront. (a two-act play by Budd Schulberg with Stan Silverman), playscript dated 3 October 1983.

Moving Pictures. (six-part miniseries based on *Moving Pictures: Memoirs of a Hollywood Prince),* Zenith Productions for American Playhouse (PBS), 1991.

Black Thunder: The Tom Molineaux-Bill Richmond Story. (a detailed outline for a motion picture about Molineaux, the African American bare-knuckle fighter of the early nineteenth century), 1984.

Back on the Waterfront. (screenplay), 1993.

A Face in the Crowd. (new screenplay based on Schulberg's short story; revised for Richard Gere, 1986; revised for Whoopi Goldberg, 1996).

UNCOLLECTED STORIES

"Old Ballad Off Key" (*Literary America*, 1936).

"Love Letters for Sale" (*College Humor*).

"Hollywood Ghost Story" (*Collier's*, 11 June 1938).

"Calling Major Adams' Car" (*Collier's*, 25 June 1938).

"Hollywood Doctor" (*Collier's*, 6 August 1938).
"Spotlight" (*Liberty*, 19 November 1938).
"Eddie Buys a Car" (*Collier's*, 7 January 1939).
"Hollywood's White Hope" (*Liberty*, 20 January 1940).
"Lovelier Than Ever" (*Liberty*, 14 February 1942).
"Bell of Tarchova" (*Saturday Evening Post*, 24 October 1942).
"The Man Who Hated Five O'Clock" (*'48*, 1948).
"The Most Romantic Couple in Town" (*This Week*, 1952).
"Hero, à la Carte" (*True*).
"Cute Kid" (*Nugget*, December 1959).
"A Latin from Killarney" (*Playboy*, January 1968).

UNCOLLECTED ARTICLES

"Nazi Pin-Up Girl" (Leni Riefenstahl) (*Saturday Evening Post*, 30 March 1946).
"The Celluloid Noose" (*The Screenwriter*, August 1946); motion picture evidence in
    Nuremberg war crimes trials.
"Why Manley Halliday Is . . . Manley Halliday" (*Theatre Arts*, December 1958).
"RFK: The Man" (*Playboy*, January 1969).

FIRST APPEARANCES IN MAGAZINES OR NEWSPAPERS

#Sammy Glick story
##Al Manheim (aka Manners) story
"What Makes Sammy Run?" *Liberty* 14, no. 44 (30 October 1937): 26–31. Fiction.#
"Love, Action, Laughter." *Collier's* 101, no. 3 (15 January 1938): 16–17, 54–56. Fiction.#
"I'll Take Care of It." *Collier's* 101, no. 8 (19 February 1938): 20–21, 49–50. Fiction.#
"Passport to Nowhere." *Story* 12, no. 70 (May 1938): 57–77. Fiction.
"Hollywood Ghost." *Collier's* 101, no. 24 (11 June 1938): 14–15, 57–58, 60–61. Fiction.##
"Calling Major Adams' Car." *Collier's* 101, no. 26 (25 June 1938): 22. Fiction.
"Romance Comes to Sammy Glick." *Liberty* 15, no. 29 (16 July 1938): 16–20. Fiction.#
"Hollywood Doctor." (aka "The Road to Recovery"). *Collier's* 102, no. 6 (6 August
    1938): 9–10, 32–33. Fiction.
"Spotlight." *Liberty* (19 November 1938): 51. Fiction.
"Eddie Buys a Car." *Collier's* 103, no. 1 (7 January 1939): 24–25, 42–44. Fiction.
"The Stars Repeat." *Collier's* 104, no. 26 (23 December 1939): 19. Fiction.

"Hollywood's White Hope." *Liberty* 17, no. 3 (20 January 1940): 20–26. Fiction.

"The Hollywood Novel." *Films* no. 2 (Spring 1940): 121.

"War Dance." *Argosy*, 299, no. 3 (25 May 1940): 91–94. Fiction.

"In Hollywood." (In Memory of Scott Fitzgerald: II) *New Republic* (3 March 1941): 311–312. Article.

"The Real Viennese Schmaltz." *Esquire* (September 1941): 68, 102–103. Fiction.

"Somebody Has to Be Nobody." (aka "A Table at Ciro's") *Saturday Evening Post* 214, no. 16 (18 October 1941): 12–13, 51, 53–54. Fiction.

"Lovelier Than Ever." *Liberty* (14 February 1942): 12–15, 46–47. Fiction.

"Third Nightcap, with Historical Footnotes." *The New Yorker* 18, no. 14 (23 May 1942): 50. Fiction.

"Memory in White." *Collier's* 110, no. 13 (26 September 1942): 52–53, 56. Fiction.

"Bell of Tarchova." *Saturday Evening Post* 215, no. 17 (24 October 1942): 12–13, 53, 56–57, 59–60. Fiction.

"The Time Is Always." (aka "The Mother of Them All") *Saturday Evening Post* (9 January 1943): 22–23, 55–56. Fiction.

"The Downfall of Innocence." (aka *"A Very Short Digest of a Very Long Novel"*) *Esquire* (July 1943): 69. Fiction.

"A Foxhole in Washington." *The New Yorker* (22 April 1944): 24–25. Fiction.

"Nazi Pin-Up Girl." (Leni Riefenstahl) *Saturday Evening Post* 218, no. 39 (30 March 1946): 11, 36, 39, 41. Article.

"100,000 Years at Hard Labor." *Saturday Evening Post* (25 May 1946): 32–33, 59, 61, 62, 64. Article.

"The Celluloid Noose." (Nuremberg War Crimes Trials) *The Screen Writer* (publication of the Screen Writers Guild of America) (August 1946): 1–15. Article.

"The Man Who Hated Five O'Clock." *This Month* (October 1946): 116–126. Fantasy.

"Typical Gesture." *Good Housekeeping* 123, no. 4 (October 1946): 22, 206–208, 210–215, 217–223. Fiction.

"The Year Santa Stayed Away" (aka "My Christmas Carol"). *True* (January 1947). Fiction.

"California Culture." *Holiday* (February 1947): 41–45, 117–119. Article.

"Movies in America: After Fifty Years." *Atlantic* (November 1947): 115–124. Article.

"Crowd Pleaser." *'48* (March 1948): 50–60. Fiction

"This Is the Fight Racket." *True* (March 1948): 25–27, 86–89. Article.

"The Frightened City." *Nation's Business* (August 1949): 36–38, 72. Article.

"The Bigger They Come——." *True* 23 (November 1948): 38–39, 85–89. Article.

"The Breaking Point." *Esquire* (December 1948): 78. Fiction.

"Hollywood: Its Life and Industry Ranging from 'Amazingly Colossal' to 'Zstinks.'" *Holiday* (January 1949): 34, 126–129. Article.

"Thirty Odd Years in Hollywood" (with B. P. Schulberg). *True* (February 1949): 44–45, 100–115. Article.

"The Road Between." (review of the book by James T. Farrell) *New York Times Book Review* (3 April 1949): 4.

"The Dare." *Esquire* (May 1949): 38. Fiction.

"The Heavyweight Championship." (review of the book by Nat Fleischer) *New York Times Book Review* (31 July 1949): 15.

"Cornelius Johnson." *Esquire* (August 1949): 27. Sports article.

"Funny Part Is, She's Happy." *Collier's* (12 November 1949): 22–23, 34, 36–38. Fiction.

"Florida Keys." *Holiday* 6, no. 6 (December 1949): 118–125, 161. Article.

"The Mike Jacobs Story." *Collier's* 125, nos. 15–16; 126, nos. 17–19; (15 April 1950): 18–19, 48, 50, 52; (22 April 1950): 30–31, 82, 84; (29 April 1950): 24–25, 82–85; (6 May 1950): 30–31, 67–69; (13 May 1950): 24–25, 70–72. Articles.

"The Legend That Walks Like a Man." *Esquire* (August 1950): 41. Fiction.

"What Made Tiger Rag?" *Esquire* (September 1950): 57. Fiction.

"Day of the Locust." (review of the book by Nathanael West) *New York Times Book Review* (1 October 1950): 4.

"Hollywood, the Dream Factory." (review of the book by Hortense Powdermaker) *New York Times Book Review* (15 October 1950): 6.

"Party" (excerpt from *The Disenchanted*). *Collier's* (4 November 1950): 26–27, 64, 66. Fiction.

"Keys to Adventure." *Holiday* (December 1950): 58–61, 63, 110–111. Article.

"Ambassadors-of-Will." (review of *East Wind over Prague*, by Jan Stransky) *Saturday Review of Literature*. (13 January 1951): 35, 63.

"The Far Side of Paradise." (review of the book by Arthur Mizener) *New York Times Book Review* (28 January 1951): 1.

"Trials of a Title Writer." *New York Times*, Section 2 (11 February 1951): 4. Article.

"See You at Dave's." *Holiday* (April 1951): 64–65, 67–70, 135, 137–138. Article.

"Chicago: City on the Make." (review of the book by Nelson Algren) *New York Times Book Review* (21 October 1951): 3.

"Tender Is the Night: A Romance." (review of the revised edition of the book by F. Scott Fitzgerald; introduction by Malcolm Cowley) *New York Times Book Review* (18 November 1951): 5.

"Dartmouth." *Holiday* (January 1952): 48–53, 71–74. Article.

"Collision with the Party Line." *Saturday Review of Literature* (30 August 1952): 6–8, 31–37. Article.

"The Indian's Answer." *This Week Magazine* (*Los Angeles Times*) (14 September 1952): 2. Article.

"Picture." (review of the book by Lillian Ross) *New York Times Book Review* (23 November 1952): 4.

"Joe Docks, Forgotten Man of the Waterfront." *New York Times Magazine* (28 December 1952): 3–5, 28–30. Article.

"Varadero Beach." *Holiday* (February 1953): 72–74, 117–120. Article.

"Prince Bart." (review of the book by Jay Michael Kennedy) *New York Times Book Review* (8 March 1953): 4.

"Formula Fighter." *Saturday Evening Post* (21 March 1953): 26, 138–140, 142–144. Fiction.

"Waterfront Priest." *Commonweal* 52, no. 26 (3 April 1953): 643–646. Article.

"City with Wings—Pensacola." *Holiday* 13, no. 6 (June 1953): 48–53. Article.

"A Free Man." *Esquire* (August 1953): 32. Fiction.

"Earthly Creatures: Ten Stories." (review of the book by Charles Jackson) *New York Times Book Review* (13 September 1953): 4.

"How One Pier Got Rid of the Mob." *New York Times Magazine* (27 September 1953): 17, 58–60. Article.

"Kiss and Forget." *McCall's* (November 1953): 40, 84, 90, 92–93. Fiction.

"A Pictorial History of the Silent Screen." (review of the book by Daniel Blum) *New York Times Book Review* (15 November 1953): 7. Part I.

"Hollywood versus Chris Samuels, Age Nine." *Esquire* (December 1953): 109. Fiction.

"Docker's Wife." *Cosmopolitan* (March 1954): 82–91. Fiction.

"Drama in Hoboken." *Holiday* (August 1954): 82–85. Article.

"Scrappy Bantams." *Sports Illustrated* (16 August 1954): 131–132, 134. Article.

"A Pay Night for Old Archie." *Sports Illustrated* (23 August 1954): 63–64. Article.

"King in the Cow Palace." (Bobo Olson vs. Rocky Castellani) *Sports Illustrated* (30 August 1954): 62–63. Article.

"Charles vs. Marciano." *Sports Illustrated* (13 September 1954): 62–63. Article.

"Rematch Is No Match." (Rocky Marciano vs. Ezzard Charles) *Sports Illustrated* (27 September 1954): 58–61. Article.

"Murder on the Waterfront." *Collier's* 134, no. 7 (1 October 1954): 82–89. Fiction.

"A Fan Fights Back." *Sports Illustrated* I, no. 9 (11 October 1954): 63. Article.

"Boxing's Dirty Business Must Be Cleaned Up Now." *Sports Illustrated* (1 November 1954): 10–11, 59–60. Article.

"The Celebrity." *The Illustrated London News* (18 November 1954) (Christmas Number): 17–18, 35. Fiction.

"A Call to Arms." *Sports Illustrated* (29 November 1954): 31–32. Article.

"It Was Great to Be a Boy in Hollywood." *Holiday*, 17, no. 1 (January 1955): 70–72, 74, 76, 107. Article.

"The Dartmouth Winter Carnival." *Sports Illustrated* (21 February 1955): 40–41, 52–54. Article.

"Old Fighters Do Die." *Sports Illustrated* (28 February 1955): 48–49. Article.

"No Room for the Groom." (Carmen Basilio). *Sports Illustrated* (21 March 1955): 44–45. Article.

"Bengal Bouts." (boxing at Notre Dame). *Sports Illustrated* (4 April 1955): 49–50. Article.

"Two Departures." (Tony DeMarco vs. Johnny Saxton). *Sports Illustrated* (11 April 1955): 56. Article.

"Boxing." (Cockell vs. Marciano). *Sports Illustrated* 2, no. 19 (9 May 1955): 48, 50. Article.

"Boxing." (Marciano's handpicked opponents). *Sports Illustrated* 2, no. 20 (16 May 1955): 44–45. Article.

"Boxing." ("Was Don Hit When He Was Down? Indeed He Was."). *Sports Illustrated* (30 May 1955): 42–43. Article.

"Boxing." (James D. Norris). *Sports Illustrated* 2, no. 24 (13 June 1955): 50, 52. Article.

"Family Night in Syracuse." (Carmen Basilio vs. Tony DeMarco). *Sports Illustrated* (20 June 1955): 22–25. Article.

"Boxing." (Archie Moore vs. Bobo Olson). *Sports Illustrated* (4 July 1955): 50–51. Article.

"Boxing." (Jimmy Carter vs. Wallace Bud Smith). *Sports Illustrated* (11 July 1955): 41–42. Article.

"Boxing." (Frankie Carbo, James D. Norris, and the IBC). *Sports Illustrated* (22 August 1955): 44–45. Article.

"Why Write It When You Can't Sell It to the Pictures?" *Saturday Review* 38, no. 36 (3 September 1955): 5–6, 27. Article.

"Boxing." (Archie Moore). *Sports Illustrated* 3, no. 10 (5 September 1955): 47–48.

"A Champion Proves His Greatness." (Archie Moore vs. Rocky Marciano). *Sports Illustrated* (3 October 1955): 36–39. Article.

"The New Florida." *Holiday* 18, no. 6 (December 1955): 42–45, 48–54, 56–57. Article.

"Boxing." (Ray Robinson vs. Bobo Olson). *Sports Illustrated* (12 December 1955): 44–45. Article.

"Counted Out: A Man's Career: Sugar Ray (Robinson)." *Sports Illustrated* (19 December 1955): 25, 37. Article.

"The Man on His Back Was Bobo Olson." (photos by Hy Peskin). *Sports Illustrated* (19 December 1955): 36–37. Article.

"Julius (Helfand) and the Beanstalk." *Sports Illustrated* (6 February 1956): 50–51. Article.

"Hollywood Hokum." (the film of *The Harder They Fall*). *Sports Illustrated* (11 June 1956): 60–61. Article.

"A Second Father." *Playboy* 4, no. 2 (February 1957): 16–18, 26, 30, 36, 38, 46, 54, 68. Novelette.

"The Story behind 'A Face in the Crowd.'" *TV Guide* (1 June 1957): 14–15. Article.

"The Barracudas." *Playboy* 4, no. 12 (December 1957): 22–24, 34, 50, 79–81. Fiction.

"Why Manley Halliday . . . Is Manley Halliday." *Theatre Arts* 42 (December 1958): 15–17, 70–71. Article.

"These for the Love of Zelda." *Saturday Review* (22 August 1959): 14–15. Article.

"The Writer and Hollywood." *Harper's* 219, no. 1313. (October 1959): 132–137, article.

"Cute Kid." *Nugget* 4, no. 6 (December 1959): 13–14, 24, 37, 64. Fiction.

"Saroyan: Ease and Unease on the Flying Trapeze." *Esquire* 54, no. 4 (October 1960): 85–91. Article.

"Taps at Reveille: A Personal Involvement in the Tragedy of the Author of Mister Roberts." *Esquire* 54, no. 5. (November 1960): 101–102, 104–105. Article.

"Sinclair Lewis: Big Wind from Sauk Centre." *Esquire* 54, no. 6 (December 1960): 110–114. Article.

"Old Scott: The Mask the Myth and the Man." *Esquire* 55, no. 1 (January 1961): 96–101. Article.

"The Night We Ate Magic Mushrooms." *Esquire,* 56, no. 6 (December 1961): 129–130, 312–316. Article.

"Sports' Greatest Event." *Esquire* 57, no. 1 (January 1962): 135–138, 140. Article.

"The Waterfront Revisited." *Saturday Evening Post* (7 September 1963): 28–32, 36, 38, 41–42, 44. Article.

"An American Family Moves South." *Holiday* (October 1962): 112, 116–118, 120. Article.

"How Are Things in Panicsville?" *Life* 55, no. 25 (20 December 1963): 79–82. Article.

"The Death of Boxing?" *Playboy* 11, no. 1 (January 1964): 151, 172, 174. Article.

"Cassius in Wonderland." *Cavalier* 14, no. 133 (July 1964): 14–16, 66–67. Article.

"My Wonderful Lousy Poem." *Family Weekly* (11 October 1964). Article.

"The Political Conventions as Show Business." *Playboy* 12, no. 1 (January 1965): 96–98, 221–222, 224–228. Article.

"Say Goodnight to Owl." *Redbook* 125, no. 4 (August 1965): 62–63, 127–131. Fiction.

"Confessions of a Hollywood Boyhood." *Los Angeles Magazine* 10, no. 3 (September 1965): 36–40, 78–81. Article.

"Senor Discretion." *Playboy* 13, no. 1 (January 1966): 140–142, 240, 244, 246. Fiction.

"Movies and Television: 50 Million Americans *Can* Be Wrong." *Los Angeles Magazine* 11, no. 1 (January 1966): 42–44, 46, 48. Article.

"The West Coast of Mexico." *Holiday* 39, no. 4 (April 1966): 46–58, 116–117, 131. Article.

"The Angry Voices of Watts." *Los Angeles Magazine* 11, no. 6 (June 1966): 32–35, 66–67. Article.

"Dialogue in Black and White." (with James Baldwin). *Playboy* 13, no. 12 (December 1966): 133–136, 282, 284, 286–287. Transcript of conversation.

"Biased Course in Cohnology." (review of Bob Thomas' *King Cohn*). *Life* 62, no. 9 (3 March 1967): 11, 14.

"Tell It Like It Is, Baby. Tell It Like It Is!" *Pageant* (May 1967): 151.

"The Watts Workshop." *Playboy* 14, no. 9 (September 1967): 111, 162, 164, 166–167, 170–172, 175–179. Article.

"A Latin from Killarney." *Playboy* 15, no. 1 (January 1968): 115, 204–205. Article.

"The Magnificent Showcase—the Museum of Anthropology." *Holiday* 44, no. 1 (July 1968): 46–47, 84, 87–88. Article.

"RFK: The Man." *Playboy* (January 1969): 176–178, 246, 248–250, 252–253. Article.

"Gentle Genius at Work in Jungletown." *Life* 66, no. 8 (28 February 1969): 6. Article.

"Who Killed Cock Robin? A Farewell to Judy." (prose-poem tribute to Judy Garland). *Life* 67, no. 2 (11 July 1969): 26–28.

"Back to the Enemy." (with excerpt from the unproduced screenplay *The Enemy Within,* based on the book by Robert F. Kennedy). *Show* (June 1970): 25–29, 68, 70, 74–76, 78, 80, 82–83. Article.

"Real Anger Was Backstage." *Life* 69, no. 8 (21 August 1970): 50–52, 55–59. Article.

"The Loser." (excerpt from *Loser and Still Champion*). *Saturday Evening Post* (fall 1971): 57, 106–107, 159. Article.

"The Chinese Boxes of Muhammad Ali." *Saturday Review* (26 February 1972): 21–26. Article.

"World Heavyweight Champions: I." *New York Times* (12 May 1972): Sports 1.

"World Heavyweight Champions: II." *New York Times* (21 May 1972): Sports 1.

"F. Scott Fitzgerald." *TV Guide* (5 January 1974): 23–25. Article.

"Journey to Zaire: A Fight That Wasn't Fought." *Newsday Magazine* (20 October 1974). Article.

"Memories of Past Rose Bowls." *TV Guide* (28 December 1974): 4–6. Article.

"'Requiem for a Nun': William Faulkner Wrote Like an Angel about His Particular Vision of Hell." *TV Guide* (1 February 1975): 31–32. Article.

"Hollywood: Through a Shot Glass Darkly." *Los Angeles Times Book Review* (29 June 1975): 1. Article.

"The Ghost of Hollywood Past." (review of *Hanging on in Paradise,* by Fred Lawrence Guiles). *American Film* (November 1975): 74–75.

"Bird Watching." *Los Angeles Times Book Review* (21 December 1975): 3. Article.

"What Makes Them Try to Write the Hollywood Novel?" (epilogue for reprint of 1930 novel *Queer People,* by Carroll and Garrett Graham). *Los Angeles Times Book Review* (3 October 1976): 3. Article.

"Where Have You Gone, Holly Mims?" *TV Guide* (16 April 1977): 6–10. Article.

"The Other Princess Grace." *Ladies Home Journal* (May 1977): 82, 84, 217–220, 222. Interview.

"The Right-Headed James Jones, 'True American Primitive.'" *Los Angeles Times Book Review* (19 June 1977): 1, 16.

"10th Avenue on the Banks of the Jumna." *American Rag* (fall 1978). First and only issue.

"Dear Ben Pleasants." *Los Angeles Times Book Review* (6 May 1979). Letter.

"The Inside Story of the 'Waterfront.'" *New York Times Magazine* (6 January 1980): 28–30, 32–34, 36. Article.

"Roberto Laid Down Law as Soon as the Bell Rang." *New York Post* Sports (18 July 1980). Article.

"Writers Always Heed the Siren Song of Boxing." *The Bridgehampton Sun* (6 August 1980). Article.

"Literary World's Passionate Love Affair with Boxing." *New York Post* (29 September 1980). Sports. Article.

"The King Is Dead; Now All Hail Holmes." *New York Post* (3 October 1980). Sports. Article.

"Duran's Hands of Stone Will Granulate Sugar." *New York Post* (25 November 1980). Sports. Article.

"Roberto Duran's Act of Disgrace." *New York Post* (28 November 1980). Sports. Article.

"Gallant Gladiators Walk with Legends." *New York Post* (17 September 1981). Sports. Article.

"Who Is the Fighter of the Century?" *Parade Magazine* (26 February 1984): 14. Article.

"Furious Eight-Minute War Will Linger in Boxing Lore." *New York Post* (17 April 1985). Sports. Article.

"In Defense of Boxing." *Newsday Magazine* (21 April 1985). Article

"Sparring with Hemingway." *Newsday Magazine* (8 September 1985). Article.

"The Jinx Hangs over Spinks." *New York Post* (20 September 1985): 94. Article.

"Historic Night in the Ring" (Holmes-Spinks). *New York Post* (23 September 1985): 31. Article.

"Beauty over Beastly Brawn—This Time." *New York Post* (7 April 1987). Sports. Article.

"'Waterfront'—More Than a 90–Minute Movie." *New York Times Book Review* 7 (26 April 1987): 1, 38. Article.

"Black Day for White Hope." *New York Post* (12 June 1987). Sports. Article.

"Cooney Questions Career after Losing to Holmes." *New York Post* (13 June 1987). Sports. Article.

"Brotherly Love Takes Its Toll." *New York Post* (15 June 1987). Sports. Article.

"Requiem for a Heavyweight." *New York Post* (16 June 1987). Sports. Article.

"Schulberg's 'Sammy' as a Role Model for Our Time." *Los Angeles Times* (3 September 1987): V, 1–2. Article.

"Reaching for Success . . . Yet Sinking in the Quicksand of Old Hollywood." *TV Guide* (31 October 1987): 26–27, 29–30. Article.

"They Fall Harder When They're Old" (Tyson-Holmes) *New York Post* (23 January 1988). Sports. Article.

"Hollywood's Full of Sharkskin." *GQ* (March 1988). Article.

"Good vs. Evil." *New York Times* (7 May 1988): I, 27. Op-ed article.

"Streetcar Named Desire." *New York Times* (22 May 1988): 21, 3. Review of Dakin Williams' parody of the play.

"Spinks' Magic Act Not Enough." *New York Post* (27 June 1988). Sports. Article.

"Books: 'Elia Kazan: A Life.'" *American Film* (July/August 1988): 55–56, 58–59. Review.

"Why Mike Tyson Didn't Make the Team in 1984." *TV Guide* (17 September 1988): 20–24. Article.

"The Heavyweight Champ—That Starts with a "C" and That Rhymes with "T" and That Stands for Trouble." *Boxing Illustrated* (October 1988): 28–33. Article.

"Quintana Roo and the Mexican Caribbean." *New York Times* 5 (26 February 1989): 14. Travel article.

"The 'Auteur' Syndrome." *New York Times* 1 (4 December 1989): 25. Op-ed article.

"You Say Auteur, I Say Author." *Writers Guild of America West Journal* 3, no. 2 (February 1990): 17. Article.

"Budd Schulberg's Take on Hollywood Ethics." *Los Angeles Times Calendar* (13 May 1990). Letter.

"A Screenwriter's Hollywood Memories." *The American Repertory Theatre Program* (1990–91): 23–26. Article.

"The Second Coming of George Foreman." *The Newsday Magazine* (7 April 1991): 10–14, 18. Article.

"Foreman-Holyfield: The Bigger They Are, the Harder They Don't Fall." *Boxing Illustrated* (6 August 1991): 30–33. Article.

"A Fighter, Not a Hater." *Parade* (27 October 1991): 4–6. Article.

"Tyson vs. Tyson." *Newsday* (12 February 1992). Article.

"Rosy Dreams vs. Harsh Truths: Do Your Values Change after 50?" *New Choices for Retirement Living* (November 1992). Article.

"The Monster I Created Is Now a Role Model." *New Choices for Retirement Living* (October 1993). Article.

"Muhammad Ali: A Thirty-Year Journey." *Image* (San Francisco *Examiner*) (19 December 1993): 14–19. Article.

"Secrets of Sinatra." *New Choices for Retirement Living* (January 1994). Article.

"Life, Not Politics, Inspired 'On the Waterfront.'" *New York Times* (14 September 1994): A18. Letter, dated September 9, 1989.

"You Was My Bruthah, Charley." *GQ* (October 1994): 240–245. Article.

"On the Waterfront." *Los Angeles Times Book Review* (11 December 1994). Letter.

"First a Movie, Then a Novel, Now a Play." (*On the Waterfront*). *New York Times* Arts and Leisure: Theatre, (30 April 1995): 5, 10. Article.

"The Tyson-McNeeley Show—'The Softer They Fall.'" *Boxing Illustrated* (October 1995): 6–9. Article.

"Watts: 30 Years Later—Progress or Doom?" *New Choices: Living Even Better after 50* (November 1995): 38–42, 44. Article.

"Bowe-Holyfield: Act III." *Boxing Illustrated* (January 1996): 4–7. Article.

"Return to the Mecca." *Boxing Illustrated* (March 1996): 6–7. Article.

"Tyson Redux: Act I." *Boxing Illustrated* (June 1996): 4–8. Article.

"Strategic Parenting: I Got a Second Chance." *New Choices: Living Even Better after 50*, (October 1996). Article.

"Re-Enter Evander: A Big Night for Him and Him." *International Boxing Digest* (January 1997): 8–11. Article.

"Bowe-Golota: A Tale of Two Losers." *International Boxing Digest* (February 1997): 14–16. Article.

"Arturo Gatti: The Manly Art of No Defense." *International Boxing Digest* (March 1997): 18–19. Article.

"The Guessing Game: Whitaker-De La Hoya." *International Boxing Digest* (July 1997): 10–11. Article.

"Requiem for a Heavyweight: Holyfield-Tyson II." *International Boxing Digest* (September 1997): 8–11. Article.

"Roy Jones, Jr.: The Mouthpiece Hamlet." *International Boxing Digest* (October 1997): 8–9. Article.

"The Oscar Express Rolls On." *International Boxing Digest* (November/December 1997): 8–10. Article.

"Lewis-Golota: The Bigger They Are." *International Boxing Digest* (January 1998): 10–11. Article.

"Evander the Holy: The Once and Future Undisputed King." *International Boxing Digest* (February 1998): 8–9. Article.

"The Little Prince: Good Hit, No Field." *International Boxing Digest* (March 1998): 10–11. Article.

"How Marlon Brando Learned to Get Along with Oscar." *The New Yorker* (30 March 1998). Article.

"Should Tyson Be Allowed to Fight Again? Yes!" *Fight Game* (May 1998): 18–19. Article.

"Lennox Lewis: The Emperor Has No Clothes." *International Boxing Digest* (July 1998): 12–13. Article.

"Holyfield, Akinwande, and Hepatitis B (for Boxing)." *International Boxing Digest* (August 1998): 12–13. Article.

"Roy Jones, Jr.: A for Ability, B for Bored." *International Boxing Digest* (October 1998): 12–13. Article.

"The Champ." (review of *Muhammad Ali and the Rise of an American Hero*, by David Remnick). *New York Times Book Review* (25 October 1998): 11–12.

"Good Night, Sweet Princes (from Benny Leonard to Roberto Duran)." *International Boxing Digest* (November/December 1998): 26–27. Article.

"Lion of Hollywood: Louis B. Mayer." (segment in "Builders & Titans of the 20th Century"). *Time* (7 December 1998): 82, 84, 86. Article.

"Hoboken Orphans in Hollywood Storm: How *On the Waterfront* Came to the Screen, Finally." *Variety* (January 1999): 40–41, 56, 58. Article.

"Evander's Home Coming and Going." *International Boxing Digest* (January 1999): 15. Article.

"Family's Cohn Connections." *Variety* (25 January 1999). Article.

"9–to-5 Plan Fells Scribe." *Variety* (25 January 1999). Article.

"The 25 Most Influential People in Boxing in the 20th Century." *Fight Game* (May 1999): 16–22. Article.

"The Welters Are Coming! The Welters Are Coming!" *Fight Game* (July 1999): 52–54. Article.

"The Competitor." (Ernest Hemingway). *P.O.V.* (30 July 1999). Article.

"Why De La Hoya Should Win." *Fight Game* (November 1999): 24–25. Article.

"The Real Main Event: King v. Arum." *Fight Game* (January 2000): 21. Article.

"Lennox Lewis: A Want of Passion." *Fight Game* (March 2000): 21–25. Article.

"Confessions of an Ex-Fight Manager." *Fight Game* (July 2000): 54–57. Article.

"Mosley-De La Hoya and My Old Hometown, L.A." *Fight Game* (November 2000): 52–57. Article.

UNPUBLISHED STORIES

"Busman's Holiday"
"The Leader Is the People"
"Parting Is Such Sweet Sorrow"
"Twinkle, Twinkle, Little Star"
"Yoo Hoo, Tyrone."

STORIES WRITTEN FOR BOOK PUBLICATION

★Collected in *Some Faces in the Crowd*
★★Collected in *Love, Action, Laughter and Other Sad Tales*
★The Breaking Point
★The Face of Hollywood
★Ensign Weasel
★The One He Called Winnie
★The Typical Gesture of Colonel Duggan

*Meal Ticket
**The Howling Dogs of Taxco
**Letter to Mac Fadden
**The Docks of New York
**The Reluctant Pilgrim
**Counterintelligence in Mexico City
**The Pettibone Plan: A Fable

REPRINTS AND CONDENSATIONS

"What Makes Sammy Run?" *Readers' Digest* 39, no. 231 (July 1941): 127–184.

"The Road to Recovery." *Avon* 33, (1946): 65–75 (originally published as "Hollywood Doctor" in *Collier's,* 6 August 1938).

"The Harder They Fall." *Readers' Digest* 51, no. 305 (September 1947): 137–176.

"Fifty Years of Movies, for What?" *Readers Digest* 52, no. 309 (January 1948): 125–128 (from *Atlantic,* November 1947).

"The Disenchanted." *Omnibook* 13, no. 6 (May 1951): 1–49.

"Calling Major Adams' Car." *Pageant* 6, no. 9 (March 1951): 74–77 (from *Collier's,* 25 June 1938).

"Murder on the Waterfront." *Ellery Queen's Mystery Magazine* 27, no. 3 (whole no. 148) (March 1956): 126–141 (from *Collier's,* 1 October 1954).

"The Harder They Fall." *Cavalier* 4, no. 35 (May 1956): 36–38, 65–90.

"Memory in White." *The Dude* 1, no. 4 (March 1957): 24–26, 28–30 (from *Collier's,* 26 September 1942).

"Crowd Pleaser." *Gent* 1, no. 4 (April 1957): 26–30 (from *'48,* March 1948).

"Party." (excerpt from *The Disenchanted*) *Collier's* 126, no. 19 (4 November 1950): 26–27, 64, 66.

"The Disenchanted." (text of the play) *Theatre Arts* 44, no. 8 (August, 1960): 21–42.

"Hollywood, Where Are You?" *Reader's Digest* 84, no. 503 (March 1964): 68–72 (from *Life,* 20 December 1963).

"My Wonderful Lousy Poem." *Reader's Digest* 89, no. 532 (August 1966): 67–68 (from *Family Weekly,* 11 October 1964). Article.

"Spotlight." *Liberty* 1, no. 3 (winter 1971): 12 (from *Liberty,* 19 November 1938).

"The Great Benny Leonard." *The Ring* 59, no. 4 (May 1980): 32–37 (excerpt from *Moving Pictures: Memories of a Hollywood Prince*).

"Growing Up in Old Hollywood" (adapted from *Moving Pictures*). *Los Angeles Magazine* (August 1981): 162–169, 385–386, 388–389, 391–392.

"Up from the Mailroom." (excerpt from *WMSR?*) *GQ* 61, no. 3 (March 1991): 318.

"1950's: Dec. 18, 1952; Joe Docks, Forgotten Man." *New York Times* (14 April 1996); (reprint of December 28, 1952, article from *New York Times Sunday Magazine*): VI, 103.

REVIEWS OF WORKS BY SCHULBERG

What Makes Sammy Run? (1941)

Ferguson, Otis. *New Republic* (March 31, 1941).

Gay, R. M. "The Atlantic Bookshelf." *Atlantic* 167, no. 5 (May 1941).

Glenn, Charles. "Novel—the Story of Hollywood Heel." *People's World* (2 April 1941): 5.

———. "What Makes Sammy Run?—Story of a Hollywood Heel." *Daily Worker* (7 April 1941): 7.

———. "News in the World of Stage and Screen." *Daily Worker* (8 April 1941): 7.

———. "Hollywood Can Be Won to the Side of the American People—Actors and Directors Respond to Criticism of Film Audiences." *Daily Worker* (23 April 1941): 7.

———. "Hollywood Vine." *People's World* (24 April 1941):

Godfrey, Eleanor. *Canadian Forum* (May 1941).

Hartung, Philip T. *Commonweal* (6 June 1941): 163.

"Hollywood Harpooned." *Time* 37, no. 13 (31 March 1941): 68–70.

Lazarus, H. P. *The Nation* (19 April 1941).

Manchester Guardian (19 December 1941).

Marsh, F. T. *Books* (30 March 1941).

New Yorker (29 March 1941): 61–62.

P.S. Times Literary Supplement (3 January 1942).

Poore, Charles. "Books of the Times" *New York Times Book Review* (4 April 1941): 18.

Van Gelder, Robert. "'What Makes Sammy Run?' and Other New Works of Fiction." *New York Times Book Review* (30 March 1941): 6.

The Harder They Fall (1947)

Gibbs, Wolcott. "The Harder They Fall." *The New Yorker* 23 (16 August 1947): 84–86.

Henderson, R. W. *Library Journal* (August 1947).

Horn, John. "The Harder They Fall." *New York Times Book Review* (10 August 1947): 3.

Jackson, J. H. *San Francisco Chronicle* (13 August 1947).

Kirkus (1 June 1947).

Kogan, Herman. *Chicago Sun Book Week* (10 August 1947).

Prescott, Orville. *Yale Review* 37, no. 1 (autumn 1947): 191–192.

Solomon, Charles. "The Harder They Fall." (review of reprint of *The Harder They Fall*) *Los Angeles Times* (13 April 1996): 10.

"The Fight Racket." *Time* 50, no. 7 (18 August 1947): 100, 102, 104.

Trilling, Diana. "Fiction in Review." *Nation* 165, no. 10 (6 September 1947): 236–237.

Tunney, Gene. "Caneravorous Fight Racketeers." *Saturday Review of Literature* 30, no. 32 (9 August 1947): 9–10.

Walker, Stanley. *New York Herald-Tribune Weekly Book Review* (17 August 1947).

Watts, Richard. *New Republic* (11 August 1947).

Weeks, Edward. *Atlantic* (September 1947).

The Disenchanted (1950)

Adams, Donald J. "Speaking of Books" (column on *The Disenchanted*). *New York Times Book Review* (19 November 1950): 2.

Alpert, Hollis. "Golden Boy of Letters Badly Tarnished" (review of *The Disenchanted*). *Saturday Review of Literature* 33, no. 43 (28 October 1950): 11.

Booklist (15 November 1950).

Cain, James M. "A Tarnished Hero of the Jazz Age." *New York Times Book Review* (29 October 1950): 1.

Chapin, Ruth. *Christian Science Monitor* (7 December 1950).

Conrad, Barnaby. "You Can Return to an Old Love" (review of paperback reprint of *The Disenchanted*). *Los Angeles Times* Part 4 (7 July 1975): 6.

Downing, Francis. "So They Tell Me: The Disenchantment of Scott Fitzgerald." *Commonweal* 53, no. 5 (10 November 1950): 117–118.

Engel, Paul. *Chicago Sunday Tribune* (5 November 1950).

Farrell, Paul V. *Commonweal* 53, no. 5 (10 November 1950): 124.

Harrison, W. K. *Library Journal* (July 1950).

Jackson, J. H. *San Francisco Chronicle* (29 October 1950).

Jones, Ernest. "Defeat of an Artist." *Nation* 171, no. 22 (25 November 1950): 487–488.

Kazin, Alfred. *New Yorker* 26, (4 November 1950): 154–157.

Lockridge, Richard. *New York Herald Tribune Book Review* (29 October 1950).

Marquand, John P. "The Disenchanted: The Story of a Gifted Novelist Whose Talent Was Outrun by Time" (pamphlet distributed with Book of the Month Club copies of *The Disenchanted;* n.d., but 1950).

Mizener, Arthur. "The King of the Enchanted World Has a Brief but Dazzling Reign." *New York Daily News* (2 December 1950): 20, 28.

Motion Picture Herald (18 November 1950).

Sandrock, Mary. *Catholic World* (December 1950).

Scott, W. T. "The Literary Summing-Up" (essay on 1950s books, including *The Disenchanted*). *Saturday Review of Literature* (30 October 1950).

"The Bottom of the Glass." *Time* 56, no. 20 (13 November 1950): 106.

"The Disenchanted." *Newsweek* 36, no. 19 (6 November 1950): 99.

Weeks, Edward. "The Peripatetic Reviewer." *Atlantic* 186, no. 5 (November 1950): 90.

Some Faces in the Crowd (1953)

Boatwright, Taliaferro. *New York Herald Tribune* (7 June 1953).

Booklist (15 June 1953).

"Books in Brief: Amusing Villainy." *Nation* 176, no. 23 (6 June 1953): 487–488.

"Briefly Noted: Fiction." *New Yorker,* 29, no. 13 (16 May 1953): 154.

Davis, Robert Gorham. "In the End, the Cost Must Be Paid." *New York Times Book Review* (17 May 1953): 4–5.

Kelly, James. *Saturday Review of Literature* (16 May 1953).

Kirkus (15 February 1953).

"Some Faces in the Crowd." *Newsweek* 41, no. 20 (18 May 1953): 119.

San Francisco Chronicle (7 June 1953).

Sullivan, Richard. *Chicago Sunday Tribune* (24 May 1953).

U.S. Quarterly Book Review (summer 1953).

Waterfront (1955)

Balmelli, Jean Michel. "Gare au changement de quai! *(Sur les quais/Waterfront).* [http:www.paru.com/redac/axxxx248.htm] (December 1999).

Booklist (1 September 1955).

Burnett, W. R. "Dockers' Dilemma." *Saturday Review of Literature* 38, no. 39 (24 September 1955): 17.

Hogan, William. *San Francisco Chronicle* (9 September 1955).

Hughes, Riley. *Catholic World* (October 1955).

Kelly, James. "Waterfront." *New York Times Book Review* (11 September 1955): 5.

Kirkus (1 July 1955).

Molly, Robert. *Chicago Sun Tribune* (18 September 1955).

Pfaff, William. "On The Docks." *Commonweal* 63, no. 4 (28 October 1955): 100–101.

Rossiter, Bernard. "Unsuccessful Reverse." *Nation* 181, no. 14 (1 October 1955): 288.

Rugoff, Milton. *New York Herald Tribune Book Review* (11 September 1955).

Time (26 September 1955).

Toffler, Alvin. "The Worker in Current Fiction." *Frontier* (October 1955): 22.

Walbridge, E. F. *Library Journal* (1 October 1955).

"Waterfront." *Time* 46, no. 13 (26 September 1955): 104, 106.
"Work for a Godly Man?" *Newsweek* 46, no. 11 (12 September 1955): 108–109.

From the Ashes: Voices of Watts (1967)

Bone, Robert. "From The Ashes." *New York Times Book Review* (4 February 1968): 36.
Christian Century (8 November 1967).
Israel, Lee. *Book World* (29 October 1967).
Margolies, Edward. *Library Journal* (1 November 1967).
Nevins, Allan. "Dateline Watts: From the Ashes, A Solution." *Saturday Review of Literature* 50, no. 38 (23 September 1967): 79.
Thomas, Piri. *Saturday Review of Literature* (23 September 1967).

Sanctuary V (1970)

Buelna, J. L. *Library Journal* (1 December 1969).
Burg, Victor. *Christian Science Monitor* (5 March 1970).
Cargas, H. J. *America* (4 April 1970).
Greenfield, Josh. "Sanctuary V." *New York Times Book Review* (25 January 1970): 40.
Greenya, John. "A Bit Hokey." *New Republic* 162, no. 10 (7 March 1970): 29–30.
Hill, W. B. *Book Sell* (15 February 1970).
Kresh, Paul. *Saturday Review of Literature* (14 February 1970): 44.
R. S. *Harper's* (November 1969).
Shea, R. J. *Book World* (18 January 1970).
"What Makes Justo Fall?" *Time* 95, no. 19 (11 May 1970): 106, 108.

Loser and Still Champion (1972)

Buck, J. E. *Library Journal* (1 April 1972).
Daly, J. G. *Library Journal* (15 September 1972).
Gardner, Liew. "Loser and Still Champion." *New Statesman* (1 December 1972).

The Four Seasons of Success (1972)

Alternative (March 1973).
Choice (January 1973).
Leggett, John. *New Republic* (18 November 1972).
Nelson, M. G. *Library Journal* (25 September 1972).
See, Carolyn. "Schulberg Goes Beyond His Image as a Lightweight." *Los Angeles Times Book Review* (25 February 1973): 1, 10.

Swan Watch (1975)

Barth, Barbara. *Library Journal* (15 January 1976).
Cosgrove, Mary Silva. "Outlook Tower" (review of *Swan Watch). The Horn Book Magazine* 52, no. 2 (April 1976): 1.
Murray, Jim. "A True Swan Song." *Los Angeles Times.* Sports (9 April 1976): 1.
Scholl, L. J. *Best Seller* (fall 1976).
Showers, Paul. "Swan Watch." *New York Times Book Review* (2 November 1975): 50.
"Swan Watch." *Los Angeles Times Book Review* (30 November 1975): 11

Everything That Moves (1980)

Gledhill, Sabrina. "'Pictures': Growing Up in Lotusland." *UCLA Daily Bruin* (7 October 1981): 14, 17–18.
Harmetz, Aljean. "Fathers and Sons." *New York Times* (31 October 1981).
Los Angeles Times Book Review (11 March 1980): 4.
Maslin, Janet. "Home Sweet Hollywood." *New York Times Book Review* (6 September 1981): 9, 22.
Moving Pictures: Memoirs of a Hollywood Prince (1981).
Ponicsan, Darryl. "Reel life with Budd Schulberg." *Los Angeles Times Book Review* (26 July 1981): 1, 4.
Schemering, Christopher. *Library Journal* (August 1981).
Schickel, Richard. "Presenting: The Missing Mogul." *Time,* 118, no. 4 (27 July 1981): 79.
Selznick, Daniel. "Motion Pictures." *Hollywood Reporter* (17 July 1981): 14.
Whitner, Dwight. "What Made Buddy Run: Schulberg Recalls His—and Hollywood's—Early Years." *Los Angeles Herald-Examiner Book Week* (30 August 1981): G-1, 6.

Writers in America (1983)

Hall, Donald. "Some Second-Act Problems." *New York Times Book Review* (17 July 1983): 9, 21.
Shepard, Richard F. "Books: Rating Authors; Writers in America: The Four Seasons of Success." *New York Times* (31 May 1983): C, 13.

Sparring with Hemingway: And Other Fistic Legends (1995)

Barra, Allen. "Sparring with Hemingway." *New York Times Book Review* (9 July 1995).
Chepesiuk, Ron. "Schulberg, Budd. Sparring with Hemingway and Other Legends of the Fight Game." *Library Journal* (15 June 1995).

'June.' "Sparring with Hemingway: And Other Legends of the Fight Game." *Publishers Weekly* (24 April 1995).

Lukowsky, Wes. "Schulberg, Budd. Sparring with Hemingway and Other Legends of the Fight Game." *Booklist*, (1 June 1995).

Roraback, Dick. "Sparring with Hemingway and Other Legends of the Fight Game." *Los Angeles Times Book Review* (9 July 1995): 6.

Yardley, Jonathan. "Sparring with Hemingway: And Other Legends of the Fight Game." *International Herald-Tribune* (5 July 1995).

REVIEWS OF STAGE PLAYS WRITTEN OR COWRITTEN BY SCHULBERG

The Disenchanted (1958)

"A Hit with Champagne." *Newsweek* 52, no. 24 (15 December 1958): 63.

America (7 February 1959).

Aston, Frank. "'The Disenchanted' Opens at the Coronet." *New York World-Telegram and Sun* (4 December 1958).

Atkinson, Brooks. "Theatre: Study of 'The Disenchanted.'" *New York Times* (4 December 1958).

Booklist (1 July 1959).

Catholic World (February 1959).

Chapman, John. "'The Disenchanted' a Fine, Adult Drama about Scott Fitzgerald." *New York Daily News* (4 December 1958).

Christian Century (24 December 1958).

Clurman, Harold. "Review of the Arts: Theatre." *Nation* 187, no. 22 (27 December 1958): 501.

Coleman, Robert. "'Disenchanted' Too Artificial." *New York Daily Mirror* (4 December 1958).

Commonweal (9 January 1959).

Freedley, George. *Library Journal* (15 June 1959).

Hewes, Henry. "Untender Nights"(review of the play *The Disenchanted*). *Saturday Review* 41, no. 51 (20 December 1958): 31–32.

Kerr, Walter. "The Disenchanted." *New York Herald Tribune* (4 December 1958).

McClain, John. "Fitzgerald 'Life' Has All It Takes." *New York Journal American* (4 December 1958).

"New Plays in Manhattan." *Time* 72 (15 December 1958): 44.

New Republic (27 December 1958).

Newsweek (27 December 1958).

Reporter (8 January 1959).

"The Disenchanted" (summary of reviews). *Theatre Arts,* 43, no. 2 (February 1959): 11, 20.

Tynan, Kenneth. "The Theatre." *New Yorker* 34, no. 43 (13 December 1958): 107–109.

Watts, Richard Jr. "The Play about Scott Fitzgerald." *New York Post* (4 December 1958).

What Makes Sammy Run? (1964)

Chapman, John. "'What Makes Sammy Run?' Runs Backward to an Old Hollywood." *New York Daily News* (28 February 1964).

Kerr, Walter. "'What Makes Sammy Run'–The New Musical." *New York Herald Tribune* (28 February 1964).

McClain, John. "What Makes Sammy Run?" *New York Journal American* (28 February 1964).

Nadel, Norman. "'Sammy' Is Off and Running." *New York World-Telegram and Sun* (28 February 1964).

Taubman, Howard. "What Makes Sammy Run?" *New York Times* (28 February 1964).

Watts, Richard Jr. "Rise of Sammy Glick, with Music." *New York Post* (28 February 1964).

On the Waterfront (1995)

Barnes, Clive. "Not a Contendah." *New York Post* (2 May 1995).

Canby, Vincent. "A Classic Film Is Transposed to 3 Dimensions." *New York Times* (2 May 1995): B, 1–2.

Gerard, Jeremy. "On the Waterfront." *Variety* (8 May 1995).

Kissel, Howard. "Pier Pressure." *New York Daily News* (5 May 1995).

Lyons, Donald. "On The Waterfront." *Wall Street Journal* (22 May 1995).

Simon, John. "Shallow Depths." *New York Magazine* (22 May 1995).

Winer, Laurie. "Nothing New in Broadway Retelling of 'Waterfront.'" *Los Angeles Times* (2 May 1995): F, 1.

Winer, Linda. "Disconcerting Preview for 'Waterfront.'" *New York Newsday* (2 May 1995).

REVIEWS OF FILMS OR TELEVISION
PRODUCTIONS WITH SCRIPTS, ADAPTATIONS,
OR ORIGINAL STORIES BY SCHULBERG

Little Orphan Annie (1938)

Film Daily (30 November 1938).

Hollywood Reporter (25 November 1938).

"Little Orphan Annie." *Variety* (24 November 1938).
Motion Picture Daily (1 December 1938).
Motion Picture Herald (3 December 1938).

Winter Carnival (1939)

Commonweal (4 August 1939): 359.
Crowther, Bosley ("B.R.C."). *New York Times* (28 July 1939): 14.
"Hobe." "Winter Carnival." *Variety* (19 July 1939).
Motion Picture Herald (22 July 1939).
New Republic (9 August 1939): 20.
Photoplay (August 1939): 54.
Time (31 July 1939): 24.

Weekend for Three (1941)

Film Daily (28 October 1941).
Hollywood Reporter (24 October 1941).
Motion Picture Herald Product Digest (1 November 1941).
T.M.P. "Weekend for Three." *New York Times* (24 October 1941): 27.
Variety (23 October 1941).
"Walt." "Weekend for Three." *Variety* (29 October 1941).

City without Men (1943)

"City without Men" *Motion Picture Herald* (27 February 1943).
Motion Picture Herald Product Digest (27 February 1943).

Government Girl (1943)

Box Office (6 November 1943).
Film Daily (5 November 1943).
Motion Picture Herald (6 November 1943).
Newsweek (29 November 1943): 78.
Time (6 December 1943): 54.
"Walt." *Variety* (10 November 1943).

On the Waterfront (1954)

A. W. "On the Waterfront." *New York Times* (29 July 1954): 18.
America (7 August 1954): 466.

Business Weekly (7 August 1954): 94.

Catholic World (August 1954): 384.

Cannon, Damian. *Movie Reviews* (U.K.) (1998).

Commonweal (20 August 1954): 485–486.

Ebert, Roger. *Chicago Sun-Times* (21 March 1999).

Farm Journal (September 1954): 140.

"Gene." *Variety* (14 July 1954).

Harper's (August 1954): 93–95.

History Today (1 June 1995).

Library Journal (July 1954): 1304.

Life (19 July 1954): 45–48.

Look (10 August 1954): 37–38.

Newsweek (2 August 1954): 78.

New York Times (30 May 1954): 5; (11 July 1954): 5; (1 August 1954): 1; (1 August 1954): 5.

New Yorker (31 July 1954): 52.

Reporter (23 September 1954): 46–47.

Saturday Review of Literature (24 July 1954): 25; (23 October 1954): 8; (1 January 1955): 63.

Weiler, A. H. *New York Times* (29 July 1954).

A Face in the Crowd (1957)

"A Face in the Crowd." *New York Times* 2 (2 June 1957): 1; 6 (2 June 1957): 17.

America (15 June 1957): 332.

Commonweal (14 June 1957): 277–278.

Coronet (May 1957): 10.

Good Housekeeping (August 1957): 70.

Holl. *Variety* (29 May 1957).

Library Journal (15 June 1957): 1665.

Life (May 27, 1957): 68.

Nation (15 June 1957): 533–534.

Newsweek (3 June 1957): 101.

New York Times 2 (30 September 1956): 7; 2 (26 May 1957): 5; (29 May 1957): 33.

New York Times Magazine (13 January 1957): 72.

New Yorker (8 June 1957): 86.

Saturday Review of Literature (25 May 1957): 23.

Time (3 June 1957): 92.

Wind across the Everglades (1958)

America (20 September 1958): 651.
Catholic World (November 1958): 153.
Commonweal (12 September 1958): 593.
Crowther, Bosley. "Wind across the Everglades." *New York Times* (12 September 1958): 21.
New Yorker (20 September 1958): 86.
Newsweek (8 September 1958): 94.
"Powe." *Variety* (20 August 1958).
Saturday Review of Literature (6 September 1958): 28.
Time (27 September 1958): 73.
"Wind Across the Everglades." *Magill's Survey of Cinema* (15 June 1995).

What Makes Sammy Run? (1959)

Shayon, Robert Lewis. "What Made Schulberg Change?" *Saturday Review of Literature* 42, no. 43 (24 October 1959): 34.

A Question of Honor (1982)

Crist, Judith. "This Week's Movies: A Question of Honor: Review of the Television Drama." *TV Guide,* 30, no. 17 (24 April 1982): A-6.
O'Connor, John J. "A Question of Honor." *New York Times* 3 (28 April 1982): 26.

ARTICLES ABOUT SCHULBERG

"A Tale of One Writer's Tale of Four Writers" ("Backstage with Esquire"). *Esquire* 54, no. 4 (October 1960): 28, 30.
Beck, Marilyn." Hollywood: From the Inside Looking Out." *San Francisco Examiner* (June 1992).
Beigel, Jerry. "Schulberg's Watts Project to Span All Showbiz Facets." *Variety* (28 April 1967): 3.
Blau, Eleanor. "'On the Waterfront' Adapted for Stage." *New York Times* (18 March 1984).
Blumenthal, Ralph. "'41 Best Seller Is Back and Clawing." *New York Times* (11 August 1998).

Brodie, John. "He Shoulda Been a Contendah . . ." *GQ* (April 1994): 109–110, 115.

"Budd Schulberg Adapting Film 'On The Waterfront' into Stage Play." *New York Times* (2 September 1983).

"Budd Schulberg to Receive B'nai B'rith 'Susie' Award." *Hollywood Reporter* (11 June 1967).

"Budd Schulberg's Aid-Watts Drive." *Variety* (8 December 1965): 5, 15.

Burns, Howard, and Anita M. Busch. "Lee, Schulberg, Sugar in Ring with 'Joe Louis.'" *Hollywood Reporter* (28 July 2000): 1, 73.

Cerf, Bennett. "Trade Winds" (reminiscence of Schulberg). *Saturday Review of Literature* (14 October 1950): 4–6.

Champion, I. "Qu est-ce qui fait courir Schulberg?" *Positif* (France) (June 1991): 81–85.

Champlin, Charles. "Novelist Schulberg Is Back Where Sammy Ran." *Los Angeles Times* 6 (1 August 1987): 1, 7.

———. "'Sammy' Keeps On Running; Next as a Movie." *Los Angeles Times* (2 February 1990): F 1, 3.

———. Column on Schulberg and Longevity of *What Makes Sammy Run? Los Angeles Times* (23 February 1990): F, 1.

Cherne, Leo. "The Businessman in America: 1. The Writer & the Entrepreneur." *Saturday Review of Literature* 35, no. 3 (January 1952): 10–11, 37–39.

Christy, George. "The Great Life." *Hollywood Reporter* (20 February 1990): 478.

Collins, Glenn. "Beneath the Glitter of Tinseltown's Golden Days." *New York Times* (1 November 1987): 35–37.

"Cosby, Schulberg to Be Honored for Work in Watts." *Variety* (28 July 1966):

Current Biography (May 1951).

"Crusading Movies Needed, Says Expose Film Writer." *Box Office* (5 May 1975).

Dalton, Joseph. "Mogul's Son Recalls the Glory Days." *Los Angeles Herald-Examiner* (13 November 1987): 40.

Davis, David. "Writin' Is Fightin': Budd Schulberg's American Century." *LA Weekly* (18–24 July 1997): 35–36.

Delatiner, Barbara. "Victim of the 50's Blacklist Gets to Tell His Tale" (Walter Bernstein). *New York Times* (20 October 1996).

Duggan, Dennis. "Schulberg—On the Stage Front." *Newsday* (9 April 1995).

Dutton, Walt. "'Voices of Watts' Subject of Special." *Los Angeles Times* (22 July 1966).

Epstein, Robert. "Schulberg Returns to the Scene of a Changed Hollywood." *Los Angeles Times* (21 March 1991): F, 9.

———. "Watts Writers Workshop: A Blueprint to Fit Today's Needs." *Los Angeles Times* (5 May 1992): F, 1.

Fotheringham, Allan. "Budd Schulberg in Great Gatsby Land." *Maclean's*, 102, 35 (28 August 1989): 56.

"Free Pix Quench Watts Flare-up; Ask More Films." *Variety* (17 June 1966).

Freedman, M. "New England and Hollywood." *Commentary* (October 1953).

Freeman, David. "The Best Revenge: Writers and Hollywood" (Schulberg and other 'Hollywood' writers). *Los Angeles Times Book Review* (23 August 1992): 1, 10.

Gallo, Bill. "Big Screen Has Share of Knockouts." *New York Daily News* [www. nydailynews.com/2000–03. . ./a-58881.as] (5 March 2000).

"Going Back to the Waterfront Before the Curtain Rises." *New York Times* (16 March 1995): D, 22.

"Going Strong at 85" ("Public Lives"). *New York Times* (31 March 1999).

Gross, Ken. "Budd Schulberg." *People,* 25 (18 December 1989): 93–94, 99.

"Happenings at Angelica 57" (Avignon/New York Film Festival, 18 April 1996) *France Telecom North America* (Online Website), 1997.

Hayden, Jeffrey. "Sammy Glick? Sure, Sammy and I Go Way Back." *Los Angeles Times Book Review* (29 April 1990): 15.

Hoffman, Irving. "Tales of Hoffman." *Hollywood Reporter* (22 August 1951): 3.

Hollinger, Hy. "Writer a Patsy in H'wood But New Era Dawning, Sez Schulberg." *Variety* (5 September 1956): 3, 18.

Humphrey, Hal. "Budd Finds Talent Jackpot in Watts." *Los Angeles Times* IV (16 August 1966): 14.

———. "Watts' Special Girls a Lesson to Viewers." *Los Angeles Times* (18 August 1966).

Jackson, James. "James Jackson Recalls Success of Watts Writers Workshop." *Los Angeles Times Calendar* (21 December 1980): 79.

Jackson, James Thomas, and Sonora McKellar, Guadalupe d. Saavedra, Jeanne Taylor, and Birdell Chew. "A Guaranteed Wage: The View from Watts." *Los Angeles Times West Magazine* (16 April 1967): 38–40.

"Kazan, Schulberg Join Stude Rally." *Variety* (5 October 1969).

Kelly, J. "World of Big Wheels." *Saturday Review of Literature* (16 May 1953).

Kehr, David. "At the Movies: Hollywood, Back When." *New York Times* (April 7, 2000).

Knapp, Dan. "Budd Schulberg Turns His Talents to a New Cause." *Los Angeles Times.* Entertainment (2 April 1970): 1, 7.

Knorr, Katherine. "Ernest and Scott Meet High Academia." *International Herald Tribune* (8 July 1994): 1, 4.

Lalehzar, Clover. "Schulberg's Lecture Shares Screenwriting Experience." *Miscellany News* (Vassar College, N.Y.) (28 September 1998).

Lee, Luaine. "What Made Budd Schulberg Run Away from Hollywood?" *Long Beach Independent Press-Telegram* (Scripps Howard News Service) (1 March 1990): B, 4.

Lescaze, Lee. "Gordon Gekko's Grandfather." *Wall Street Journal* (19 December 1989).

Long, Robert. "'Sammy' To Run On A Big Screen." *East Hampton Star* (N.Y.) (4 June 1998).

Loynd, Ray. "Looking Back at the Birth of Watts Writers Workshop." *Los Angeles Times* 5 (27 April 1987): 4.

Lumenick, Lou. "New Jersey's Home Movie." *The Record* (Bergen County, N.J.) (24 July 1994).

Lyman, Rick. "The Long Run of Sammy Glick." *New York Times* (7 May 2000).

Magida, Arthur. "What Really Makes Sammy Run." *Jewish Journal* (Los Angeles) (27 April–3 May 1990).

Makefield, Wallace, and Merle Miller. "All Talking! All Singing! All Aggravation!" *New York* (17 August 1981): 37–38.

Mallozi, Vincent M. "Theater; Taking a Drama to the Docks Where It Was Filmed." *New York Times* (New Jersey Weekly Desk) (30 July 2000).

Markel, Dan. "Budd Schulberg, Film Writer, Claims Red Link Now Broken." *Los Angeles Examiner* (24 May 1951).

Marx, Andy. "It's Finally Time for Sammy Glick, the Ultimate Player." *Los Angeles Times* (26 April 1992).

———. "Again and Again: Another Face, Another Crowd." *Los Angeles Times Calendar* (7 June 1992): 22–23.

Melton, Mary. "There's Something about 'Sammy.'" *Los Angeles Times Magazine* (6 September 1998): 12–15, 33–34.

"New Schulberg Novel in October." *Hollywood Reporter* (21 August 1969).

"New Writers." *Publishers Weekly* (22 March 1941).

Nichols, Lewis. "Talk with Budd Schulberg." *New York Times Book Review* (24 May 1953).

Nystedt, Bob. "Budd Schulberg." *The Players* (fall 1964).

Olson, Dale. "Schulberg, Wife Ask Volunteers for Watts Project." *Variety* (2 December 1965): 1, 4.

Ornstein, Bill. "Budd Schulberg Seeking $12,000 for Watts Writers Workshop as Talent Here Contributes." *Hollywood Reporter* (16 August 1966).

Pace, Eric. "The Writer Is the Forgotten Man." *New York Times* (25 April 1982).

Pirie, David. "How to Write Films and Influence People . . . How to Lose Friends and Still Win." *The Independent on Sunday* (U.K.) (31 May 1992).

Pleasants, Ben. "Son of Cinema, Man of Activism." *Los Angeles Times* West View (15 November 1981): 3.

"'Problem' Pix Not Always That at B.O., Argues Schulberg." *Variety* (29 June 1962).

"Raise $1,500 for Watts Project." *Variety* (7 December 1965).

Reeves, Richard. "Sammy Glick, Yuppie Hero." *San Francisco Chronicle* (7 August 1987).

Reidel, Michael. "Musical 'Crowd' Pleaser . . . Classic 1957 movie being reworked for B'way." *New York Post* (June 29, 2001): 41.

Reiner, Jay. "Harrowing tales of Fitzgerald in Hollywood." *Los Angeles Herald-Examiner* (23 July 1982): D, 28.

Richler, Mordecai. "The Famous Sammy G." *GQ* (February 1990).

Rosenberg, Howard. "Schulberg Removes Name from 'Jacobo Timerman.'" *Los Angeles Times* 6 (6 May 1983): 1.

———. "'Face in Crowd' Saw the Danger." *Los Angeles Times* (14 August 2000): F1, 14.

Rosenthal, Sharon. "Is Sammy Glick Ready for Another Run?" *Buzz* 1, no. 2 (December/January 1991): 24.

Rothman, Cliff. "Shud He Have Been a Contendah?" *Nation* (5–12 April 1999): 57–60.

"Rotten Business in the Ring." *Life* 40 (16 April 1956): 103–104. Preview of the film *The Harder They Fall*.

Scaduto, Anthony. "Name-Dropper Budd Schulberg Says He's Behind Kazan." *Newsday* (18 March 1999).

Scheiderer, David. "Life or Script, 'Waterfront' Retains Drama." *Los Angeles Times* VI (30 December 1988): 8.

Scheuer, Philip K. "Writer Liberated, Schulberg Claims." *Los Angeles Times* (5 October 1959).

"Schulberg Feels H'wood 'Treats Writers Worse Than Civil War Slaves.'" *Variety* (5 September 1956): 1, 4.

"Schulberg Pushes Watts Aid Plans." *Hollywood Reporter* (5 October 1967).

"Schulberg Ponders a Return to Watts Project." *New York Times* (3 March 1980): B, 6.

"Schulberg Running Watts Workshop; Says Need Big for Every Aid Available." *Writers Guild of America West Newsletter* (April 1966): 3.

"Schulberg to Revisit 'Waterfront' for Trilogy/Col." *Variety* (1 September 1992): 19.

"Schulberg to Stay with 20th's 'Enemy.'" *Variety* (23 July 1962).

"Schulberg Would Bring 'On The Waterfront' to Stage." *Los Angeles Times* 6 (30 December 1988): 8.

Schwager, Jeff. "What Makes Buddy Run." *Village View* (Westwood Village, Calif.) 4, no. 34 (30 March–5 April 1990): 18–19.

Scott, W. T. "The Literary Summing Up: A Personal Winnowing of 1950s Books" (*The Disenchanted* discussed). *Saturday Review of Literature* (30 December 1950): 6–8, 28–29.

"Screenwriter in the Ghetto." *Time* 88, no. 4 (22 July 1966): 53–54.

Seidenbaum, Art. "Buddy's Back, and Bitterness Is Gone." *Los Angeles Times* Entertainment (4 August 1964): 1, 6.

Shanley, John. "He Made Sammy Run: Budd Schulberg Discusses Adaptation of His Novel for Television." *New York Times* (27 September 1959).

"$6,500 to Westminster Neighborhood Assoc. to Build Day-Care Center in Watts." *Hollywood Reporter* (22 June 1966).

Smith, Cecil. "Budd Schulberg." *Los Angeles Times* Entertainment (5 May 1957): 1, 12.

"Something to Write About." *Life* (4 June 1951).

Spiegel, Meryl. "Schulberg Tackling Fitzgerald Play Anew." *New York Times* (1 December 1996).

Thomas, Bob. "The Novel That Shook Hollywood." *Richmond (Va.) New Leader* (Associated Press) (13 April 1991).

Thomas, Kevin. "Susie Award Given to Budd Schulberg." *Los Angeles Times* (13 September 1967).

Time (13 November 1950).

Torre, Marie. "TV Won't Whitewash Budd Schulberg's Sammy." *Beverly Hills* (Calif.) *Citizen* (10 August 1959).

Van Gelder, Lawrence. "At the Movies: 'What Makes Sammy Run?' Hasn't Been Filmed, Yet." *New York Times* (12 April 1991).

"What Made Schulberg Run? Red Writing Code Disenchanted Him." *New York Daily News* (Associated Press) (24 May 1951): 4.

"What Makes a Communist?" *New York Herald-Tribune* (16 June 1951): Editorial.

Wilson, Earl. "Oscar-Winning Pair Map Film Play on Advertising." *Los Angeles Mirror-News* (31 March 1955).

Zahradnik, Rich. "Schulberg's 'Face' Attracts Goldberg." *Hollywood Reporter* (12 August 1986).

INTERVIEWS

Bernstein, Fred. "Budd Schulberg Remembers How Hollywood Was Run—and What Made Him Run from It." *People* (21 September 1981).

"Budd Schulberg—Conversation at Vassar College." *Euroscreen* [http://www.geocities.com/Hollywoo . . . /artbudd.htm] (28 September 1998).

Colmenares, J., ed. "It Could Happen in the Schools." *NEA Journal* (December 1967).

Georgakas, Dan. "The Screen Playwright as Author." *Cineaste* Vol. 11, No. 4 (winter 1982): 7–15.

"Is Sammy Glick Ready for Another Run?" *Buzz* (December–January 1991).

Nichols, Lewis. "A Talk with Budd Schulberg." *New York Times Book Review* (24 May 1953).

Pace, Eric. (Schulberg's role as Screenwriter on 'Question of Honor.') *New York Times* 2 (25 April 1982): 29.

Van Gelder, Robert. "An Interview with Budd Schulberg: The Author of 'What Makes Sammy Run?' Discusses Hollywood, Writing and Glickism." *New York Times Book Review* (10 August 1941): 2.

"Waterfront." *New York Times Book Review* (August 1955).

"Writers and Writing." *New York Times* 2 (3 March 1980): 6.

MISCELLANEOUS

Cover photo: Jason Robards Jr. and Rosemary Harris in *The Disenchanted*. *Theatre Arts* (January 1959).

"Odd Flock of People to See in Everglades" ('Speaking of Pictures'). *Life* 45, no. 12 (22 September 1958): 14–15.

The Budd Schulberg Papers are deposited in the Harvey S. Firestone Memorial Library at Princeton University. They consist of thirty-three boxes covering the years 1937–1985. Included are holograph and typescript manuscripts and galley sheets of Schulberg's novels, plays, screenplays, radio scripts and scenarios, as well as other holographs, signed holographs, signed typescripts, telegrams, and clippings. A typescript guide is available in the Firestone Library. A microfilm copy of the papers, on twenty-five reels of 35mm positive film, is in the Jones Microtext Center of the Baker Humanities and Social Sciences Library of Dartmouth College in Hanover, N.H. Other Schulberg books, manuscripts, and albums are on deposit in the Rauner Special Collections Library at Dartmouth College and in Baker Library. As of February 2001, an additional amount of Schulberg archival material [correspondence, manuscripts, clippings, and miscellaneous files] comprising approximately 150 linear feet in about 120 boxes, was destined for an unspecified university library.

INDEX

191

ABOUT THE AUTHOR

Nicholas Beck was born in Hollywood, attended Hollywood High School, Los Angeles City College, Los Angeles State College, and UCLA, where he earned a doctorate in education in 1975. Between 1957 and 1968, he served several tours of duty with United Press International, as overnight manager of the Los Angeles bureau, and as boxing writer at the Tokyo (1964) and Mexico City (1968) Olympic Games.

He taught journalism and English at Pasadena (Calif.) City College and was professor of journalism and department chairman at California State University, Los Angeles, from which he retired in 1988. He is an avid book collector, with outstanding collections of F. Scott Fitzgerald, Ernest Hemingway, Christopher Isherwood, and not surprisingly, of Budd Schulberg.

Dr. Beck served in the U.S. Army during the Korean War and did some amateur boxing. He lives in Sherman Oaks, California.